A few words ab

A very informative memoir on
enjoyed reading about some of the events I had heard about
growing up as well as learning some new ones.

Hannah Halliday
(Tim's very most favorite child)

It was such a joy to read "A Journey" written by my dad. It
helped paint a picture of all of the stories I had been told
growing up. He is and will always be my hero.

Thanks for writing this book about your life!!! :]

Abbie Klein
(Tim's very most favorite child)

I very much enjoyed reading my father's memoir. It provided
me with the opportunity to learn some new stories, some I
had perhaps heard over the years; along with some details I
could have gone my whole life without knowing. In the end,
who wouldn't want dirt on their father? After reading this
book, one of the biggest things I can walk away with is his
admirable commitment to both Jesus and his family. For this
reason I can say I'm truly fortunate to have him as a father
and he is easily one of my heroes! Love ya bud!

Philip Gates
(Tim's very most favorite child)

Tim has been a friend of mine since we were children. I found
Tim's "A Journey" to be a very honest and surprisingly detailed
account of a life well lived. Tim's humor and optimism shine
through on almost each page. His lack of hubris is refresh-
ing. From his foggy and randy teenage ramblings through the
Irish countryside to the development of lifesaving medical
skills and genuine lifelong compassion to help those in need,
a few hours spent accompanying Tim on the pages of this
journey is time well spent for anyone. I'm proud to call Tim a
friend! Thank you for sharing this with me!

Roy Rutherford
(aka Rinaldo, or Rizwan, or maybe Ruben)

Copyright © 2018 Timothy Gates
All rights reserved
First Edition

PAGE PUBLISHING, INC.
New York, NY

First originally published by Page Publishing, Inc. 2018

ISBN 978-1-64138-414-8 (Paperback)
ISBN 978-1-64138-448-3 (Hardcover)
ISBN 978-1-64138-415-5 (Digital)

Printed in the United States of America

A Journey

An Attempt (and Sometimes Struggle) at Being Real in This World

TIMOTHY GATES

Dedicated to Frank and Peggy Gates with love.

CONTENTS

Journal entry:

Friday, 10/9/2015

Good morning, God. It's been a long time since I wrote in a journal. Think it's time to start doing it again. Yesterday really took the wind out of my sails. Still don't know what to think about the whole thing. Still don't know whether to laugh or cry. I've done both. It looks like I lost about six months and 35,000 words worth of writing. On the one hand, I'm not really a writer, so what difference does it make? On the other hand, I don't know if I've ever been so passionate about doing anything as I am (or at least was) about writing the memoir. It's so hard to know if this was some kind of divine intervention or just me being a total bonehead and losing all the data. Maybe a little bit of both. I really don't know. Carol and each of the kids have all been super supportive and encouraging, and they all want me to keep on writing and not be discouraged. (They are looking forward to reading a finished story someday.) Right now, I am very discouraged. In the big scheme of things though, I've got as long as it takes to do this. I will definitely be more careful about backing everything up. Oh yeah,

Carol greeted me this morning with a verse from the song "You Can't Roller Skate in a Buffalo Herd." It goes like this: "You can't roller skate in a buffalo herd. But you can be happy if you've a mind to. All ya gotta do is put your mind to it. Knuckle down, buckle down, do it, do it, do it." I think that's just what I needed to hear. Carol is the greatest. Until next time.

Around three years ago, I started looking at a couple old journals from the '70s and then one written between 2003 and 2005. While rereading what had been recorded about forty years and then more than ten years from the past, I developed an overwhelming desire to start writing a memoir. Unquestionably aware of the privileged and wonderful life I have been given, I wanted to put together some kind of written record of it. Something at least my wife and kids could have and maybe even a few others might like to read if they found it interesting. Who knows, some folks might even find that they could relate to a few of the adventures I'd had the good fortune of experiencing. Well, after having put pen to paper (actually fingers to computer keys) for several months, I was having lunch in a wonderful little Vietnamese restaurant near our home and was also doing a little work on the notes. I saved my document both to the computer and to a thumb drive as I'd been doing all along. This time, however (having absolutely no idea how), I somehow saved not the document I'd just being working on but a version from about six months and thirty-five thousand words prior. I had overwritten my current copy with this old transcript and then saved it. All the work from the previous six months was gone. A bit later in the day, while trying to squeak in a little more time on the computer, it became evident to me what had happened. Talk about wanting to throw up. For the next few days, I certainly did. So here we were, deciding whether or not the last several months had just been a giant waste of effort and wondering if maybe it was time to bag the whole idea of writing a memoir. Or should I just consider this as part of the "great adventure" and press on. I ended up trying to go with the latter. In the words of Roger Miller, as Carol lovingly sang to me, "All ya gotta do is put your mind to it, knuckle down, buckle down, do it, do it, do it." (Kind of corny but pretty good advice all the same.) Who knows, maybe this little story will actually get written. My bonehead mishap versus journalistic reboot from God has even given me some motivation to start journaling again. I'm so glad there have been times in life over the last forty years when I saw the value of writing things down. It has helped to re-recognize what a wonderful adventure life really is. If it weren't for those old journals, I wouldn't have had anything to help refresh so many wonderful memories today. I'm a fortunate guy to have so many good memories—to remember.

INTRODUCTION

It was 1974, the summer after our junior year in high school. A sunny, beautiful, perfect day for a few high school buddies to be cruising Point Defiance Park in my 64 Jeep Willys mail truck with, mind you, the steering wheel on the right side. (What an undeniably awesome truck. Cream yellow, a black stripe across the sides, shag carpet throughout and very cool astro mags.) Drinking beer, most assuredly smoking pot (it was the '70s after all), and taking turns sharing BAs with those poor unfortunate and unsuspecting drivers and passengers in the cars behind us. (That's a bare ass for anyone from a younger generation.) Suddenly, the Indian tapestry curtains hanging across the back windows of the truck would part, and voila, a bare butt to greet you. Life, as most of us have found, is so full of unexpected surprises—some welcome, some not so.

We thought this was hilarious.

I would have to say that I grew up a privileged kid. The youngest of four boys, I was the baby of the family. Mom and Dad were two of the—no, they were the two finest people I have ever known. They were kind and generous and honest. They were real. What you saw is exactly what you got. Dad grew up during the depression on a farm in Deming, Washington, one of six kids born to Guy and Katie. They didn't have a lot. As was true of many young men of that time, Dad joined the military and was a veteran of WWII. His areas of military service included Pearl Harbor, Australia, North Africa, Palestine, India, China, and I'm not sure where else. On December 7, 1941, my dad was aboard ship having left Pearl Harbor just six days prior. (Thank You, God, the unit he was with left Hawaii when they did.) Dad was awarded the Air Medal by General H. H. Arnold, commander of Army Air Forces during WWII and a pioneer airman who was personally taught to fly by the Wright brothers. The Distinguished Flying Cross was also pinned onto Dad's chest by WWI Flying Ace Captain Eddie Rickenbacker. My father retired from the Air Force as a chief master sergeant and I believe was among the first group of individuals to receive that distinguished rank. Dad was a hero. (I never knew about my father's military history until I became a young adult and saw some of the newspaper clippings that Mom had kept. He just never talked about it.) Dad by the way seldom went to church while we were growing up. He used to say that he "didn't want to be a hypocrite." I never really understood just what he meant at the time.

One of my father's most notable accomplishments was to catch the eye of Miss Peggy Sharp. That's my mom. Mom grew up one of four kids in Mt. Vernon, Washington, the daughter of Melburn and Bessie. Grandpa was the bridge tender for a long-since-dismantled bridge that crossed the Skagit River in Mt Vernon. Grandma was from Ireland and had come to the United States on the *Olympic*, sister ship to the *Titanic*. The story goes that she was booked to sail on the *Titanic* but for some reason had to change plans and make the voyage on the *Olympic*. (Thank You, God, for unexpected changes in our plans.) And to think that she was probably disappointed and maybe even upset about not getting to sail on the *Titanic* as originally scheduled. Mom was the greatest example of "Jesus with skin on" that I have ever met. If you knew my mom, you know that she had a supernatural love, the kind that puts other people first. The kind that the Bible talks about where Paul says, "If you've gotten anything at all out of following Christ, if his love has made any difference in your life, if being in a community of the Spirit means anything to you, if you have a heart, if you care, then do me a favor: agree with each other, love each other, be deep-spirited friends. Don't push your way to the front; don't sweet-talk your way to the top. Put yourself aside and help others get ahead. Don't be obsessed with getting your own advantage. Forget yourself long enough to lend a helping hand" (Philippians 2:1–4, The Message). That is the way my mother was with everybody, the way she lived. Although there have been many wonderful people who have influenced my life, Mom is by far the biggest reason I was ever motivated to embark on this spiritual journey that life has to offer. Mom was a hero.

Strange Stuff

The late '60s and '70s were a very interesting, significant, and some-times crazy time to be growing up. With the assassination of beloved leaders and politicians, the Vietnam War, drugs, rock-and-roll music, the sexual revolution, hippies, the Jesus movement, there was no short-age of ideas, ideologies, philosophies, and adventures to consider and to participate in. I always wanted to be a hippie. It was probably the summer of '66 when my folks decided to take a car trip down the west coast of Washington, Oregon, and California, bringing along my brother Pat and me. Our visit to San Francisco was my most memora-ble part of the trip. Never had I seen so many of these *exceptional*-look-ing people. In particular, I will never forget the long, frizzy, red-haired mailman who was happily making his way down a hilly San Francisco street with his mailbag. I decided then that not only did I want to be a hippie but also a mailman. (While at a Chinese restaurant in the City by the Bay, the nice owner of the place taught Pat and I how to use chopsticks. Given my love for Asian cuisine and gluttonous nature, this has been a skill I have always been grateful for.) Alas, I was born a little too late in the twentieth century to really be a part of those strange and wonderful people called hippies. Sure, in later years, I did grow my hair a bit longer, and I did live in a school bus, along with a friend David and our three dogs during the senior year of high school. And there was the mail truck. Still, I was more of a wannabe hippie.

As mentioned earlier, I was the youngest of four boys. Frankie, the oldest, was twelve years my senior. He had already spent a stint in the Air Force and become a state patrolman by the time I was in my teens. (Frank was responsible for our family owning a horse when I was just an elementary school lad. What a wonderful gift to grow up with Prancer, our gentle part Quarter Horse part Arabian mare.) Before I wanted to be a hippie or a mailman, I wanted to be a cowboy. Frank rode Prancer to my kindergarten class one day so I could give all the kids a ride for show and tell. I remember the principal even taking a little spin. A few years later, while in the fourth grade, I was asked by Mrs. Roe (my old kindergarten teacher) to bring Prancer to her class-room again and give all the kids a ride. What a great excuse to get out of class in the fourth grade. Prancer didn't even mind making the trip to school on a road and across a freeway overpass that could sometimes have quite a few cars zooming by.

Michael, who is ten years older, took a little different direction in his career path. He was drafted into and spent two years in the Army. A few years after military service, he and a business partner opened Strange Stuff, one of the first if not the first "head shop" in Lakewood, Washington. Strange Stuff didn't market itself as a head shop but rather a place where one could purchase modern home decor—pillow furni-ture, waterbeds, air furniture, various pretty, and colorful items from Mexico to decorate your home with, artwork, candles, incense, Kama Sutra pleasure balms and oils, jewelry (to include spoon rings which were very cool), and of course, pot-smoking paraphernalia. Some of the artwork sold in the shop was the result of Michael's partner and his friends getting together all night with paints, canvases, and acid (the Timothy Leary kind.) Not sure if they sold a lot of those paintings. The shop was within walking distance of the junior high I was attending.

A few days a week after school, I would walk to the store and work, doing anything from building waterbed frames to selling hash pipes. Although I had never used a pipe at that time, I was getting my wannabe hippie fix just by working in the store. We typically had music playing in the shop. It was here I became better acquainted with bands like Iron Butterfly, the Stones, Moody Blues, Cream, Sly and the Family Stone, and let us not forget the Velvet Underground & Nico. Sly and the Family Stone was in fact the first concert I ever went to, and it was during the Strange Stuff days. It was very cool to be seeing Sly and the Family Stone, but we were at the University of Puget Sound

Field House, sitting in wood bleachers, and rumor had it that Sly and the band were about an hour late because they were in the back, watching Sanford and Son. I hoped that wasn't true, but regardless, except for the feedback from the base, it was a great concert, and I was glad to be there. With the music mingled with smells of scented candles and incense, Strange Stuff was a very '70s kind of place to be. By the way, just last week, I was invited to and attended a Moody Blues concert in Seattle. They still had three of the early band members, and I believe a couple of those guys are in their seventies. They have been together as a band for over fifty years. It was a great concert.

Patrick is my brother the closest in age. We are two years apart. After he decided that I was perhaps more than just a nuisance little brother, we grew to be very close friends. Pat has influenced my life in more ways than he knows. By going before me, he was able to provide an example of some do's and don'ts, some things to avoid and some things to embrace. (Also, with careful study of Pat's methods, I learned how to not get caught when embracing those things that I should have been avoiding. He sometimes got caught.) I think it was probably Pat's love of travel and stories of his adventures that sparked the same wanderlust in me. Because my brother did quite well in school academically and due to our parent's graciousness in providing a big chunk of the needed finances, he was able to travel to Europe as a student ambassador with the People to People program. People to People is a student exchange program that organizes groups of high school kids going to and coming from other countries. The program gives the students an opportunity to live with local families as well as to see some of the sights that a visitor really shouldn't miss.

Pat had a more-than-wonderful time on his trip, and as a result, I too wanted to try and experience a similar adventure. (He traded a ballpoint pen with a Russian soldier in Moscow for an awesome hammer and sickle belt buckle. How cool is that?) Brother Pat was also fortunate enough to somehow, over the years, own some of the most beautiful old classic cars of anyone I know. All of my brothers seemed to have a love for cars. Frankie, for instance, once had a 1940 LaSalle convertible (beautiful) and later a 32 Ford Model T. Michael owned a 56 Chevy, a 1953 Mercury Monterey and a 66 Corvette Stingray to name a few. I still remember when Mike and his then girlfriend, later to become wife, Sharon brought me to the Puyallup fair in the Monterey. (I also remember thinking Sharon was way too pretty and nice for Michael.) Pat, however, definitely took the cake when it came to cars. It started with him driving to high school (a punk kid in high school) in an orange 1957 MGA convertible. The MGA may have originally been Frankie's before Pat took possession and put some work into it and until Michael later confiscated it and made it his own. Michael did teach me how to drive a stick shift in that car (which Pat probably wouldn't have done), so his managing to obtain ownership did work out pretty nicely for me.

Michael also managed to get his hands on my Honda 305 Superhawk motorcycle with a sidecar, which I had purchased from brother Frank and which Michael totaled when he crashed it into a fence. I have to admit that being about fourteen years old and owning a Honda Superhawk with a sidecar, until Michael "obtained" it and crashed it, was pretty amazing. But back to Pat. After the MGA, there was an absolutely beautiful 1948 Nash, a super clean 65 VW bug, a cherry 1950 Dodge, a 65 VW (party bus), a 54 Nash Metropolitan, a super unique 47 Jeep Willy's Overland, a 54 VW bug with sunroof (totaled that one), a classic 56 VW bug, and a 57 VW Karmann Ghia, which also unfortunately got totaled. (Thank You, God, that Pat wasn't hurt worse than he was in that accident.) The car ended up flipped over, crashed through a fence, and lodged into a house trailer. Oh, I forgot the 72 VW Station Wagon, the 48 four-wheel-drive Jeepster, the 72 Opel GT, and a '50s something beautiful black convertible Mercedes. Patrick definitely had some cars. But then I had a 64 Jeep Willys mail truck with astro mags.

Once again, due to my parents' gracious willingness to finance the lion's share of the trip and due to my adequate grades in school (how bad can you do when areas of study include band, leather works, physical education, and an English composition class called It's Magic?), I too was privileged to take part in an amazing trip to Europe with the People to People program. Our It's Magic English teacher Mr. Fleming was actually a gifted magician and taught a great class. Also, Mr. Fleming had a bumper sticker on the rear of his car that read "God Bless Bob Fleming." I always liked him.

A Disturbing Dream

Probably a big reason that my brothers loved cars so much is that my father was also a car guy. After retiring from the Air Force and before he and Mom opened an auction house (what a fun business to grow up a part of that was—the stuff reality TV shows are made of these days), Dad was a car dealer. I would often spend time at the car lot with my dad after attending elementary school. Sometimes he would bring me with him for meetings with other car dealers. Sometimes he would bring me to lunch at the counter of Woolworths. (I still remember ordering a cheese sandwich with mayonnaise.) During that time, I think Mom was the secretary for the chaplain's at American Lake Veterans Hospital. And that's right, one year I was an angel at the VA Chapel Christmas play. (Just sayin'.) Whether it was the car business or the auction, we all participated. Mom and Dad were very hard workers, and I know that they tried to instill that quality in their kids. From a young age and about as soon as I found out that if you worked you could sometimes even get paid and have money to do fun stuff, I held some kind of job. As a senior in high school, I was working after class and on weekends at a grocery store as a box boy, whatever needs to be done boy. (In order to keep my "longer than acceptable for the grocery store" hair, I actually wore a short hair wig for this job. It looked terrible, and I can hardly believe they let me get away with it.)

My friend David had worked very hard the summer before our senior year converting an old '50s school bus (brother Mike had obtained somewhere) into a place where we could actually live. I helped a little, but Dave was pretty much the guy responsible for the plans and the bulk of the work. (Dave's dad, I should add, was later the defense military attaché in Iran and a hostage when the American embassy was taken in 1978. It was wonderful to later see Dave's dad come home.) I think we paid about $80 a month to park the bus in a guy's backyard, where we hooked up to his water and electricity and where the toilet emptied into a big hole in the ground. We put a blue chemical into the hole to reduce the aroma (the kind they use in an RV holding tank.) Dave and I shared the bus with Bart, GJ, and Smokey (good doggies all three). The little bathroom in the bus was walled with thin cedar shakes. It was always an entertaining experience for one of our guests to use the facilities as you could just about hear them breathe while they were inside the little cedar shake room, contemplating life. It all added to the adventure.

I think my folks, although probably a little hesitant about allowing their youngest child to live on his own while still in high school, also appreciated my desire to be independent. By this time in life, I had definitely learned how to use a pipe or rolling paper or whatever was handy and was also becoming much more acquainted with what the world had to offer. At the same time, however, I still had a longing to know Jesus better. Mom was the one that always brought us to church (South Tacoma Baptist Church), and with my mother's loving example, which she demonstrated daily, together with a loving church family, I honestly did believe that Jesus was very real and that he really cared about me. I still remember Pat and me praying as little kids each night with Mom at the bedside, "Jesus, tender shepherd, hear me. Bless thy little lamb tonight. Through the darkness, be thou near me. Keep me safe till morning light." Followed by reciting John 3:16: "For God so loved the world that He gave His only begotten Son, that whosoever believeth in Him should not perish but have everlasting life." And finally, "God bless Mom and Dad and Frank and Mike and Pat and aunts and uncles and cousins and everybody else in need of blessing." I believed that it was possible to talk with God at a very young age and also believed that He was listening.

While in elementary school, I had a little dog named Pug. She came with me pretty much everywhere a boy could walk or ride his bike. Pug even came with me, delivering papers on my paper route. On a few occasions, I also delivered the papers on Prancer, our horse. The manager of Fir Acres Trailer Court was more than a little ticked when on one occasion Prancer left a gift on a street in the court (and which I didn't clean up). I was not a responsible horse-riding paper boy. The next time he saw me delivering papers on Prancer, he made sure that I understood not to ride my horse in his trailer court ever again.

And speaking of Prancer, just yesterday, I saw a post on Facebook from the brother of my old friend Warren. Unfortunately, their dad was in the hospital due to a very serious medical condition. I posted back to let them know that their dad was in our prayers and that I had so many great memories that included their family. The return post I received was that he and his dad had just been talking the night before about the time Warren and I rode Prancer through their house in the front door and out the back. I really can't remember why we thought that might be a good idea at the time. I am quite sure that Warren was there on that beautiful summer day at Point Defiance Park when we were flashing BAs out of the back of the mail truck. Come to think of it, he might even have instigated that little adventure.

But let's get back to Pug. One day some of my friends stopped by to visit and see if I would like to make the walk down the railroad tracks to the B & I circus store (home of Ivan the gorilla). Unfortunately, I was not home, but Pug my dog was. For reasons I never understood, they allowed Pug to make the walk to the B & I without me. (It was about a three-mile walk by way of the railroad tracks.) They all went into the store and left Pug outside. When they came out, she was nowhere to be found. My friends made it back to our place only to let me know that Pug was lost. Well, what was a boy to do? I decided to pray, really pray. The kind of prayer that little kids who have no reason to believe God could not or would not answer their prayer prays. My dad came home from work that night with a surprise. At that time, he owned a car lot located a mile or two from our home and about three miles from the B & I circus store (home of Ivan the gorilla.) Pug, who had never been to the car lot, made the three-mile trip down Pacific Highway on a busy road where she had never walked, and lay down next to my dad's desk in an office where she had never been. No lie. Do we have a Father God who even cares about a little kid and his dog? I believed that I did.

So here we were—two teenage boys and three dogs living the high life in a school bus and able to make whatever decisions and do just about whatever we wanted to do. Then I had this dream. It was later in the afternoon, and I was taking a nap in the bus. The dream was very short but also very vivid. I saw a white-haired man wearing a robe that looked as if it was flowing in the wind. (Quite biblical-looking.) He appeared to be up and among the clouds, and he was speaking to me. He said, "Tim, come with me, it's all right." While speaking, he was also gesturing with his hand to join him. That was it, and I woke up just after. What was so disturbing is that when I did wake up, the first thing that came to my mind was that this white-haired, ancient-looking old man inviting me to join him was actually Satan. (No, I hadn't been doing drugs.) This grandfatherly old man was someone you might even envision when trying to picture what God could look like. It was clear to me though that he wasn't God. It was kind of an "evil versus good" sort of thing, where evil was trying to make me think that it was good. He was trying to fool me into thinking that following him would be a good thing. (This is at least how I ended up interpreting the dream.)

I don't know for sure why I had this dream. I don't know what part God may or may not have played in the whole thing. I do know at that time I was a young man who would have told you he was a Christian if you asked. I remember as a little boy (probably about seven years old) the morning at Sunday school when I "asked Jesus into my heart." I remember as a young teen when I decided to be baptized (although truth be told, I probably wasn't really clear on why I was doing it). Here it was the senior year of high school, and I was still even going to church on most Sundays. At the same time, however, I was making just about zero effort to really get to know this Jesus I claimed to believe in. The dream brought to mind a verse in 2 Corinthians, where it says, "Satan disguises himself as an angel of light." It kind of scared me. Not long after, I decided that maybe it was time to make some changes. Also, not long after, I packed up Smokey, GJ, an old antique rocker, and whatever other few possessions I had and headed back to my folks' house.

Making Promises to God

God, I'm going to stop getting drunk. I'm going to stop doing drugs. I'm going to stop obsessing about pretty girls. I'm going to stop hanging out with friends that are doing all the things that I'm going to stop doing. I'm . . . I'm . . . I'm . . . I'm . . . blah, blah, blah, blah. Although I think that my intentions were genuine and although I did want to know God better, it wouldn't take too long to find out that trying to be good was not necessarily a formula for knowing or pleasing God. In fact, trying to make those changes under my own power and by my own strength was impossible. Trying to "be good" my way to God would prove to be a difficult and, in the end, unsuccessful effort. Not to mention, my friends would probably tell you that I wasn't the most pleasant person to be around during that part of the journey. (Trying to work your way to God's favor is a frustrating task and can make some people grumpy.)

It took some time and some serious lessons learned before I became aware of a few basic truths that have made and I hope are continuing to make a difference in my journey to know Jesus better. But because I had not yet learned these fundamental facts of life, I would just have to settle for not getting drunk, not doing drugs, not obsessing over pretty girls, and not hanging out with my friends who were doing all the things that I had (at least temporarily) stopped doing. Also and unfortunately, because trying to live a spiritual life without a relationship with the Spirit is not possible, I also settled for being kind of a frustrated and grumpy (so-called) Christian.

Come New Year's Eve of 1975, I was trying to get closer to God the best I knew how. I had determined to participate in the December 31st festivities drug and alcohol free while still getting together with friends and family. These particular friends and family had not however made the same commitment to "get high on life" that evening without the addition of intoxicating party favors. My brother Pat's longtime and dear friend David was having a party at his mom and dad's house. David was much like a brother. I remember when we were little kids, him spending the night at our place on many a Saturday, and just like Pat and me, he would be lying next to one of the big flat wall heaters in his underwear on Sunday morning reading the funny papers. Also, just like Pat and me, I am sure he experienced rolling back too close to the big glass panel in his jockeys and getting burned. (I can't believe they allowed you to have these things in your house.) David's parents had become great friends with my mom and dad. For many memorable summers, both of our families would travel up to the Aurora Lakes in British Columbia, Canada. We stayed in cabins (I told you I was a privileged kid) and spent our days fishing for rainbow and brook trout in one of the many lakes. Mostly I would just fish on Lake Carol, named after Carol, the lovely wife of Miles. The Aurora Lakes were operated by my folks' friends Miles and Carol. As was true of many of my parents' close friends, Miles was a prior military serviceman who had served with my dad. Here we were swimming and fishing in beautiful Canadian lakes and even sometimes catching big trout.

What an incredible place for Pat, David, sometimes David's brother and sometimes a friend that I would bring along to spend a couple weeks during the summer. Just now, I'm remembering when a big black bear was right outside our cabin door, and we had to yell at it and make a bunch of noise until it finally left. And the time when Pug got her leg caught in a bear trap. Because she was so little, Pug was actually okay, and her leg wasn't broken. We were all pretty amazed. Or the time I rigged up a wonderful little gizmo out of twine and a piece of cardboard. The cardboard was carefully placed on top of a beam just above the bed where David slept. The twine was attached to the cardboard and strung up above the rafters and down the wall next to my bed where I could pull it at the opportune time. On the piece of cardboard was a carefully placed horse turd (just dry enough on top to pick up but moist enough on the bottom to still be "just right"). The plan was to wait for David to lay his head on his pillow, pull the twine, and the rest would be history. After we had all gone to bed, I started thinking too much and began to worry that David's surprise might end up landing in his mouth and how that wouldn't be very cool. (What was I thinking, that would have been great). So still wanting to land a turd on David's head but not wanting it to land in his mouth, I first gave him a verbal warning before pulling on the string. He had moved his head a little (and probably shut his mouth) when the turd bomb fell, and it landed on his pillow. Oh well, he didn't get the full effect, but it was still kind of funny. I should probably add that I only came up with this idea in the first place after having woken up a night or two before to find my hand in a bowl of warm water that David and Pat were holding. They had apparently heard that if you put a sleeping person's hand in warm water it would cause them to pee the bed. I'm happy to report that it didn't work with me.

I had decided to spend New Year's Eve partly at David's parents' house and partly over at the home of my brother Mike and his wife. Mike and Sharon were having a get-together along with some of their friends. I celebrated the coming New Year at Dave's house long enough for somebody to start throwing up in the toilet. I recall the girlfriend of Dave's oldest brother commenting at that time, "That's why I prefer drugs." I was definitely seeing the benefit of not imbibing at that moment. After enjoying the extra added New Year's Eve bonus of someone ralphing their guts out, I decided it was time to head for Mike and Sharon's. The atmosphere at Mike's was a little different than what I had experienced at David's. Some of the guests at my brother's place were not only well "primed" but also very eager to make me the topic of discussion. Particularly, my decision to try and better know Jesus. A couple of the guys were in agreement that I was using Jesus as a "crutch" and that trying to know God was only something that weak people did, not something for the truly thoughtful and enlightened. Truth is, I didn't really know how to respond to Michael's friends. I wasn't confident enough about my own worldview and spiritual beliefs to give a reason for the path I was attempting to travel. It shook me a little. If given the opportunity to have that conversation again, I would so like to let them know that Jesus is not at all a crutch. He is, however, for me a complete and total life support system, without which I am toast. I don't need a crutch. I need the life that comes from the one whom I believe is the life giver. It took some years though to come to that realization.

Bon Voyage

For the remainder of the senior year, I tried to play my B-flat eupho-
nium skillfully, tool my leather projects with care (I did make a pretty
cool backpack), participate in PE class with vigor, and eagerly learn
magic tricks in the It's Magic English composition class. (I must have
completed a few writing assignments as well.) Then came summer, and
it was time to head for Europe with People to People.

Before we journey on to talking about the trip, I would like to
mention that there really did seem to be a movement in the '60s and
'70s taking place where people, many people, were seeking to be a part
of something greater than themselves, seeking to have a deeper relationship with God. Although what was called the Jesus Movement was
primarily known as a late '60s and early '70s phenomenon. Even in
1975, I believe we were fortunate enough to still be experiencing a little
breeze from the spiritual wind that had been blowing. Like many and
perhaps most graduating classes, we had both a baccalaureate service
and a graduation program. I guess it was customary at the baccalaureate service for the graduates to sing a song together. It's pretty amazing
to me that we as a class sang the song "Day by Day." It was from the
musical *Godspell* and was later recorded by the Fifth Dimension. The
lyrics go like this: "Day by day, day by day, oh, dear Lord, three things I
pray—to see thee more clearly, love thee more dearly, follow thee more
nearly, day by day."

Keeping in mind this was a public school, I feel privileged to have
been a member of that class and applaud the folks who were behind

the song choice. It still surprises me that we sang it at all and love that we did. (I'm thinking it would be totally and completely politically incorrect for a song like this to be sung in public school today.) At graduation, I don't recall singing any songs, but I do remember traveling together on buses to the Seattle Center after the program for a senior party. We had an all-night dance that ended with breakfast in the morning. I also remember the band not being very happy when we were all dancing around in a big circle and knocked over one of their big expensive speakers.

Our People to People trip started with a couple days in Washington, DC, where we received some refresher US government history and also saw the sights (to include—"let me make this perfectly clear"— the Watergate Hotel). The boys in the group stayed in Calhoun Hall at George Washington University. One afternoon, I thought it might be fun to throw a Frisbee out of a top-story window of Calhoun for a friend below to catch (one of the old big Frisbees called a Sailing Satellite, made in the late '50s). What a dumb idea. It's amazing just how incredibly fast a Frisbee can fly when thrown from several stories up. Fortunately, I didn't take anybody's head off or shatter a car window.

Having the opportunity to visit our nation's capital was a huge privilege. Funny that what I remember most about that part of the trip had really nothing to do with the capital or how our government operates or the remarkable historical landmarks found in Washington, DC, or any of that. What I remember most is the wrestling match I had out on a big grass lawn with Dina. Dear Dina was a beautiful young lady and girlfriend to my longtime neighborhood buddy Mike. It was to be my responsibility to keep an eye on Dina during the trip. Lovely Dina was a little feisty, and she liked to wrestle (a beautiful girl in a tank top that likes to wrestle . . . oh my. . .) Things never went farther than a wrestling match, but I must admit that the whole concept of not obsessing over pretty girls was definitely being challenged.

Our trip to Europe included enjoying the hospitality of *homestays*, which just meant that we lived together with families in some of the countries we visited. The group's homestays were in Holland, Denmark, and England. The program also included traveling within England, Denmark, Holland, Austria, and Germany, with visits to Prague, Czechoslovakia, and Moscow, Russia. Prior to leaving on the trip, I had determined that I would be taking full advantage of the cultural exchange being offered to include the consumption of European alcohol if the opportunity were to arise. It did, many times. Travel within Holland and Denmark even included visits to both Heineken and Carlsberg breweries. So much for my "promise to God" about that one.

Our first stop on the European continent was Holland, and after a day in Amsterdam, we headed for our first homestay. I had the incredible pleasure of staying with a lovely girl named Willy along with her mom and dad and a nice doggy named Sita. Willy and her friends were also on break from school. They were enjoying summer much like we were in the States. This included going to several parties where—surprise, surprise—people were enjoying the inhaled smoke of something that had the very familiar aroma of hashish (which it was). I remember the night at one of these parties when my no smoking "promise" was scrapped. I also remember when late that night, after returning to Willy's house, I attempted to spend some time reading the Bible. (After "the dream," reading the Bible had become at least a little more of a regular practice in my life.) I had to admit that getting stoned that night didn't open my mind up to any fresh and inspired spiritual insights.

The week with Willy and her family was wonderful. They lived in Zuidlaren, a quaint little town in Friesland, Northern Holland. Willy and a couple of her friends owned horses, so we were even able to go horseback riding in the incredibly beautiful northern Dutch countryside. I remember not feeling very much like a rootin'-tootin' cowboy when, after having been at a gallop and even jumping the horse over a couple logs (hadn't done that before), I couldn't get my trusty steed to stop. After some serious yanking on the reins and finally slowing down enough to jump off, I ended up walking in front of my nice horsey for the remainder of the ride. Ye-ha! The village center of Zuidlaren was just a bicycle ride from Willy's house. One day we rode on the tandem bike into town and visited the old village church. Some guys were working on the building and, at Willy's request, allowed us to climb up into the top of the bell tower. While there, Willy thought it would be fun to ring the old church bell—so she did. We later found out that when the bell was rung, the priest or pastor or bishop or whatever (I'm not exactly sure what flavor the village church was) thought something was wrong and came to the church building. He must have either believed we were already gone or just didn't want to climb the tower because we managed to somehow miss him when we came down. We then learned from the workers (who had just been advised by the good padre) that it was forbidden for anyone to climb to the top of the tower. Forbidden though it may have been, the view from the top of the bell tower was pretty awesome. On the ride back to Willy's house, we stopped at a lake and rented a row boat. The water was so rough that after about a half hour we came in and switched to a canoe, thinking it might be easier to maneuver. We were able to better handle the canoe and had a great time, but the waves were so high that Willy and I both got absolutely soaked. Willy by the way, just in case I haven't mentioned it, was really beautiful.

From Holland, we travelled by train to Copenhagen Denmark. After a day of seeing the sights in Copenhagen, we all headed for our next homestay. I spent a week with a lovely couple and their three teenage children—two boys and a girl. I got to know the kids right off the bat by pulling out the Frisbee. That good old Frisbee was always a great ice breaker in any country and in any language. (Don't leave home without it.) Also, it didn't hurt having learned a few magic tricks from Mr. Fleming in the English class. Magic tricks are also a great international ice breaker. My Danish homestay family lived on and managed a working farm with lots of animals but were primarily raising pigs. Much like Holland, the countryside was beautiful, and I was able to enjoy it with the kids, often by bicycle. On one occasion, the whole family went to the beach for a swim. I swam to a rock offshore where I could climb out of the water and up onto the rock. I was a little surprised when a beautiful girl with no top on also swam out and joined me for a short time next to the rock. We exchanged pleasant greetings, and she then swam away as quickly as she had come. (I don't believe I ever did see this young lady's legs and remember thinking that she was perhaps a mermaid, like the little mermaid in Copenhagen.) My journal for that day reads, *Some of the women around here don't believe in wearing tops to the beach. It was a little different. I'm not complaining however.* While in Denmark, I learned from my homestay family that because I was the youngest child in my house that made me "the raisin in the sausage." I never knew if this was a common Danish phrase or only among folks involved with the pork industry.

During our visit to Prague, Czechoslovakia, a small group of us decided one night to go out with our lovely guide Helen and try some dark Bohemian beer. Unfortunately, the place with dark beer had no electricity due to a recent storm. We went to another establishment where we did drink Czechoslovakian beer, just not the dark Bohemian kind. On the way back to our hotel, a young man named Gordy and I thought it would be fun to pretend like we were fighting while walking down the road. We were swinging at one another and, at the same time, hitting our own chests to make a sound as if we were hitting each other. I even fell to the ground at one point as if Gordy had knocked me down. Suddenly, we heard the sound of a whistle blowing. Turns out we were right in front of a police station. Gordy and I had lagged a little behind from the rest of the group, so we were calling out for our guide Helen as the policemen brought us into the station. Helen did show up and try to explain the situation, after which time both she and Gordy were given breathalyzer tests. The police wanted to keep Gordy and I in the station (I'm guessing they had a cell in the back) for twelve hours. After much discussion and Helen's pleading in our defense, they decided that we could go. The words of advice that they directed to us and that Helen translated were "Do not play stupid American games late at night in Czechoslovakia." Okay, won't do that again. After resuming our walk to the hotel, dear Helen actually apologized to us for what had happened and stated, "They were drunk. They are not police but silly donkeys." Also, while in Czechoslovakia, I believe I may have witnessed the near electrocution of one of my friends and fellow People to People people. Paul and I found ourselves being roommates at several of our hotel stays. One day, while getting onto the elevator at the hotel in Prague, we noticed that when the doors were open you could see what looked like a positive and a negative connection on both the right and left doors. When the doors closed, these connections came together, and the elevator would then move up or down. For some reason, Paul had the idea to put one of his fingers onto a connection on the door on the right and also put a finger from the other hand onto a connection on the left door. (Thus completing a circuit.) He suddenly crumpled to the ground. I wasn't sure if he was playing with me or not. When I saw the dark rings under his eyes and realized that he really did need help getting up, I knew that he had actually been zapped. In all our wisdom, we went up to the room and never did get a proper medical evaluation for Paul.

Paul and I not only discovered how to receive a shock that will knock you off your feet from an elevator door in Czechoslovakia, but we also invented a game while drinking wine in Austria. Vienna is the home of a giant ferris wheel (the world's tallest from 1920 to 1985) known as the Wiener Riesenrad. Most of our group had decided that they were going up on the gondola-style Ferris wheel, but Paul and I decided to instead spend some time in a wine garden. While enjoying delicious bread, cheese, and wine, we also found ourselves discovering things to do with toothpicks. I think Paul used to carry toothpicks in his pocket, so this provided us with our needed game equipment. To play, each participant holds a toothpick in his or her teeth. At the ready, set, go, each player manipulates their toothpick using teeth, tongue, and lips only (no cheating, no hands) until the distal end—the one not in your mouth—ends up in one of your nostrils. First one wins. Depending on how much bread, cheese, and wine you incorporate in the game (not included), the fun just waiting to be experienced is unlimited. When I recently told my wife, Carol, about this marvelous wine-drinking game (also compatible with beer), she wasn't very impressed. I'm guessing that Milton Bradley probably won't be interested in the rights.

One night, while in Moscow, Russia, a few of us managed to sneak away from the hotel. There was definitely a tighter rein on the group during our stay in Russia. We made our way to a bar in another hotel and had a fun time talking with some folks from Hungary who were in Moscow for holiday. We also met and spent a long time chatting with a young lady from Paris. I can't remember her specific circumstances, except that she told us a very complex but at the time very believable story (at least believable for a group of teenage boys) of how it was she had no place to stay that night. The female member of our little group that had snuck away with us may not have found the story quite so believable. Why we thought we could invite our lovely new friend from Paris to come and stay at our hotel in one of our rooms I don't know, but we did. I'm sure it had crossed our minds that this beautiful young French girl could possibly experience evenings like the one she was having now for a living but that didn't sway our decision to invite her.

It hadn't occurred to us that the security at our hotel was a little more diligent than to allow an unknown young lady to just slip by the desk and stay the night in the room of a male, hormonal, teenage People to People student ambassador. We had to reluctantly bid her adieu.

The last country we visited on our incredible trip was England. After a day touring London, we spent that same evening at a Broadway-style musical theater and saw John, Paul, George, Ringo, and Bert. The story of the Beatles as told by Bert. It was so good, and being able to experience the play while in London was so very cool. The next day, we were en route to our final homestays. I was incredibly fortunate to be able to spend the week with our cousin's (on my mother's side) that lived in Congresbury, Somerset, not too far from Bristol. My brother Pat also had the privilege and pleasure of staying with our relatives while he was in England on his People to People trip. I took a train from London to Bristol and was there met by my cousin Les. (Les is actually the husband of Em, who is originally from Ireland and a cousin to my mom.) The next week was full of wonderful stories about my Grandma Bessie, sightseeing all over that part of England to include Bath and Cheddar and also a trip north to Shropshire and the town of Bridgenorth, where more family lived. I had a marvelous time. One memory that stands out in my mind is the evening that Les, Em, their daughter Pat, her boyfriend Ken, and Kevin (a friend of Ken's) all went to the Cadbury Country Club, where we were planning to have a bite to eat and a swim in the indoor pool. We got to the club; however, Les and I were turned away because we weren't wearing a dress jacket. Both tie and jacket were required to enter. After a quick trip back to the house, we returned with the appropriate apparel. When it came time to take a dip, Ken, Kevin, and I decided that as this was such a formal establishment, it would only be fitting to also wear our neckties into the pool. While swimming and splashing and just having a good time, it was brought to our attention that two young ladies who were carefully paddling around the pool were in the entertainment industry—one performing on stage in the theater and the other a TV personality. When we attempted to engage them in the festivities, they made it quite clear that they did not want to get their hair wet. We made quite certain that they did. Hooligans!

By the time the People to People trip was over, I was no longer so worried about doing the right or not doing the wrong things (my promise didn't last long) and wasn't thinking much about the old-man dream. I still knew though that something was not right. My spiritual life was definitely not what it should or could be. I'm glad when looking back at my journal from the summer of 1975 that although most of what I read is about a wholehearted effort to have fun, there are some entries that simply say thank you to God. That young man writing in his journal, although certainly not participating in an intimate relationship with Jesus, did at least have some sense of the incredible blessings that he had been and was being given.

CHAPTER 5

Wanderlust

Upon return home from People to People, I knew that my first order of business would be to earn enough money to leave on another journey. Many of my friends had decided on college or university, and some of them even knew (or thought they knew) what course of study they wanted to pursue. I knew that I wanted to travel. As mentioned earlier, my brother Pat had done some travelling, which in addition to People to People also included returning to Europe in 1974 to hitchhike and camp around Great Britain. He even camped at Stonehenge for two or three days along with about ten people that were living in a little make-shift commune. Stonehenge is an ancient and very mysterious group of rock structures that are located on Salisbury plain in England. There are lots of theories about the origin of Stonehenge. I think what is known for sure is that it is thousands of years old and that there doesn't seem to be a definitive answer as to who built it and why. Pat also pitched his tent inside of St. Michael's Tower, which sits atop the Tor in Glastonbury. The Tor is a huge mound that overlooks the county of Somerset. Saint Michael's Church built in the fourteenth century once sat on top of the Tor, but now only the tower remains. Legend of the Tor includes it being a place where the fairy folk live. (Pat and I were no stranger to fairy folk.)

Growing up, we had Jilly and Jolly (two Irish fairies) living in our kitchen cupboard. They were responsible for any of those annoying little mishaps or lost items from the cupboard that couldn't be explained. They had lived in my mother's house growing up and in her mother's house in Ireland before her. My kids have grown up with Jilly and Jolly living in our house. I'm pretty sure they will live in the kid's houses. (What I'm not sure about is how they manage to live in multiple houses at the same time. That's okay though—there are just some mysteries in life that we will never know.) Before making his hike up the hill to set up camp for the night, Pat first stopped at a pub in the village below. There was a sign posted outside the door which read, "No Hippies." He didn't go in.

While staying at a cheap hotel in London, Pat traded a book he was carrying for a paperback on the hotel book table. His new read was about sailing. Some days later, he traveled to the Isle of Wight, and after reading this little book and becoming an "expert sailor," he managed to talk himself into a crew position on a sailboat that was heading for Barbados. If I remember correctly, the sailboat was originally built in the early 1900s and actually had a grand piano on board. He was hired on and had a spectacular time and I'm sure really did learn an enormous amount about sailing. Unfortunately, when they reached Barbados, he or the captain or both failed to jump through the proper hoops where paperwork was concerned, and Pat found himself fearing that he was going to end up in jail. I don't know all the details, but I do remember my mom and dad being terribly worried and making phone calls to people or agencies or whoever that could help. Pat ended up flying home out of Martinique and was able to avoid jail time. So with travel tales like this, how could I not want to strap on a backpack and hit the road?

I was able to obtain employment at the same grocery store where I used to work as a box boy with a short hair wig. This time as a night stocker (not stalker), and no wig was required. I was in fat city with a $7-plus hourly wage. It was a night job, so this allowed the opportunity to enjoy the day, sometimes with not a lot of sleep and then work at night. (These days, I so appreciate a good night's sleep.) I was able to find an inexpensive little one-bedroom house that was actually attached to the office of a driving range. My backyard was the driving range, and the front yard was asphalt. Yard maintenance was great. I think the rent for this little piece of heaven was about $95 a month. (Mom and Dad graciously spent several hours helping me to clean it up before moving in.) I'm sure I would still recognize the smell of the musty, moldy carpet and the old oil heater. I would sometimes open the door of the oil heater and look at the little flame it produced, pretending I had a wood-burning stove. Occasionally, friends and I would go out back and hit a bucket of balls. The goal was to direct your drive so that you hit the little caged Volkswagen that was out on the range picking up golf balls. Good times. And with $7-plus per hour from the night stocker job, I could purchase the rare album, buy the occasional bit of smoke, eat on a budget, and still stash away a little savings for the future trip. Probably my biggest expense was trying to keep gas in a 1957 Chrysler New Yorker. It was beautiful but such a gas hog. By the time the summer of '76 rolled around, I had sold the New Yorker and was ready to hit the road.

Rod was a longtime friend from elementary and high school. He too was a cool-car enthusiast and used to drive a beautiful 1941 Ford to school. (He still owns that car today.) Rod and I would sometimes venture to the Pearl Street Antique and Sandwich Shop, which was located just outside of Point Defiance Park, a wonderful place for incredible rich and creamy cheesecake. On more than one occasion (and after spending a little time with his meerschaum pipe), Rod and I may have even eaten a whole cheesecake. We may have in fact used that same method to down one of their delicious carrot cakes. (Oh, to be young and slim with a rapid metabolism.) I remember the day I stopped by the sandwich shop just to show my airplane tickets to Tammy and Shirley, the two lovely, earthy sisters that owned the establishment. The Antique and Sandwich Shop was also home to Victory Music. Victory Music was an organization that brought together local musicians, great musicians, who played their music in a variety of venues around the region. One of these venues was open-mic night at the sandwich shop. I enjoyed many a Tuesday evening listening to great music along with a good cup of coffee and maybe a toke. Before moving their Tuesday nights to Pearl Street, Victory Music used to be located in underground Court C in Tacoma. I can still recall the lovely hippie waitresses with hairy armpits at the coffee shop where the musicians played. I also remember an open-mic night when a gentleman was playing Bob Dylan. He really did sound just like Bob Dylan. I decided that night that nobody except Bob Dylan can pull off sounding like Bob Dylan. Rod decided that he too was ready for an adventure and that he would like to join me on the trip to Europe. We purchased open tickets to fly into London with a return good for a year. Upon arrival to Heathrow Airport, we were pretty much ready and willing to go wherever the wind blew.

Journal entry:

> *"Thank You, Lord. It is now about 7 in the morning of May 31. We are in Earl's Court London at a hostel. We arrived yesterday morning at around 9:30. A van with three American girls and an English guy gave us a ride into the outskirts of London. We later received a ride from a man in a tiny little fiat. He was from Egypt and worked at the Egyptian embassy.* [This would be our first lesson about trying to hitch-hike with two people both carrying large backpacks in a country with several compact cars on the road.] *Later yesterday, we met a guy in Hyde Park named Rayad, who was from Saudi Arabia. We got high with him in the park.*

Our flight to England included a stop in Chicago. (It was a windy city that day.) While waiting at the airport, we met a young guy named Ralph. Ralph was en route to his mom and dad's home located about thirty-five miles outside of London. His dad held some kind of government position, I believe, with the American embassy. Mom and Dad lived in a beautiful big home with tennis court and pool. They were having a giant party on May 30, and Ralph was kind enough to invite us. I think the celebration was for Memorial Day in addition to being our nation's bicentennial with July 4 only a month away. If I remember correctly, they were going to be celebrating both. It probably would have been considered bad form for a US government official to have a huge party in Great Britain on the Fourth of July to celebrate our nation's independence, so thus the Memorial Day gathering. At any rate, for some reason, Rod and I decided not to try and make it for the party but to instead wait a day before paying Ralph and family a visit.

As I write this, I am sitting in a hotel room in Sequim Washington. For the last two days, I have been attending a CISM or critical incident stress management class. The training provides instruction and certification in assisting persons, primarily medical and law enforcement persons who may be struggling after experiencing a traumatic event while on the job. Earlier this evening, I went to a cool little bistro in town that also had live music on Thursday nights. I had such a great time listening to acoustic music that so reminded me of Tuesday night open mic at the Antique and Sandwich Shop. It was a really good time.

So Rod and I did make our way to the house of Ralph's parents. His folks were kind enough to invite us to spend a couple days with them as well as to help them get rid of some awesome leftovers that still remained from the party. (It must have been a huge party. I was a little sad that we didn't make more of an effort to get there when all the festivities were taking place.) We had a great time nonetheless and thoroughly enjoyed their gracious hospitality and generosity as well as the hospitality of some nearby pubs. (There really is something about the atmosphere of an old English pub.) From Ralph's place, we returned to London and spent a couple more days sightseeing and girl-watching and pub-crawling and pretty much just basking in the realization that we were in London Town. We then decided to make our way to Bristol and to the home of my wonderful relatives, Les and Em. Looking back, I am a little surprised and embarrassed that I would be willing to just drop in on my cousins without even giving them some kind of warning first, but that's exactly what we did.

Journal entry:

Sunday, 6/6/76

We arrived in Bristol shortly after 2 on Friday. From there we were directed across town to the motorway. After about an hour, we were able to hitch a ride into Congresbury. I felt like I was going home when we got into town, and I was happy to find that I remembered the way to the house. Fiona [one of Les and Ems lovely daugh-

ters] *was the only one home when we arrived,
and she was very surprised to say the least.*

Not only was I willing to impose on my dear family in England, but I was willing to bring along a friend when I did it. And just like the year before when I had stayed with Les and Em during the People to People program, these wonderful folks displayed a hospitality that was totally over the top. Rod and I ended up spending about a week with the family and couldn't have felt more at home.

Journal entry:

Sunday, 10/11/2015

Hello, Lord. So I have started looking over what was left of (A Journey) and plan to start continuing the story from where it left off. There was so much of it I don't think I can possibly remember. Hoping that you will help bring back to my memory the things that were written. Seems like as the years go by, my memory gets worse and worse. Half the time, I can't even find my wallet or my keys. Guess we'll just see how this goes.

This is the place in the memoir where I managed to misplace about thirty-five thousand words. It's both a little discouraging and at the same time kind of exciting to think that I get to try and write some of those things again. It was fun the first time. And so the journey continues.

After our week of enjoying the hospitality of my family, along with the beautiful countryside of Congresbury, Rod and I decided it was time to start looking for some kind of employment. It was the hay season, and we were hoping to find work on a farm either in England or Wales. Congresbury was quite close to Bristol, and just north of Bristol was the Severn Bridge. We were only about twenty-five miles from the bridge that would bring us into the area where England borders Southern Wales.

Journal entry:

Wednesday, 6/9–

Yesterday Rod and I went hiking up in the woods and then went to a few pubs in Congresbury. Today we set out for the Severn Bridge. We walked to the roundabout (stopped for a nice lunch along the way) and got a ride from a young guy who was going to travel with his wife as far as Bristol. We were then picked up by a couple guys in a double-decker bus. They had just been living in teepees. There was a little boy [probably about two years old] *sitting in the sink. (Poor little guy had a diaper full.) We then had a three-paper ciggie, which did me in. They gave us a ride to the bridge, which we walked over.* [After being dropped off by the bus, both Rod and I ended up needing to lie down in the grass. That three-paper ciggie our double-decker tour bus so graciously provided was a giant joint loaded with tobacco and hashish. Not being a big cigarette smoker, just the tobacco would have probably made me dizzy, but mixed with the hash, I needed to lie down before I fell down or hurled. We never did get the full story as to why our bus driver and tour guide / herbalist had been living in a teepee. Sounds like hippies to me.] *Not far on the other side of the bridge, we got another ride from a guy that works for Rolls-Royce. He ended up bringing us through the Wye Valley* [a beautiful rural part of southern Britain that straddles the border between England and Wales] *almost to St. Briavels, which is way up on a hill, and the area is unbelievably beautiful. I have to remember to keep in mind that God made all of this. We are now camping in a cow field for 25P* [less than 50 cents], *and we had a nice dinner in the owner's house. He runs a bed and breakfast. Good night for now.*

The village of St. Briavels rests within the Royal Forest of Dean in West Gloucester. Probably the most famous feature of the village (at least for the typical visitor) is St. Briavels Castle. Built between the late eleventh and early twelfth centuries, this moated fortress is apparently regarded by some as the most haunted castle in all of England. In addition to being haunted, this old English castle has also been home to a popular youth hostel since around 1950. Next to the castle sits another famous historical site, St. Mary's Parish Church built in the twelfth century. As mentioned in the journal entry, Rod and I were able to find a place to camp in a kindly farmer's field. Not only were we pitching our tents in an incredibly beautiful setting that was within a stone's throw of two famous English historical landmarks, we were (more importantly to the two of us) also just a short walk from the George. The George was (and I'm pretty sure still is) a wonderful old pub right next to St. Briavels Castle. It also happened to be the only pub in the village. As such, it became our go-to place while residing in the Forest of Dean.

Journal entry:

Wednesday, 6/16/–

Friday, we walked around the area, looking for work on one of the local farms. We went to the Willsbury Farm, and that's who we are working for now. Saturday we went to the town carnival and had a good time. [Rod and I were fortunate enough to be in St. Briavels at the same time as their annual summer carnival, also known as the fete. One of the carnival highlights was the wellie wanging competition. Wellie wanging is the art of heaving a Wellington boot as far as you can. It really does require a little technique; I'm afraid I didn't represent the good old US of A very well when attempting to compete by giving a wellie a wang.] *Sunday we stayed around the area, and that night we went to the George and met two young guys who were singing and playing guitar. Their names were Berry and James, and they were really great. They dropped by our tents after the pub closed and got high for their first time. I felt a little guilty contributing, but they seemed to enjoy themselves.*

James and Berry truly were excellent musicians. They played all sorts of late '60s early '70s favorites (in addition to the classic pub tunes—Wild Rover etc.) but were especially gifted at classic Simon and Garfunkel. They became good friends to Rod and I and were kind enough to show us all around the St. Briavels area and even invited us to join them to a couple of their music gigs. I did feel genuinely guilty being a part of James and Berry's first encounter with marijuana. Our new friends had made it known to us that they would like to try pot, and although at this time in life I wasn't demonstrating any sort of restraint when it came to herbal inhalants, it also wasn't something that I was recommending to others. That would be the only time we had a toke with Simon and Garfunkel, mostly because it was the last of what little bit of herb both Rod and I had brought with us on the trip.

As noted in the journal entry, we obtained employment on the Willsbury Farm. This large dairy farm was managed by a very nice couple named Mike and Rosemary. In addition to managing the Willsbury, Mike also owned another farm which he had recently obtained from his brother. Between the two farms, there was plenty of work to keep Rod and I busy for over two weeks. As part of our working conditions, Mike and Rosemary invited us to camp in their yard and also have access to a bathroom and shower in the house. After only a few days, we were graciously upgraded to rooms in the house. Before finishing our time working on the farms, Rod and I had enjoyed more than a few great meals in the house and even an after-dinner brandy or two. Because it was hay season, our primary job was to bring the bales in from the field. This meant picking up and throwing them (sometimes over your head) onto a trailer. It was great exercise and good healthy work. Something every teenaged lad should have a chance to experience. In addition to throwing around bales of hay, we also had opportunities to drive around on big farm tractors (first time I ever drove a tractor) and also to drive from one farm to the other (on the wrong side of the road) in the work jeep. I even had kind of a significant "life moment" one night on the farm when we had to help a momma cow give birth. Her calf was positioned in such a way that it needed some help delivering, and we had to hook chains on its legs and pull him or her out. (And I'm talkin' both Rod and I pulling really hard.) Growing up, we always had dogs and cats and as a result lots of puppies and kittens born in the house. Seeing new creatures being born had always been an awe-inspiring experience, but now seeing this calf—one minute struggling to come into the world, the next standing up on wobbly legs and then not long after, learning to walk and starting to nurse from its momma—was all pretty amazing.

Journal entry:

Friday, 6/25/-

It's a beautiful day. Thanks so much! Today we're leaving for the Lake District with James and Berry. Up until now, everything has been fantastic. I thank God that life can be so good. Well, I guess I'd better go start packing.

After having thoroughly enjoyed the privilege of being a working guest in the village of St. Briavels in the Royal Forest of Dean, Rod and I accepted an invitation that we couldn't refuse. Our musical friend James had a brother who lived in the north of England in an area known as the Lake District. The Lake District is that part of Northwest England famous for its lakes, forests, and mountains. These "mountains" include the largest mountain in England at 3,209 feet, Scafell Pike. (I must admit that having been born in Washington State with Mt. Ranier at 14,411, Mt. Adams at 12,281 and Mt. Baker at 10,781 feet, I wasn't terribly impressed with Scafell Pike.) Having said that, although we ended up camping at the foot of Scafell Pike, we managed to find some lame reason not to climb it. Looking back, I so wish I'd taken the opportunity to scale the highest mountain in England. We ended up spending about a week with Nick and his lovely wife, Wendy.

(I will always remember Wendy in her singsong voice reciting, "Eat your macaroni, Joe." My mother used to say, "Eat your minestrone, Joe, every bloody day." We stayed over a week in the Lake District, enjoying the wonderful lakes, the very cool nearby waterfall, the swimming and hiking, and most importantly, the pubs.

Journal entry:

Friday, 7/2/-

Well, we never hiked up the hill on Monday, but instead went to a lake and swam. We left that night and got back to Nick and Wendy's about ten. Nobody was there so we had a few drinks at the nearby pub (whose owners by the way once lived in Florida.) The next day, Rod and I gave a hand at a farm down the road. It belonged to a really nice couple and their daughter. That afternoon Berry, James, Rod, and I went to a fantastic waterfall in the woods about twenty minutes from Nick's. It was fantastic. I dove off a rock up the ledge a few times, and it was great. We left that evening about seven, heading for Sammy and May's. The car was overheating every twenty minutes, so we didn't make it to Bridgnorth until about 1:00 AM. Sammy and May were surprised to say the least when I knocked on their door at that time.

Without question, I have been blessed with the most wonderful (and tolerant) relatives that any person could ever ask for. Near the town of Bridgnorth, in the county of Shropshire, lived Sammy and May. May was sister to dear cousin Em. The summer before, during the People to People trip, Les and Em had brought me up to meet and visit with Sammy and May. They made me feel so incredibly welcome and a part of the family during that visit that I felt comfortable enough to knock on their door at one in the morning a year later along with three other people they had never met. (What an incredibly rude young fellow.) Sammy and May greeted us with open arms. James and Berry were traveling back to St. Briavels, so the next morning they headed out—but not until after enjoying the lovely breakfast that May prepared. If I'm not mistaken, Sammy was even able to help the guys with the car's overheating problem before they left. Rod and I enjoyed about a week with my wonderful family in Bridgnorth. Some of that time we spent working over at the farm of their daughter June and her husband Keith. June and Keith ran a dairy farm, and once again, Rod and I were given an opportunity to work with the hay harvest. We were very glad to find that it wasn't all work and no play at the farm when Keith showed us the supercharged go-cart he had made and that he allowed us to scream around in a little. In addition to working and playing at Keith and June's, Rod and I also spent quite a bit of time with Sammy and May's daughter Christine.

Journal entry (continued):

Friday, 7/2/-

Wednesday night, Sammy brought us out for a drink. Thursday we hitched into Bridgnorth and that afternoon we went to Ludlow on Christine's school bus and saw a fantastic production of Hamlet. It was actually done at an old castle and was really fantastic.

(I guess it must have really been "fantastic.") Christine was about the same age as Rod and I and, I'm guessing, must have been involved with some kind of summer school program. We were fortunate enough to be invited to join Christine and her class on a school trip and ride on the school bus to the beautiful Old English village of Ludlow. Sitting atop a small hill and surrounded by the medieval walled part of town stands Ludlow Castle. It was at the site of this wonderful old castle that we enjoyed a theater production. Nobody would have accused me of being a huge fan of Shakespeare at that time in my life. My perspective managed to change a little after experiencing a presentation of *Hamlet* within the walls of an eleventh-century English village at the foot of a stone castle. (It was truly amazing.)

It was during our visit with Sammy and May that Rod and I decided it was time to go our separate ways. Traveling with a friend had been a great experience, but I was now looking forward to heading off on my own. (It had also been fun to have an ongoing cribbage match with Rod during our travels. He ended up being the grand champion in the end.) I had decided that Ireland would be my next destination, and Rod planned to head for the European continent.

Journal entry (continued):

> *Friday, 7/2/-*
>
> *Last night we went out with Christine and her boyfriend, Lester. Later we went to a small party at Chris Yate's house (Chris and her sister Carolyn are both very beautiful, and I've fallen madly in love with both of them.) Thank you so much, Lord.*

Alas, madly in love with two beautiful sisters or not, it was time to go.

CHAPTER 6

Emerald Isle

Journal entry:

Monday, 7/5–

Today Rod and I left Sammy and May's and have now gone our separate ways. He has headed for Great Yarmouth and is then going to the continent, and I headed off for Stranraer. [Great Yarmouth is a seaside resort town on the east coast of England and Stranraer is a port town in southwest Scotland from where I would be taking the ferry to Larne Northern Ireland.] *I got very many really nice rides—one by a lady whose son is going to travel Europe, another by a man who owns seven shoe stores, one quite long ride by a very nice guy who bought me a cold drink at a service stop, and the last, just a few exits by a young guy. After the last ride, I walked up to a house to ask if a nearby town had accommodations. I am now camping in their field. I spent the evening watching Bonny & Clyde in their house. I can't believe how fantastic people can be.*

After a couple days and several rides (the last one being a commercial truck that brought me over one hundred miles) I arrived in Stranraer and was able to catch a boat to the Emerald Isle. That first night in Northern Ireland, I spent camping in a field in the seaport town of Larne.

The year Nineteen Seventy-Six would prove to be an incredibly violent year in Northern Ireland with nearly three hundred deaths due to "the troubles" and over two hundred of those killed being civilians. I must admit that I arrived in Ireland without a clear understanding of just what was really behind this violence. I had hoped that after spending some time traveling throughout both the north and south I would have a better handle on what was actually going on. The truth is, even after nearly two months, I never did.

From Larne, I was able to hitch a ride from a nice gentleman in a dairy truck. (Riding in the milk truck brought back great memories of my youth when Marty the milkman would sometimes give me a ride in his truck from our house up the gravel road to our mailbox.) As I recall, however, Marty and I never did discuss religion during our short ride up the bumpy gravel road. One of the first questions that the kindly Irish milkman asked during our trip was whether I was Catholic or Protestant. Although I had grown up in a Baptist church, I had never given a lot of thought about being a Protestant or a Catholic. Truth is, I simply considered myself a believer in Jesus. That's what I told Mr. Milkman: "I'm just a believer." Thankfully, this answer was enough to satisfy his question, and we went on to talk about some simpler things.

My lift from the kindly milkman ended in the village of Ballymena, where I hoped to make contact with another wonderful relative, cousin George. George was married to Sadie, sister to Em and May, my delightful motherly cousins in England. Ballymena was at that time a town where coal was converted to gas at the gasworks and where cousin George was employed. Before trying to get in touch with George, I first made a stop at the logical place to pause when arriving at a new Irish village—the pub. While at the public house, I met a guy named Pete. Pete was careful to point out a small group of long-haired gentlemen who were playing pool, one of which according to Pete was "a really bad guy." Wouldn't you know it, it wasn't long before Matt (the really bad guy) and his friends had invited me over to play pool and were buying me pints and sandwiches. No question about it, Matt was an interesting character. He told me how he and his mates would load up into a van and go down south for "a good punch up." When I asked why they would do this, Matt gave a lame excuse about disliking Catholics because "they prayed through a priest instead of directly to Jesus." Yeah, right. I suggested to Matt that he and his buddies just liked to have a good punch up—they just liked to fight. He didn't disagree. By the time I finally made it over to the gasworks, George had already gone home for the day. The nice lady in the office was kind enough to give George and Sadie's house a call, and not many minutes later, dear cousin George was there to pick me up.

Journal entry:

Saturday, 7/10/-

Well, just like at my relatives in England, I'm being treated absolutely fantastic here in Ireland. Yesterday George, May, and Winifred [May and Winifred are two of George and Sadie's five kids] *brought me out for a look at the country, and it's really beautiful.*

For the next several days, I had a chance to see much of Northern Ireland's spectacular countryside and unique sites—places like the Giant's Causeway, an amazing natural wonder along the northern coast of county Antrim. It's made up of about forty thousand interlocking basalt columns, the tallest nearly forty feet high. The tops of the columns form stepping stones that lead from the cliff foot out into the sea. You really have to see it to believe it. In addition to having a chance to travel around a little, I also had an opportunity to work alongside George out in the peat fields. We cut and stacked bricks of peat moss, which were used in the home to heat and cook. We also brought in a couple trailer loads of the bricks that George had already cut and that were already dry. George pulled the trailer to and from the peat field and the barn with a wonderful old crank start tractor that amazingly was still up and running. (I felt like I was participating in some genuine Irish culture.) Another piece of Irish culture that I so thoroughly enjoyed and so genuinely miss is an evening out to the Irish pub. English and Irish pubs are such a unique experience and are unlike anywhere else in the world. George and Sadie were parents to Ann, May, Winifred, Barbara, and wee George. Barbara was married to Roy. Dear Roy definitely went out of his way to make sure that I had every opportunity to experience and enjoy the wonderful pubs in county Antrim and vicinity. What made an evening to the pub even more memorable was coming back home to George and Sadie's and enjoying a late-night hot cup of tea along with some kind of wonderful fresh baked scone or biscuit or griddle bread or maybe even a bite of each. So good!

Journal entry (continued):

Saturday, 7/10/-

Barbara and Roy came over, and we all went out to the local pub. I really had a great time. I even had the honor of meeting lovely Molly, the infamous barkeep at the pub.

Molly was famous for, among other things, her rare and beautiful presentation of the Swan Dance (something I believe only a chosen few were given the honor of experiencing). She didn't grace us with dance that night, but fortunately, this would not be my only visit to sweet Molly's.

Journal entry:

Saturday, 7/17/-

I am now at Bessy and Henry's house. Wednesday I helped George collect a couple trailer loads of peat from the field. We had quite a day of it. (This trip is really fantastic. Thank You, Lord, very much.) First of all, we got stuck in the moss for about an hour. Then when we got home again, the tractor wouldn't start, and then when it started, it quit on our way back from the field. That evening we came here to Bessy's. Their children are Tilly (who is in London working for the embassy), Alfy (who is here doing more work than I ever want to), Emma, and Melva. Friday, I worked with Henry, Alfy, and a guy named Wally bringing in the hay. Today I also brought in the hay. I don't think I could be a farmer because I wouldn't want to work every day as hard as I have the last two.

Not only did I have the privilege of staying with George and Sadie, but I was also invited to spend some time on the dairy farm belonging to cousin Bessie and her husband, Henry. Bessie was sister to Em, May, and Sadie. Bessie was also, by the way, named after my Grandma Bessie. I ended up spending about a week at Bessie and Henry's and was able to have one more opportunity to "bring in the hay." I also had an opportunity to see why I would never choose to own a dairy farm. What an unbelievable amount of work—all day, every day, forever and ever, amen. Cousin Alfy was the one and only son to Bessie and Henry. As such, it was a given that he would be inheriting the farm. I remember asking Alfy if he really wanted to be a farmer and felt a little bad for him when he responded, "It's all that I know how to do." I was hoping that Alfy really loved to be a dairy farmer, because if you didn't, it would be really, really hard. I was almost surprised that he even found the time to take a rest on Sunday, although it was pretty much just long enough to go to church. The cows still had to be milked—twice a day.

Journal entry:

Sunday, 7/18/-

Well, today Henry, Bessie, and I went for a drive around the area. First, however, I went to church with Alfy and Emma. Alfy locked his keys in the car, so it was quite comical after church to see about twelve men trying to open the door with their keys. I gave them a hand with a piece of wire and opened the door.

[Always was pretty good with a coat hanger.] *During our drive we went to Oatlands, the house where Grandma Sharp* [Bessie] *was brought up.*

I had heard stories from cousin Sadie about how she remembered attending large parties at Oatlands as a child, sitting on the staircase with the other kids and watching the guests coming around the circular drive by horse-drawn carriage and being dropped off. I could imagine it being a pretty grand place in its day. At the time of my visit, it was a working farm, and the owner was kind enough to allow me to have a little look around the inside. There was something very cool about being able to visit the house where your grandmother grew up in Ireland. (Over the years to come, I would have a couple more opportunities to visit Oatlands, once with my parents and then also with my wife and kids.)

Journal entry:

Sunday, 7/25/-

Well, on Monday the 19th we finished up with the hay that was ready, and that evening, Bessie and Henry brought me to George and Sadie's. Saturday evening, Barbara and Roy brought me to their friends named Ken and Roberta. Ken had some moonshine (potcheen) made by his friend Fred, and I had a glass. It smelled a little like a doctor's office, but I didn't think it tasted bad. Roy, on the other hand, thought it was awful. We then went to a pub and managed to get quite messy. [Only the boys mind you.] *Fred played his flute on stage and was very good.*

As was often the case in an Irish pub, there was traditional Irish music being played that night. It just so happened Fred was one of the great musicians performing. In addition to being a skilled potcheen distiller and a great flute player, Fred was also known to make very special walking sticks out of black hawthorn. On our way home, after closing the pub down, we all stopped by Fred's place where I was presented with one of his wooden creations. He had taken a branch from a black hawthorn bush and apparently soaked the head of it in rutabaga juice (that's what I was told, really) until it became pliable. He then formed that part of the stick into what looked like a duck's head. The little walking stick traveled with me into several countries and remains one of my prized possessions today.

Journal entry:

Friday, 7/30/-

Hello again. Well, it's now Friday, and I've ended up staying here at George and Sadie's a little longer than I expected. Monday I helped with peat a little and that was about all. Tuesday George Jr. and I painted some and later went to the peat field. [Cutting and collecting the dried peat bricks was a pretty important part of life for a family that depended on them for fuel.] *The next few days were pretty much the same until last night (Thursday) when Barbara and Roy brought me out. We went out of town to a couple of places, both of which turned out to be closed. We then made a mad dash to try and get to Molly's before she closed. We raced and got there just before 11:00. As it turned out, we didn't need to fear her closing at all. Among the people there were the chief of the CID (Criminal Investigation Department), one of his detectives, and the detective's friend who was the champion bagpipe player of Ireland* [that's what I was told]. *It was fantastic. Both the detective and his friend played the pipes while Molly and some others, including the chief, danced. It was really a lot of fun.*

It was pretty hilarious to see the chief get more and more loosened up throughout the night and watch him trying to dance with my lovely cousin Barbara, who was very pregnant at the time. Barbara, who was not imbibing due to her delicate condition, was a great sport and even graced the well-primed chief of the CID with a dance. And speaking of dance, sweet Molly did not disappoint. I am privileged to say that on this very special night I witnessed her rare and beautiful swan dance. Thank you, Molly.

Journal entry:

Sunday, 8/1/–

The time I spent at George and Sadie's and Northern Ireland in all has really been fantastic. Today though, Barbara and Roy and May and I came down into the South with Greg, Ann, and Winifred behind us. [We came down in two cars.] *I am now near a town called Sligo. I was let out very near a big waterfall and am now staying just up a hill beside it. It's really a beautiful place, and I just hope I don't get too wet because it's been raining. Things are really too good to be true, and I really thank the Lord for it.*

Journal entry:

Monday, 8/2/–

It's now about 12:30 in the afternoon of the 2nd. After getting up this morning, I packed up and headed for Sligo. That was around 10:00, and I made it about a mile down the road. It's pouring down rain, and I'm inside what looks to be an old mill of some kind. Hopefully, the rain will stop soon, and I'll be on my way. (After looking around, I'd say this building wasn't a mill but possibly a coal- or ironworks.)

Journal entry:

Wednesday, 8/4/-

Well, I finally made it into Sligo and went just a few miles outside of town when I stopped for the night. The next day (yesterday), I went into a little shop to pick up a few things and ended up getting a ride from a guy who was selling confections. He brought me into Ballina with a few stops on the way. After Ballina, I was picked up by a really nice couple named Patty and Phillip. They were on their way to Castlebar for Patty to get a checkup because she's due to have a baby in couple of weeks. Well, Phil and I had some pints while we waited for Patty, and then we went on to Westport. Phillip is a policeman, and two days ago, he went on a big raid of an IRA camp up in the middle of nowhere outside Westport. We went and looked at the place where it was, and it was really pretty incredible to be able to see this. Well, after leaving this place, they decided to bring me all the way to Achill. On the way, we picked up two more hitchhikers named Rita and Anne. We all then went to Keel on the island and stopped for a couple pints. I hope Phillip and Patty made it home okay because we had more than a couple.

[Phillip and Patty were such incredibly kind people and couldn't have been nicer to me. It became very clear, however, after Phillip and I enjoyed some pints while Patty was at her appointment with the obstetrician, that alcohol caused him to lose any sense of "how fast is too fast when driving?" On the road to Achill Island, we were going very, very fast on roads that were way too narrow and way too windy and way too dangerous to be driving really, really fast on. Lovely Rita and Anne and I were all more than ready to reach our destination of Keel on Achill Island and get out of the car. Looking back, I wonder if Patty, who hadn't been drinking any alcohol, was someone who just never drank or if she was a little ahead of her time with considering possible problems with drinking alcohol while pregnant. I don't think it was until 1981 that the Surgeon General began warning women about drinking alcohol during pregnancy. Whatever the case, I just hope that she was the designated driver when they finally started for home.]

After we finally left the pub, I offered my tent to Anne and Rita, and that's where they slept.

Travelling with a tent on your back would prove to be a pretty great way to get around without having to worry so much about where you were going to sleep that night. It could be set up pretty quickly and just about anywhere that didn't cause the landowner a lot of grief. And not only did it provide me with a place to stay, but on several occasions, I was given the opportunity to share my little shelter with new friends who were also needing a place to spend the night. As mentioned, it could be set up *just about anywhere.* On this occasion, I choose a field not far from the pub and just off the village road. Everything was fine until quite early the next morning when we had cows stepping on the corners of the tent and trying to poke their heads into the door. They may have been being coaxed on by the farmer who was just outside and who was making it pretty clear that he didn't appreciate my choice of campsites. Oh well, lesson learned—sort of. This wouldn't be the only time I would need to quickly pack things up and vacate a location.

Achill is the largest island off the west coast of Ireland, and I had heard that it would be a good place to enjoy some traditional Irish music. After that first night in Keel, I found a nice secluded little spot next to a bog lake where I could enjoy a lakeside campsite with a place to bathe and still be close to a local hotel/pub with lots of guests also enjoying some vacation time on the island. (Because the bottom of the lake where I stayed was peat moss, the water was almost black to look at. When bathing or paddling around in the water, I sometimes wondered a little if some cousin to the Loch Ness monster was going to have me for lunch.) In addition to this little lakeside resort, I also spent some time camping on the coast near the village of Dooega. I think it was while listening to some traditional music at a pub in Dooega that I noticed how many old guys had yellow fingers from cupping their cigarettes. (I must say that it was a huge surprise to me when in 2004 Ireland became the first country in the world to ban smoking in closed public spaces.) When thinking about Irish pubs, I can't help but remember the pints of Guinness and cider, the wonderful traditional Irish music, and the cigarette smoke. Truth is, I even started to roll my own during that phase of life.

Journal entry:

Saturday, 8/14/-

From Achill Island, I headed for Killorglin and the Puck Fair. Made it to Galway the first night where I met some people from Dublin. They were Lowell, Patty, and their three children. I was very happy I met them because they ended up picking me up again in Clare, where I wasn't getting any rides. My first really bad thing happened this day because when I was tying my pack on their car, I set my hat down and then forgot it. I didn't care about losing the hat, but I feel really awful about losing the Mizpah pin that Mom gave me. They brought me to the Shannon Ferry.

One of the many beautiful natural features that you see when traveling down the west coast of Ireland are the wild fuchsia bushes that line the coastal roads. Unfortunately, when Lowell and Patty picked me up in county Clare, I set my hat on one of these lovely hedges but forgot all about it until we were several miles away, too far away to go back. *Mizpah* is a Hebrew word that is associated with a phrase found in Genesis 31:49, where it says, "The Lord watch between me and thee, when we are absent one from another" (KJV). I believe the pin had originally belonged to Grandma Bessie, who gave it to my mother, who in turn gave it to me. My brother Pat had also worn the pin during his travel adventures. I can only hope that it went to a good home. I also hope that the hat which the pin was attached to also made it to a good home. Although it didn't have the sentimental value of the pin, it had been hand made by a wonderful old Greek hatter that used to have a shop in downtown Tacoma. (It was cool.) After taking the ferry across the Shannon River and going from county Clare into county Kerry, I finally made it to Killorglin. Killorglin was home to the Puck Fair or "Fair of the He-Goat" one of Ireland's oldest fairs and a great place to hear some traditional music. (I was blessed to hear so much wonderful music in Ireland that I almost feel a little guilty.) What makes the Puck Fair a little more than just an excuse for three days of beer and music is that the reigning king of the fair is a goat. A goat catcher goes up into the mountains where he (or perhaps she) catches a wild goat and brings it back to the village where it is crowned King Puck. Some say that the Puck Fair is the oldest fair in all of Ireland. It can apparently "officially" be traced back to 1603, when King James I issued a charter granting legal status to the existing fair in Killorglin. Another little something about the fair that makes it even more unique (and that doesn't set real well with animal rights activists) is that King Puck reigns over the festivities from atop a caged pedestal that's raised about sixty feet in the air. I got the impression that with the exception of having to witness all the drunken antics going on below, it wasn't such a bad gig. The good king seemed to be treated very well and probably enjoyed a much better diet (at least for a few days) than most any other wild goat on the Emerald Isle. While enjoying the music, beer, and overall festivities of the Puck Fair, I became friends with a group of people who had come over from Brittany. Brittany is located in northwest France and is bordered by the Bay of Biscay to the south, the English Channel to the north, and the Celtic Sea and Atlantic Ocean to the west. Although Ireland and Scotland were pretty much the only places that came to my mind when thinking of Celtic music and languages, it turns out the Celts apparently dominated much of western and central Europe in the first millennium BC. As a result, they brought their language and customs along with them. Even today, in addition to French, the Celtic language Breton is still spoken in Brittany. And where there is Celtic language, it only makes sense that there would be Celtic music. My new friends from France had also come to enjoy the great music to be found at the Puck Fair.

Journal entry (continued):

Saturday, 8/14/-

Well, I finally got to Killorglin. I met some people from France (Brittany rather). They are Herve, Elizabeth, Bridgett, Henry, John Pier, and Pascal. They were really nice, and I will be meeting Herve, Elizabeth, Bridgett, and Henry on the 21st or 23rd and going to Brittany with them. They invited me to Herve's sister's wedding. I left on Friday and came here to Dingle, and that's where I am now. It's really beautiful country. Today I've moved my tent to a really beautiful place along the water. Last night was really great because when I went to bed there was someone in a tent nearby playing folk music on a fiddle. Things are really going great.

Dingle is a wonderful little village found on the westernmost point of Southern Ireland on the Dingle Peninsula. I would so encourage anyone visiting Ireland to try to make a stop at this incredibly beautiful part of the country. Not only was the scenery magnificent, but there was also more wonderful Irish music to be found. One evening, I accompanied some newfound friends to a local pub where we stumbled into an impromptu Irish music jam session that (so we were told) included a couple guys from what was becoming a popular Irish folk group, the Fury Brothers. After closing down the pub, just about the whole place headed to the beach for a bonfire.

Journal entry:

Saturday, 8/21/-

During my stay in Dingle, I became good friends with two brothers named Martin and Lance, also Lance's girlfriend, Anne. I also met up with two Germans named Martin and Andrae. We all had one really good night last Sunday when we had a big fire on the beach with about forty other people. There were also some beautiful girls from Dublin camping nearby, and I had a nice swim in a nearby pool with one named Fiona. [Near to where we were camping, there was a beachside guesthouse that had an outdoor pool. Lovely Fiona and I were able to enjoy a clandestine middle-of-the-night dip in their pool. However, I can still remember the water being so cold that my teeth were chattering.] *Well, I left Dingle on Tuesday and made it to Cork. I stayed in the hostel for two nights and visited with Lance and Anne both nights because they live in Cork. Thursday I got a lift from a really fantastic guy named Lynn, and he brought me to his parents' house, where he, his wife Mary, and their two children are staying for the summer. They are really great people, and I ended up pitching my tent in their backyard. Lynn and Mary even brought me out for a movie. I left yesterday and made it here to Rosslare last night. I had a bit of a shocking experience yesterday when I got a lift from a Catholic priest.*

Up to this point, I had hitchhiked several hundred miles throughout England, Scotland and Ireland and met many wonderful people along the way. My ride from a Catholic priest, however, although it got me a few miles closer to my destination, turned out to be a strange one for sure. Long story short, this man of the cloth tried to put his hand down my pants. Actually, while telling me how "fit" I looked, he tried to slip his hand into my bib overalls. (Hey, I get it—a young, shirtless, tanned, sinewy American boy wearing old bib overalls—how was this dedicated servant of the Lord to be expected not to act like a creepy old pervert?) I wasn't sure whether to punch him in the throat or what. Although that was my first thought, I figured since he was driving, it probably wasn't the best plan, so I simply told him to "pull over now." He did. No question, it was a pretty weird experience to be hit on by a Catholic priest. Probably most troubling was that here I was, a young seeker who would have truly appreciated and could have benefited from a heartfelt conversation about things that matter. It made me wonder how many people had come to this (most likely) very respected, so-called man of God in search of spiritual counsel and instead encountered someone with something very different than their spiritual well-being on his mind. I must admit that this very unexpected encounter did significantly skew the Father Flanagan image I had of what an Irish Catholic priest should be like.

The Vendange

Journal entry (continued):

Saturday, 8/21/-

I met up with Herve, Elizabeth, Henry, and Bridgett last night, and I will be leaving on the boat with them in a few hours. (Life is really good.)

From Southern Ireland, I would be traveling with my Puck Fair friends on a boat to Le Havre, France. We all met up in the village of Rosslare and, from there, walked to a spot near the Ferry Landing, where we could sleep on the beach. From our waterfront campsite, we were also able to enjoy a late-night skinny dip in the Irish Sea before leaving the beautiful Emerald Isle. Although it was a cold swim, the water felt warm compared to the teeth-chattering dip I had enjoyed with Fiona in Dingle.

Journal entry:

Tuesday, 8/24/-

Well, the boat ride was nice with the exception of feeling a little rough.

[Although the cruise across the Celtic Sea and English Cannel did turn my stomach a little, it wasn't so bad that I couldn't enjoy a bowl of French onion soup that someone had left on a table in the dining area. It seemed like such a shame to waste a perfectly good bowl of soup. Given the same circumstances today, I probably wouldn't eat someone else's leftover soup, at least not someone I didn't know. Life was a lot simpler then; at the time it seemed like the obvious thing to do. And the soup was delicious.]

We got into Le Havre Sunday, and Henry left for Paris. Herve and I then hitched together, and Bridgett and Elizabeth went together. Herve and I got good lifts on that night by two guys and a girl who smoked with us and also bought us sandwiches. We arrived at Herve's grandmother's yesterday around 3:30. I have met many, many cousins, and they're all really nice. Today I'm writing this from a nice little patio in the backyard.

Journal entry:

Saturday, 8/28/-, approx. 1:45 AM

Thank You, Lord, so very much for such a really great life.

While in Killorglin at the Puck Fair, I was invited to attend the wedding of Herve's sister Swaziek. The wedding was to be held not far from the port town of Brest in northwestern France near the Breton peninsula. For the few days prior to the wedding, we stayed in a wonderful old farmhouse belonging to Herve's grandmother, where Herve had visited often while growing up and where he had spent many days exploring the beautiful rocky beaches. One afternoon, we went to the nearby shore of the Atlantic and played on a beach that was totally made up of huge rocks. The game that Herve showed me was how to leap from one giant rock formation to another without falling off and breaking your neck. It really was fun. More than once though,

I half-considered just what bones would likely break if I didn't quite make a jump.

The wedding of Pat and Swaziek was held in a wonderful old stone castle. What an amazing thing to have been invited to be a guest at this very special event. Although I couldn't understand everything spoken in the vows, it really was a beautiful ceremony. Even more than that—it was an amazing party. Barrels full of French wine, lovely female cousins of Herve who loved to dance, and a Celtic band providing the awesome traditional music that we danced to. Not only did the band play great music, but they also (and on more than one occasion) invited me to join them during their breaks for a toke.

Journal entry:

> *Saturday, 9/4/-*
>
> *(Beautiful day.) Well, Swaziek and Pat had a very beautiful ceremony. I met so many really nice people while staying in Kersaint* [the area where Herve's grandmother lived]. *The night of the wedding, I met four people that played in the traditional folk band (Phillipe, Jean-Eve his brother, Patrick, and Fabea). I ended up getting a lift to Lorient on Sunday by some friends of Pat* [the groom]. *There I met up with Phillipe, and we took a boat to the Ile de Groix* [the Island of Groix].

While at the wedding, Phillipe had told me that he and some friends would be hitchhiking to the Bordeaux region of France to make a little money working the vendange, or grape harvest. Knowing that I was in search of some seasonal work, Phillipe was kind enough to invite me to join them. We would first rendezvous with a group of his friends on the beautiful Ile de Groix, Brittany's second largest island located just a ferry boat ride from Lorient. Phillipe and I arrived in Groix in the evening and met up with the folks that we would be picking grapes with. Our little group included Dominique, Olivia, another Phillipe, and Maryvonne. Oh my goodness, Maryvonne . . . I fell in love with her the first time I saw her. As it turned out, she was girlfriend to my friend Phillipe from the wedding. Oh well, c'est la vie. We spent a couple days camping on the island, and during that time, I was introduced to their amazingly delicious regional crepes. I had eaten crepes before, but these were made with a special buck wheat flour and filled with all kinds of local yummy ingredients—so delicious.

Journal entry (continued):

Saturday, 9/4/-

Phillipe, Maryvonne, Phillipe [the other one], *Dominique, Olivia, and myself headed off for the grapes. That's where we are now. We are on a farm just outside of Rauzan. The last few days have really been great. Phillipe is a chef, and Maryvonne is also an excellent cook, so we have been eating fantastic food. Last night, we had rabbit, and it tasted great. (It was the first time I had ever eaten it.) It would have tasted better, however, if I hadn't gone up to the rabbit cage and watched the rabbits the day before. I found out later that we would be eating some of the bunnies. (Last night, a hedgehog came into our house. He was very shy, however, so I don't think he will be back.) Lately, I have been giving some thought as to where I'll be going after here. The way I'm thinking now, after Paris it will be toward Israel.*

[While hitchhiking in England, I was picked up by a young lady in a little convertible (I think it was an MG) who had spent some time on a kibbutz in Israel and suggested that it might be a nice place for me to spend the winter. As the weather was cooling a bit in Europe, Israel was sounding like a real possibility.]

> *We'll just have to wait and see though. Just now, I am sitting in a beautiful little field (very near the cement pool where we wash our clothes) and drinking a bottle of wine. It's very nice because we get all the wine we want.*

We *did* get all the wine we wanted, that is until we sort of exploited the privilege. Not only was wine provided in the fields so you could quench your thirst while picking grapes, the kindly proprietors of the farm also gave us free and open access to the wine cellar for after-work. We had been provided with a big plastic pitcher that was meant to be used for washing up. Lo and behold, it also made an excellent container for evening wine. (It held a whole lot.) It didn't take too many nights of quaffing giant plastic pitchers full of wine for Mr. and Mrs. Vineyard owner to give us a pretty clear message that we had lost our privileges. It was my turn to make the run for wine with the blue plastic pitcher. What was this? The door to the wine cellar was locked. Nobody mentioned that we no longer had an open-door policy to the cellar. Surely, they didn't mean to lock us out. Surely, this was a mistake. Surely, I was able to justify climbing through the open window above the cellar door to gain access. Not only was I able to justify climbing through the open window on that occasion, but I also agreed to make a return trip the following evening. This time, I was joined by a lovely Scottish lass who was part of a group of Scott's that were working at the same vineyard. My plan was to climb through the window and then open the door from the inside so my cohort could help fill containers. (We had a large group of vendange workers back at our quarters and would need more than just the blue plastic pitcher.) I did climb through the window and did open the door for my helper. Before filling our containers, however, we were totally and thoroughly terrified by the grandpapa who was waiting in the shadows of the cellar and who jumped out at us, holding what I think was a pitchfork. (Guess he figured we would be coming.) We ran away without our evening ration of wine. (I think I saw a little smile on the grandpapa's face while we were running away.) We understood very clearly after that night that our wine privileges were gone.

The seasonal workers at the vineyard were all provided with a place to stay, a place to cook, unlimited wine (for a while), and access to a shower. Unfortunately, we all had to share one shower that was set up in a barn. One day after work in the vineyard, I may have jokingly suggested to Maryvonne that by showering together we could both preserve water (just trying to be ecologically responsible) and also cut down on the total time in the shower, thus benefiting the whole group. Much, much to my surprise, she thought this would be a great idea. Talk about my wildest dreams coming true. This insanely beautiful French girl (girlfriend to Phillipe) that I fell madly in love with the first time I saw her (girlfriend to Phillipe) wants to shower with me (girlfriend to Phillipe). What a weird and wonderful and ultimately uncomfortable situation to get myself into. Our first couple showers together, we were paid a visit by Phillipe. He wandered into the barn, spoke a little together with Maryvonne in French, and then wandered out the way he came. He must have decided that he could trust his beautiful naked girlfriend to my capable hands because our following showers together were uninterrupted. No question about it, the thought of making mad passionate love to Maryvonne did enter my head—a bunch. What would also come to mind, however, was the sound of Phillipe's voice telling me how much he loved Maryvonne. I felt like she and Phillipe were a very loving couple together—with the exception of her being very amenable to sharing the shower with me, which did add an element of confusion to our simple life on the grape farm. It was all very cool and very hippy-ish, but after a couple weeks of washing one another's backs, I suggested to Maryvonne that it would perhaps be better for all of our friendships if she and I stopped conserving water. She agreed. I know for sure Phillipe was a much happier man.

Just a short walk from the farmhouse was the village of Rauzan. In the village of Rauzan was a cafe that, in addition to being home to a wonderful big black Bouvier, also happened to be where we would often go for a night out on the weekends (and maybe on rare occasion during the week). It was here that I met many people from all over Europe who were also working the vendange. Among those were a group that had come over from Scotland and who ended up working on the same farm that I was on. Tommy was sort of the leader of this little band of crazy people from Scotland. Someone in the group had referred to Tommy as "mad with it," and it was so true. One evening, Tommy was in "mad with it" mode as he wore a rubber mask of the then president of France (Valery Giscard d'Estaing) and tried to dance with just about everyone in the room. That wouldn't have been so bad, but he also felt compelled to grab some of the people he was dancing with by the crotch. Fortunately for Tommy, it was a friendly (and forgiving) crowd in Rauzan that night who understood his drunken condition. Nobody knocked his head off. (Although come to think of it, Tommy would probably have loved a good punch-up.) One night at the cafe, I was introduced to two young Scottish lassies who were enjoying an evening out and who managed to give me quite a lesson in the English language. Honestly, I couldn't believe what I was hearing come out of these young ladies' mouths. Having grown up the youngest of four boys, having grown up near two military bases, and not having grown up in a bubble, I wasn't immune to smutty language. For the most part, however, the people I knew—and in particular the young ladies I knew—could all carry on an engaging conversation without feeling the need to throw in all kinds of four-letter nastiness. Not so with our lovely ladies from Scotland. In the short time we were together, I experienced more feminine foul mouth than I ever had in one sitting. I may have jokingly mentioned to them how unusual it was for me to hear two girls talking the way they were and how it didn't seem so very ladylike. They may have jokingly (or not) told me to f—— off.

Journal entry:

Sunday, 9/24/-

Hello. Well, it's now Sunday, and tonight we eat our first meal in the farmhouse. I can hardly wait. [The little group of folks that I had come to the farm with were invited to start taking breakfast and supper meals in the farmhouse—in spite of our being winebibbers.] *As have been the last few months, the last few days have been beautiful. Yesterday was very special. Last night, we went to the cafe and met three people (two from Versailles and one from Paris). They were very nice, and after leaving the cafe, we all had a smoke. Maryvonne, Phillipe, and I then started our journey home. We had the most fantastic* [actu-

ally it was pretty strange] experience when we got here. We were just heading for the door when we all saw Adolphine [Maryvonne's nice kitty that had traveled with us from the Isle de Groix] *sitting on the stone wall. I was just about to pet her when I realized that it wasn't Adolphine but just a bottle and a plastic wash pan. We had all seen Adolphine at exactly the same time and then suddenly the bottle also at the same time. And I really did see, and we all saw the cat. I think because we were all thinking that Adolphine was sitting on the wall, our heads put her there.*

This was to be sure a very unusual experience that none of us were able to explain. While reaching to pet Adolphine and then realizing that it was a bottle and plastic wash pan that I was about to pet, I looked over at Phillipe and Maryvonne and saw the same surprise in their faces that I was feeling. Coincidence? Power of suggestion? ESP? (Probably not.) I don't know. It did make me consider though just what kind of things our minds might be capable of. I know that unusual occurrences happen all the time, and if I'd only had one of this kind of experience in my lifetime, I probably wouldn't even have given it a second thought. It just so happened, however, that I had another "coincidence" occur just about a week prior while on a little day trip with Phillipe. We had decided to hitchhike into Bordeaux one Saturday with the intention of buying something to smoke. Phillipe seemed to think that if we went to a particular park in the city, we would be able to meet someone from whom we could make a purchase. Phillipe was right, and we did meet an overly friendly, purplish henna-haired young man in the park who indicated that he could help us with our quest. We followed him to an old apartment building in what appeared to be kind of a sketchy part of town. Phillipe and I were asked to wait on the street while he went inside to let his associate know that we would like to make a transaction. After what felt like a very long time, our new friend came down accompanied by a young lady. She instructed us to follow her inside the kind of creepy-looking old building and up the dark stairway to where the exchange would take place. (This whole thing was feeling more and more wrong all the time.) We followed her upstairs to a dark hallway where another guy was standing. They insisted that we give them the money after which time they would go inside an apartment and bring us back our herb. We were left standing in the hall while they walked around a corner out of our sight. That was the last we saw of any of our new friends and the last we saw of the money we had given them. So looking back on that whole encounter, I guess we should have just been grateful that we weren't robbed of any other money or valuables (which wouldn't have amounted to much) while upstairs in the hallway of a dark, creepy, old apartment building with some sketchy folks that were all about ripping people off.

After our attempt at buying some pot took an unpleasant twist, Phillipe and I decided it was time to forget that plan and return to the vineyard. Which brings us back to our little "coincidence." We caught a ride in a van and were on our way back to the farm. Neither of us was very talkative, probably because we were both feeling incredibly stupid for losing our money the way we did. In addition to thinking about how stupid I was, I was also thinking about how hungry I was and how much I was looking forward to eating something when we got home. In particular, I was thinking about how much I would like to eat pizza. The only problem was, we didn't have the capability of making pizza back at our quarters, and the cafe in Rauzan wasn't in the business of making pizzas. It was just what I would have liked to eat at that moment. I asked Phillipe what he would like to eat when we got back, and he responded with this question. Do you know pizza? I realize that this was no big deal and that these sorts of things happen all the time. Had there not been the unusual evening with Phillipe and Maryvonne (and Adolphine) about a week later, I probably would have forgotten all about it. I might have still forgotten about both incidents had there not been another strange thing happen in Israel in the months to come. I'll say more about that a little later.

Journal entry:

Monday, 10/4/-

Well, we're all finally finished at the farm. I can honestly say that I was ready to go. It got

*to be really fun the last few days. All in all, I
think everybody had a pretty good time at the
grapes. Friday night, they even left the cellar
door open because they knew we'd be going in.*

Our gracious employers and owners of the vineyard really did
display a huge level of tolerance to our little group of grape pickers.
Especially when you consider it wasn't just our little group but also
the totally crazy bunch from Scotland as well. All things considered
though, I think we were all (even the totally crazy Scott's) hard workers.
We played pretty hard, but I think that we all worked pretty hard too.
We did get the grapes picked. And when all was said and done, we were
even given back our wine privileges for the last couple days. My biggest
regret about the time on the farm is that after running out of film for
my camera, I didn't make an effort to buy more until it was too late. I
don't even have pictures of many of the unique and colorful and great
people I was fortunate enough to meet and spend several wonderful
weeks with.

One of the many people I became friends with while at the
vineyard was a young lady named Veronique. Vero had come from
Cognac to work the grape harvest and try to make some money. She
lived in Cognac with her husband Patrice and sweet baby boy Jeremy.
Veronique left the harvest a little early but, before going, invited me to
come and stay with her, Patrice, and Jeremy and to work the vendange
with Patrice at a vineyard just outside of Cognac.

Journal entry (continued):

Monday, 10/4/-

*Now I am at the house of Veronique, whom
I met at the other farm. She is at home with
her husband, Patrice, and their son, Jeremy.
They are really beautiful people. Maryvonne,
Phillipe, Olivia, and I came here with Jon Louie
yesterday.* [Jon Louie was a fellow vineyard worker who
had a car and who was going to Cognac.] *I will be starting the vendange here tomorrow and staying*

with Patrice and Vero. I really can't believe how fantastic everything has been. Thank You, Lord, very much for making life so great.

Sunday, 10/10/–

Well, things are really fantastic. Phillipe and Maryvonne and Olivia left on Wednesday. Since then I have been working with Patrice and getting to know he and Vero very well.

[Patrice and I were working on a farm that was a few miles from their house. The farm was far enough away that we would often end up with frosty eyebrows after the early morning commute to get there. Each day one of us would ride the moped, and the other would ride a bike while at the same time hanging onto the shoulder of the guy riding the moped, thus letting it pull him along. After a few weeks of going back and forth to work like this, I almost started to feel like a local boy going to a regular job.] *Patrice and Vero are very strong believers in God, and it's really great to be with them. They hope that in the near future they'll be able to start a community in the country. I pray that it happens for them. I might even end up helping them out.*

Friday, 10/15/-

Well, it's been a wet week at the vendange. It's all right though. Today I was given a change of clothes because my coat and shirt were so wet. The people at the farm are really fantastic. A few nights ago, we went to the house of Anika and Pierre [friends of Patrice and Vero]. *It was really fun. There was a guy named Patrick, who spent about four years in the States. He has an amazing dog named Ash that eats fruits and nuts. I couldn't believe it when she ate some of my walnuts and then some pineapple. Yesterday Patrice and Vero received a letter from Maryvonne and Phillipe. For some reason, Maryvonne said to say happy birthday to me* [My birthday is actually in January], *so tonight I was surprised with a little cake and a little clown made in Austria. His name is Joshua.*

Tuesday, 10/26/-

Well, many things have happened in the last week. I've become friends with Jack and Stella. They're really nice people. They have invited Patrice and Vero, and I to come to their home for a week after the vendange, so it looks like that's what we'll do. A few days ago, I painted a picture on Jeremy's bed, and I'm really happy with it. [It was a painting of a teapot being used for a vase and holding a bouquet of flowers. I was in my Cognac period.] *Yesterday we began working on Mr. Buzanga, a man for Stella and Jack. It should be good.*

Mr. Buzanga was a life-sized man made of hay that we were planning to bring to Jack and Stella's as a thank-you gift for inviting us to stay with them. I had been tasked with painting Mr. Buzanga's face. Unfortunately, my interpretation of what he should look like turned out to be more of a scary guy in a dark alley than a friendly straw man. Vero walked into the dark living room one night (forgetting about Mr. Buzanga) and had a nasty fright when she was surprised (unpleasantly) by Mr. B sitting there in a chair. The next day, he went through some changes and was transformed into more of a big lovable clown version of Mr. Buzanga. (Fortunately, neither Jack nor Stella had a fear of clowns.)

Journal entry:

Saturday, 10/30/-

Yay! The vendange is finished! We finished yesterday. After work we had a fantastic feast at the farmer's house. It was really great.

Sunday, 11/7/-

Since Wednesday, Patrice, Vero, Jeremy, and I have been at Jack and Stella's farmhouse in the country. [They really liked Mr. Buzanga by the way.] *Jack is an amazing artist, and he and Stella are both very nice. Stella keeps a garden, and they have some excellent homegrown that she grew. (It's scary nice.) Yesterday I took a long walk, and it was really great. I saw a flock of wild geese going south. I also found a little bird but was afraid to try and bring it all the way back, so I just put him in some shelter. (Flash: tonight Stella and Vero gave Jack, Patrice, and I each a sack, and inside mine was a really fantastic sleeping shirt and some sleeping shorts (right out of Little House on the Prairie). The shorts aren't really my type, but the shirt is great.*

Jack and Stella lived in a great, old country farmhouse. Although I think I remember a fireplace in the house, my bedroom did get pretty chilly at night. The wonderful vintage nightshirt I was given was thoroughly appreciated.

Much of the time with Jack and Stella (and Mr. Buzanga) was spent simply enjoying the country, though we did try to pitch in and participate with chores wherever we could. One afternoon while Patrice and Jack were in town, I thought it might be helpful to try and replace some of the broken clay tiles on the roof of the barn. Many of them were really old and really brittle. Although I did replace a number of tiles, I may have broken about as many while crawling around on the roof. If I remember correctly, that was my only day of "helping" with roof repair.

CHAPTER 8

Paris

Journal entry:

Sunday, 11/13/-

It's now Sunday night, and Patrice, Vero, Jeremy, and I came back about an hour ago from the film Barry Lyndon [apparently a very popular movie when it came out]. *The film was okay. It was surprisingly easy to understand in French.* [When it wasn't obvious what they were trying to say, I would just use my imagination.] *We came back from Jack and Stella's on Friday. It was nice staying with them. Tuesday (if things happen this way) I'll be going with Jon Christopher* [a friend of Patrice and Vero's] *to Paris. He drives a truck and goes a few times a week.*

Back at the vineyard near Rauzan, I was introduced to a gentleman named René. René had come to the vendange from Paris. I think his connection with our little group was that he knew Maryvonne through her older sister. René must have been a bit too late in the harvest to obtain employment because I don't remember him ever picking any grapes. He did, however, stay on the farm for a couple days, and in addition to sharing his hash with us, René also graciously offered me a place to stay if ever I was in the City of Lights. With the weather getting colder, I was more and more thinking that Israel would be a good destination for the winter. I also started thinking that this might be a great opportunity to take René up on his offer and spend some time in Paris before heading east.

Journal entry:

Sunday, 11/27/-

First of all, I might have written this before, but it doesn't matter. While in Rausan, I had a very fantastic dream. I was cutting the grapes, and it was very wet with much mud. I began to sink in the mud all the way up to my neck and then over my head. It was very fantastic because in the dream I just thought that's okay. It's time for me to go. It was a surprise for me to have this attitude. I hope I have the same when the time comes.

[I don't know if it had anything to do with the dream or not, but I really don't feel like I've had any kind of fear of dying since that time. Come to think of it, I don't think I remember ever having an overwhelming fear of death.]

For the last couple weeks, I have been staying with René in his home. Also with his cat Bull and two friends, Jean Marie and Vivian. We visited Pigalle, which is a street with many nasty clubs. We also visited the Champs-Élysées, which is like the fifth avenue of Paris. (Very expensive.) Also while here I've visited Bridgette and Elizabeth from the wedding.

[It was wonderful to spend a little time with Bridgette and Elizabeth, the lovely girls I met at the Puck Fair in Ireland and then accompanied to the wedding in Brest. During one of our days together, the ladies thought it would be a good cultural experience for me to assist them with a little job they were involved with. I would be helping to distribute posters that advertised cultural events (things like concerts or plays or maybe a world-famous Lipizzaner Stallion show). The poster is called an affiche. I was given a stack of posters and instructions to go from business to business and just say, "Acceptez vous les affiche?" This was a short way of asking if they were agreeable to posting one of the advertisements on a window or on a wall in their shop. It was no problem when a business owner responded with a simple yes or no, oui or non. The problem occurred when someone wanted to know more about the event or wanted to talk about the weather or discuss the price of peaches or whatever. My mastery of the French language was embarrassingly nill even though I'd been in the country for a few months. Gratefully, all the folks I spoke with in the shops maintained a good sense of humor even though after I asked them a question in French, I couldn't carry on any kind of conversation. That was probably about the time I started to realize how important it is to try and make an effort to learn some of the language in the country where you are a guest.]

A few days ago, Jean Eve [brother to Phillipe, member of the band at the wedding in Brest, and resident of Paris] *and I went to Bridgette's house and stayed the night. The next day Jean had to go to work, so we parted company on the metro. Well, naturally I forgot the name of the station near René's place, so I spent about three hours in Paris just walking around and riding the metro. René and friends seldom pay for the metro but instead just jump over the machine. I was feeling very brave, so this morning I jumped over the machine and thought everything was really groovy until I heard a whis-*

tle and noticed the three policemen just across the tracks. They told me to go up and buy a ticket "toot sweet," so I did. [I was very grateful that the kindly policemen didn't arrest me for being a stupid boy.] *Oh yeah, I didn't mention that I've visited the Louvre twice now. It's very big and very beautiful.*

[Although I couldn't possibly take in all that the Louvre had to offer, even in two days, I did have an opportunity to see and say hello to lovely Mona Lisa. She does have a compelling smile.]

Lately, for the last day or two, I've been thinking about heading directly for Greece and Israel. I think it would be very nice to be in Israel for Christmas. Oh yeah, I went to an English bookshop in Opéra. I bought two books, I Heard the Owl Call My Name and Oliver Twist.

Sadly, I was probably more of a reader back in '76–'77 than I am today. Although I wasn't expanding my mind with anything terribly deep, I was enjoying some light reading of things like *Watership Down* (purchased in England), *I Heard the Owl Call My Name*, *Oliver Twist*, and a few others thrown in between. I ended up spending about a month at the flat in Paris, and truth be told, it sometimes felt a little like something out of *Oliver Twist*. I was not the only wayfaring stranger to benefit from René's incredible hospitality. We were often joined by a few extra visitors finding a place on the floor to crash for the night.

In addition to visiting all the must-see sights (the Arc De Triomphe, Champs-Élysées, Eiffel Tower, Notre-Dame, the Louvre to name a few), I also had a chance to do some things that were a little off the beaten path. One day for instance, René, Katherine (a friend of René's who sometimes stayed at the flat), Jean Marie, Vivian, and I all took a little day trip to the Père Lachaise Cemetery. The cemetery was resting place to a friend of René's who had died from a heroin overdose. We spent a quiet, spiritual moment at the grave side (actually we smoked a joint) and then made our way to another burial site. This second grave—although often visited as evidenced by the flowers and notes and other assorted memorials left around the graveside—was unmarked. We were at the grave of Jim Morrison, lead singer of the Doors. I had always been a Doors fan, and it did feel pretty cool to be able to visit his grave. I had been enough of a fan to do a comparative study of Jim Morrison and Walt Whitman for an English project (the name of the class was Grandfather Rock) during my junior year in high school. As part of an oral presentation, I played a song by the Doors for the class and was able to borrow a huge powerful stereo system (with big speakers) from my friend Terry. It was gonna be great. I was going to rock the halls. But then after all the work of picking up the fancy big stereo, delivering it to the school (in my mail truck), and setting it up in the room, my teacher wouldn't let me crank it up (not even a little). The class next door hardly even knew I played the song. I could have used my portable 8-track instead of Terry's awesome turntable. Although I still enjoy the music of the Doors today, truth is, after doing the research about Walt and Jim, I came away from the assignment thinking they were both pretty weird guys. Much like at the graveside of René's friend, we spent a quiet, spiritual reflective moment (actually we smoked a joint) and then said au revoir to Mr. Morrison. In 1976 the grave was unmarked. Apparently, several markers have since been placed and then stolen from the site over the years. I believe the gravestone that currently marks the spot was placed there by Jim Morrison's parents at the twentieth anniversary of his death.

While in Paris, I started asking questions and trying to figure out what might be the best way to get to Israel. I wanted to ultimately find a way to Athens and from there fly or maybe take a boat to Tel Aviv. Somebody suggested an organization called Provoya. Provoya was in the business of putting travelers with cars together with travelers needing a ride in a car to a like destination. Driving and the cost of gas were shared. My encounter with the gentleman at Provoya would help to reinforce for me the truth that it's so important to at least try and use the language of the country you are visiting. I walked into the office to find kind of a philosophical-looking long hair sitting behind the desk. He appeared to be rather engrossed with a book he was reading. Upon approaching the desk, rather than make any effort to converse with him in French, I asked in English, "Excuse me, do you speak English?" He looked up and in English responded, "Do you speak Russian?" Obviously he did, as well as probably six or eight other languages. What I could hear him really asking was "So you can't even try to speak a little French?" My new friend from Provoya did ultimately hook me up with a ride to Belgrade, Yugoslavia, with a gentleman that was traveling home to visit his family.

Journal entry:

Sunday, 12/12/-

I will be leaving Paris with a man named Lubo for Yugoslavia. I got this ride through Provoya, and at this moment, I'm waiting for a call from Lubo so we can see each other and talk about the journey. [I did hear from Lubo, and we set up a rendezvous in a cafe where we were able to meet and check each other out and determine that the other guy didn't look like a crazed axe murderer.] *Now I've met Lubo, and he seems like a nice guy. The way it stands now, we'll be leaving at about 6:20, Tuesday morning. Or at least we think we're leaving then.*

Yesterday, Katherine, René, and I went to Versailles and to the palace. We didn't go inside, but we went in the big park just behind it. It was really nice. We went to one place that may have been a bath. It had a high fence all around it with barbed wire. When I went to the gate, it was open. It was a beautiful place for a doodie.

[I am certainly not an advocate of pooping in public, and had there been a toilet available that didn't charge an unreasonable fee, I wouldn't have chosen to relieve myself in the gardens behind the palace of Versailles. Under the circumstances however. I was very grateful for this secluded little spot.]

After leaving the park, we went to a cafe for a coffee, and after that, we started walking toward the train station. On the way, René "obtained" a little chicken from an oven outside of a shop. It was a little greasy, but it tasted good.

[It was a surprise to me when René started breaking off and passing around pieces of a cafe rotisserie chicken that he had snatched while we were walking. Although I didn't approve of the stealing, I also didn't say no when invited to eat some of the goods.] *We then took the train to the Champs-Élysées, where we ate a hamburger at McDonalds. (It was just as bad as it is in America.) We then went and saw The Lady and the Tramp. It was really good.*

Classic Disney movies are great in every language.

CHAPTER 9

Kibbutz

Journal entry:

Thursday, 12/16/-

Well, at the moment, I'm sitting in (really its outside) the train station at Belgrade Yugoslavia. We left from Paris on Tuesday morning as was planned but we were a little late. Monday night we all went to a concert— Caravan and Kevin Ayers & Soft Machine. [I wasn't familiar with either of these bands prior to the concert.]

It was really great. I must admit that I was a little surprised at myself, however, because I bought a "petite trip" for Katherine and me. [For some stupid reason, I decided to take up an offer from a guy standing in the concert line who was selling acid.]

It was nice, but I don't think I'll make a habit of it. We arrived home about 1:30 or 2:00 and then talked until probably about 4:00. I was supposed to meet Lubo at 6:30 but managed to fall asleep about 5:00 and didn't wake up until he called me at 10 minutes to 7:00. He was a little upset to say the least. I raced to the station, but when I got there, I didn't see him. I was sure he had gone alone. He didn't though because I'm now in Yugoslavia, waiting for the train to Greece.

[After Lubo's phone call, I frantically hightailed it to the agreed-upon location only to find that he wasn't there. I looked around and waited for twenty or thirty minutes, the whole time becoming less and less hopeful that I still had a ride. Just when I was about to leave, Lubo came out of the cafe where he had been enjoying a cappuccino and watching me become more and more sure that he was gone. But he wasn't bitter.]

Tuesday we drove from Paris to a town about 190 kilometers into Austria. I drove a few hundred kilometers with Lubo telling me how to drive all the way. We stayed in a guest house that night and the next morning continued on through Austria and Hungary, finally arriving here in Belgrade about 4:00 this morning.

Lubo was more than willing to have me drive, which I was happy to do. Between all the snow throughout Austria and Hungary and Lubo's incessant commentary on my driving, it did however prove to be a little stressful. Lubo made sure to let me know that if I were to be in a car accident or run into a farm animal that wandered into the road (which wasn't out of the question considering the horrible driving conditions) I would probably end up in jail regardless of the cause. He shared this encouraging news as we were driving in the pitch dark of night during a heavy snowfall just outside of Budapest. We had stopped I think twice by this time to knock off the snow that had covered our headlights. Good fun.

With the exception of some pretty horrible weather and a couple intimidating Hungarian border guards, the road trip from Paris to

Belgrade was good. I even received a little geography lesson when driving across a bridge that spans the Danube River in Budapest. Turns out that Buda and Pest are actually two cities that weren't joined together to become Budapest until the late 1800s. I never knew.

As mentioned in the journal entry, we arrived to Belgrade about 4:00 AM. Lubo was in a hurry to get to his folks home, so instead of bringing me into the city center, he dropped me off on a road a few miles outside of town and pointed me in the right direction. (I think Lubo was still a little ticked about me causing us to get a late start from Paris.) I started walking in the direction of town and, along the way, noticed a little working man's cafe next to the railroad tracks in what appeared to be a train yard. Inside were a few guys who looked as if they might work for the railroad. My hope was that someone in the cafe would be able to tell me how long it would take to walk to the train station. I definitely didn't speak any Serbian (or whatever dialect the gentlemen in the cafe were speaking), and none of them seemed to know English. After trying some words like *locomotive* and even *chuga, chuga, chuga* and then pointing to my pocket watch, one of the fellows communicated to me that I was about forty-five minutes from the station. (Turns out I really was.) Before leaving the cafe, I ordered a cup of coffee and had my very first encounter with the Turkish kind. I wasn't aware that there were fine coffee grounds in the bottom of the cup until I ended up with a mouth full. Lesson learned.

Journal entry:

Friday, 12/17/-

Well, I caught the train at the station, and when I was just getting on, I met a boy from Yugoslavia. He was with a group of students who were going to the town of Skopje for a grammar contest. I sat with about seven of them, and it was really nice. One guy played the accordion very, very fantastic. I drank some rum and talked a lot and fell asleep. In Skopje, I had to change cars, and once again, as I was getting on, I met two brothers from

France. They were also traveling to Athens, so we came together.

[It's almost unbelievable when thinking of all that has occurred in Yugoslavia since my brief visit in 1976. I certainly never expected to one day be hearing about the brutal fighting between Serbs and Croats or to see the breakup of the country into Slovenia, Croatia, Bosnia-Hercegovina, Serbia-Montenegro, Kosovo, and Macedonia. Did I miss anyone? I would have never thought that the future of Yugoslavia would take all the turns that it did, not while laughing and drinking rum and listening to accordion music on a train with a group of fun-loving young Yugoslavian students.]

We arrived about 12:00 this afternoon. As I was changing money, I met another boy from Switzerland. His name was Beet. We spent the afternoon together, and then I came here to the airport. I arrived at the airport about seven, and it's now around 11:00. My flight is at 12:45 tomorrow, and if I'm not asked to leave, I'll be spending the night here. Once again, as always, I must thank the Lord for making everything so fantastic.

Sunday, 12/19/–

All right! It's really great. Before I get into what's happening now, I'll continue with the night at the airport. At about 12:00, I met a guy named Roger from New York. He was going home after a year's travel in Europe. Well, he left about 4:00, and I went to sleep. The next day, I left on the plane as was scheduled.

Flying to Israel from Greece in 1976 was my first experience with serious airport security. While traveling I always carried a Buck Knife in my pocket. Back then it really didn't occur to me that trying to get on the airplane with a pocket knife was going to be such a huge issue. In the case of flying to Israel—it was. I have ever since been grateful to the kindly security folks that were willing to let me run back to the baggage area and put my knife in the back pack. I still have that trusty Buck Knife today.

> *We arrived in Tel Aviv around 3:00. There were about six people from America also going to a Kibbutz. We all went to the youth hostel together. I couldn't change my Greek money at the airport, so I didn't have any money when we got to the hostel. Luckily, it was possible to make a deal with the man behind the counter. He kept my camera as insurance and let me stay the night and eat. This morning, I found out how difficult it is to change Greek money in Israel. There were two banks near the hostel, both of which wouldn't take it. As it turned out, I had to go into the center where there was one bank that would take it. Well, after getting back my camera, I headed in the direction of Jerusalem.*

I don't know what it's like today, but in Israel in 1976, it was nearly impossible to exchange Greek into Israeli currency. It was nice of the guy at the hostel to allow me to stay the night and have some dinner with the promise to pay him the next day. I'm pretty sure he knew the cheapie little camera I left with him as collateral wasn't even worth the cost of my bill. After settling up at the hostel and getting back my little Polaroid, it was time to hit the road and stick out my thumb. Actually, at that time in Israel, proper hitchhiking etiquette was not to stick out your thumb but to point at the ground.

I was picked up by one really nice guy named Mark, who was originally from Israel but went to New York when he was fifteen. He now lives here again with his wife and three children. He invited me to his house for lunch, and it was really nice. My destination today was kibbutz Nachshon the place that Teri, the girl in England, told me about.

I had always been interested in the idea of communes and communal living. I never really had an opportunity however to pursue that interest while in the States. Now, in the land of Israel, I was being given a chance to do just that. Kibbutz refers to the communal settlements that can be found scattered throughout Israel. The first of these communities were established in the early 1900s, and I believe that today there are around 275 of the settlements in the land. It's my understanding that the residents of the first kibbutz were Jewish pioneers from Eastern Europe wanting to return to the land of their forefathers. Understandably there was a significant increase in the number of kibbutzim after the establishment of the state of Israel in 1948. Many of those wanting to become residents were refugees from Europe and the Arab world, and many of those ended up on kibbutz. Nachshon, I believe, was originally established by immigrants from Eastern Europe around 1950. Because I had been given an address for a kibbutz, and because Teri, the nice young lady driving the convertible in England, had also given me her name to use as a reference, I choose to make Nachshon the first place I would try to become a volunteer.

I finally made it here about eight this evening, and I think that it's really going to be nice. Once again, the Lord has pulled a few strings for me. I think everybody here (the volunteers) had to go through the office in Tel Aviv to get here. Had I done that, I'm sure I wouldn't have gotten to come because they really don't need anyone. As it is though, it's possible that I'll be staying for quite a while. Thank you so much.

*Well, I think I'll go to bed now because I want
to get up early for breakfast.*

Turns out that just showing up at kibbutz Nachshon was perhaps the best way for me to go about it. Had I gone through the agency that handles the placement of volunteers onto different kibbutz, they would have told me that Nachshon wasn't in need of any additional workers. Thinking about it now, that would have been just fine too because I would have likely found a place on another kibbutz; it was pretty cool though to be able to stay in the community that had been recommended by Teri in England. Like most kibbutzim of that time, Nachshon was truly a share and share alike community where everybody was in the same big social boat. Everything was the property of the whole community. Fortunately for me (and for the countless volunteers from all over the world that had lived on a kibbutz), kibbutzim were often places in need of extra manpower and, as a result, in need of volunteers to help do the work. In return for being a volunteer, you received a bed (sometimes two to a bungalow, sometimes a private room), all of your meals which were eaten together with the whole community, and I think what worked out to about $35 a month. You could maybe even get a ration of cigarettes if you were a smoker. Also, there were occasional bus trips for the volunteers where they would bring us to some very cool place in the country. (Living on kibbutz was a pretty great gig.)

From what I understand, the first kibbutzim in Israel were primarily agricultural settlements that over the years have branched into various kinds of industry. Nachshon was a farming community where in addition to growing crops they raised turkeys and chickens. They also operated a small glass-making business with a gift shop and a factory where simulated star sapphires were made. My work in the community varied from repairing kerosene heaters to working with the groundskeepers to catching turkeys and chickens for market. I also spent a week or two washing dishes in the kitchen where the kibbutz kids went to high school. My favorite job was definitely working outside on the grounds and in the gardens.

Journal entry:

Monday, 12/27/-

I can't believe how fast time is going by. It's already after Christmas, and it seems like I just got here. (Actually, I did just get here.) Well, today I telephoned Mom and Dad, and every-thing is good. They also said that they're talking about Mom coming with Jack and Olga. We'll talk more about that though. [Turns out my mom was considering coming to Israel along with her brother Jack and his wife Olga.]

The last week has really been great. Friday we had a Christmas party, and it was fun. Yesterday I began working on the kerosene heaters. I really like this job. The man who showed me how is named Avi.

Avi was a Jewish gentleman originally from New York. He was an older guy and, I believe, may have been one of the early settlers of Nachshon. He, like other Jewish folks who immigrated to Israel from other countries, had made what was called Aliyah, which loosely trans-lates to the act of going up toward Jerusalem. He, like those settlers of the early 1900s, wanted to return to the land of his Jewish forefathers.

Journal entry:

Thursday, 1/12/-

The work I've been doing has varied from chickens to kerosene heaters to washing dishes at the high school, which I've been doing for the last week. It's not bad, but I'll be happy to change. Today I missed the bus and caused a bit of havoc. [Oops.]

Friday, 2/4/-

First of all, thank You, Lord, for making things so great. At the moment, I'm at the St. George Hotel, and here also is Mom, Jack, Olga, and Ethel. All with a tour group of Christians. It's fantastic. They arrived last night, and so did I. It was so good to see them all, especially Mother. She brought all kinds of beautiful homemade goodies to eat. Life is good. Today I went on the tour with everyone to Bethlehem, the Garden Tomb, and the Sheep Market to name just a few of the places we went. [It was a full day.] *Tomorrow Mom is coming to the kibbutz and is staying the night.*

It was an unexpected and wonderful surprise when I received the news that mom was coming to Israel. Until then I didn't even know my Uncle Jack and Aunt Olga were involved with bringing tour groups to the Holy Land. Mom and my Aunt Ethel (wife to Mom's brother Pat) would both be joining one of these groups with Jack and Olga as their guides. I was able to meet up with everyone in Jerusalem and got invited to join the group for a day of touring. Jerusalem, by the way, might just be my favorite place in the entire world. The colors and smells and sounds of the Arab market, or *souk*, in the old city along with the flavors of a Turkish-style cup of coffee with a piece of baklava (oh yes). That will forever be etched in my brain. Throughout the course of the day, my mom made sure to introduce me to all the nice church people on the bus. I can still remember her referring to me as "one of the pillars of the church back home." I also remember feeling sick to the stomach when she said that because it was so not true. The love of a mother can sometimes definitely be blind.

Mom and I took the bus back to Nachshon, and she had a chance to see, at least a little, what kibbutz life was like. Everybody made sure to make my mom feel more than welcome. We even had a bonfire the night she stayed, which meant hearing some really great music. Inevitably when we got together around the fire, someone would pull out a guitar and sing. (Truly good times.) I'm so glad that Mom had a chance to visit kibbutz and to see the land of Israel. Although she was only in the community for a couple days, she met some really great folks from all over the world. One of the people who took extra time and effort to make my mom feel at home was an Irishman named Sean. Sean was one of those people who befriended everyone. He was in Israel enjoying some time away from his job in Great Britain by taking a working vacation as a volunteer on kibbutz. Sean was a gifted storyteller. In my mom's words, he was someone who had "kissed the blarney stone." Although I think Sean's stories were all true, they were sometimes a little hard to believe. For instance, he told me about a time when, while managing a hotel in Europe, one of his frequent guests was Rock Hudson. Mr. Hudson apparently had a favorite brand of champagne, and Sean was on several occasions called upon to bring a bottle of this bubbly to the hotel room. It was when Sean told me Rock Hudson was, without a doubt, gay that I had some trouble believing his story. (The Rock, gay—no way.) Keep in mind, it was early 1977 when I was hearing this very unexpected news. It wasn't until 1985 when tragically Mr. Hudson died of the complications of AIDS and his sexuality became openly known to the public. Sean had become privy to this information several years prior. Not only was Sean someone whom you were compelled to listen to, but his genuine interest in people also made him someone who you felt like you could freely talk to. Perhaps even Mr. Hudson experienced that freedom.

In addition to meeting some really great people at the kibbutz, Mom also had the privilege of meeting Punky and Eddie. Punky and Eddie were the two nice doggies that lived along with the volunteers. Often I would allow both of the dogs to come into my room, so it wasn't such a surprise to come home one day and find Eddie lying on my bed. (Guess I left the door open.) I didn't mind that Eddie was in my room or even on my bed until sometime later when I noticed the bump on my head. Well, turns out that bump was actually a tick. A tick! This big, fat, nasty thing was sucking the blood out of my head. Fortunately, someone nearby was skilled at removing a nasty bloodsucking tick off your head with the use of a burning cigarette. Although I still loved Punky and Eddie, they were no longer welcome in my room. (I never did find more ticks on the doggies, so it's possible that Eddie wasn't the culprit. He and Punky still weren't coming back into the room.)

Journal entry:

Saturday, 3/5/-

It's really about time I got my act together and wrote something. Many things have happened in the last few weeks. At the moment, there's a new guy in the room named Paul from California. Tonight he played some really nice guitar and sang some songs he wrote. It was great.

Paul and I became pretty good friends and, on one occasion, traveled together into Jerusalem, where we spent the day with some nice, young California girls. These three Jewish princesses were friends of Paul's from school and were now attending Hebrew University in Jerusalem. During our visit, Paul and I took over occupancy of the little dorm kitchen and kicked out some pretty fine eggplant parmesan. (I love the way that sometimes where you are and what you're doing and what you're smelling and what all your senses are saying come together with what you're eating and make it taste extra good.) That was probably the best eggplant parmesan I have ever had. Also, while visiting with the girls, I decided to have my ear pierced. It just seemed like the thing to do at the time. The only dilemma was that, depending on which ear you chose, it might imply that you were gay or a convict or a whatever. I just wanted to have an earring. We went with the left ear. I'm not sure how they do it at the ear-piercing place in the mall, but at Hebrew U, it's a big needle and a cork and a camera case to smack the needle so it goes through the ear (my ear) and into the cork. My lovely ear-piercer did use ice to numb up the ear first, which I was very grateful for. Also, it helped that there was wine with the delicious eggplant parmesan. After saying goodbye to the ladies, Paul and I went into the old city souk where a silversmith made a little silver stud earring while I waited. It was all very cool. Although I haven't worn an earring for many years, the hole created by smacking a big needle with a camera case never has closed.

Living on kibbutz meant that you would likely meet and work with people from all over the world; it also meant you would likely never see most of those people again. This was not the case with Paul. About twenty-five years after living on kibbutz Nachshon and while on holidays at Disneyland with my wife and three kids, I was waiting in line to buy tickets for the Indiana Jones ride. I looked over at a guy who was buying tickets for another ride, and lo and behold, it was Paul. How cool was that. Time didn't allow us to reminisce for very long, but it was such an unexpected and wonderful surprise to see him.

Journal entry (continued):

Saturday, 3/5/-

About a week ago, Andy and I [Andy was a fellow volunteer, originally from England] *went to Tel Aviv, and while there, we met a very nice young lady on the beach, Ronnie. Since then I have spoken with her on the phone and invited her to the Purim party, which was last night.*

Purim, as recorded in the Bible in the book of Esther, commemorates the deliverance of the Jewish people living in Persia in the time of Esther, somewhere between 331 and 460 BC according to the introduction to Esther in my Bible. In a nutshell, Ahasuerus was king of Persia. Ahasuerus had a big party and got a little drunk. Vashti, the king's wife, had a little party of her own. Ahasuerus wanted his wife, the queen, to come and join him at his party so he could show her off. Vashti said no. Ahasuerus got ticked. Ahasuerus dumped Vashti. Ahasuerus held a beauty pageant so he could choose a new queen. The winner of the pageant was a lovely young maiden named Esther. Esther was beautiful. Esther was Jewish. Haman was the prime minister of Persia. Haman hated the Jews. Haman had a plot to kill all of the Jews. Esther learned of his plan. Esther told the king. The king was not pleased. The king had Haman hung on a gallows. Esther and all of the

Jews of Persia were saved. A holiday was established to commemorate these events. Jews worldwide celebrate this holiday today.

The word *purim* I think just means "lots," like in casting lots. Haman had cast lots when he chose the day that he was going to destroy the Jews. Thus, the celebration called Purim and thus casino night. Nachshon, like probably many nonreligious kibbutzim in Israel, celebrated Purim with a casino night. On this particular night, I was selected to be the cashier. Actually, it was a demanding job handing out the allotted amount of fake money to gamblers hungry to lay their play money down. And it wasn't just one denomination. We're talking a variety of bills. But it's okay. I held strong. There was wine with Purim.

> *Her parents told her she couldn't come but being quite determined she came anyway. It was a great surprise, but unfortunately, her father wasn't far behind. She didn't get to stay for the party, but we plan to see each other again. The party last night was lots of fun. I was the cashier who gave everyone money to gamble with.* [The person who asked me to be the cashier seemed to think that because I was from America, I would know something about casinos. I didn't.] *I don't know if I ever mentioned our volunteer trip to Mt. Hermon. We all took the chair lift up and played in the snow. It was a good time.*

One of our volunteer trips was to the Golan Heights and in particular to Mount Hermon. It was a unique experience to be in sunny Israel and at the same time have a snowball fight. That same day, we visited Mivzar Nimrod, a twelfth-century crusader castle. Like I said earlier, living on kibbutz was a pretty great gig.

Most of my friends on the kibbutz where volunteers like myself. Two of my closest friends, however, were official members of Nachshon. Steve was originally from Chicago, and his lovely wife, Freda, was from South Africa. Steve was a mechanic by profession but had also been in a rock-and-roll band back in Chicago. During those nights around a kibbutz campfire, it was often Steve who would pull out a guitar and share his great musical talent. Whenever there was need to repair one of the many machines or vehicles in the community, Steve was the man. On occasion, you would find him working on one of the beautiful Harleys that he had brought with him to Nachshon. One of the bikes was chopped and looked like it was right out of Easy Rider. That's the one that I took a ride on to Tel Aviv. Although I was only riding on the back, 120-plus miles per hour (even from the back) felt really, really fast. (I've been okay never to go that fast on a motorcycle again.) It was never clear to me if Steve was able to retain ownership of his beautiful Harleys or if in the true spirit of kibbutz they had become the property of the community.

One day while paying Steve a visit at the mechanics shop, I was reminded of the two unusual occurrences that happened during the grape harvest in France. Steve and I were chatting outside of the shop, and I noticed this cement trough sort of thing that was full of water. I think it was used to check for leaks in big tires. I was thinking to myself, you could take a bath in that thing. While thinking this, Steve looked over and said "What? You could take a bath in that." I was thinking it, but I hadn't said it. What was this? I didn't know then, and I still don't know. I've decided it's just one of those mysteries of life. Kind of like how Jilly and Jolly manage to live in multiple houses at the same time.

I think I will mention here that, with the exception of those occasional instances when my wife and I seem to be on the same page and thinking the same thing, there have not been any more "occurrences" like the ones in France or the one with Steve. That is until just this last Christmas season. I had gone to the annual Christmas party, which was being held at the home of one of the physicians from the clinic where I worked. When entering the front door of the home, there was a little table with labels and markers laid out. Everyone was asked to put their name on a tag and also to write what kind of profession they would like to be involved with if they weren't doing what they were doing. I spent several minutes thinking what I would like to write and had just about settled on "lion tamer." Before writing anything down, a gentleman who was standing by the table said to me, "You could just put lion tamer." Honest to goodness, that's what he said. And I thought I had pretty much seen the last of those "occurrences." Maybe Jilly or Jolly will have to explain to me what that's all about. In the end I didn't write lion tamer on the tag. I went with cowboy instead.

Journal entry:

Saturday, 3/26/-

Hello. At the moment, I'm at a Moshav in the South called Ir Ovot. Left the kibbutz about two weeks ago and stopped here to see Peter.

Peter was another kibbutz volunteer who, much like myself, came to Israel because it was a great place for a traveler to find work, have a roof over his head, and receive three squares a day. We ended up becoming very good friends and would ultimately find ourselves doing a little traveling together. Peter and I both worked in the chicken houses. (Since leaving Israel, I have never had a great desire to do that job again.) Shavook is what I think we called it when catching chickens and turkeys for market. (I say "think we called it" because I have since tried to find correct spelling for this term and haven't been able to anywhere, except for in my journal.) If you've never had the pleasure of catching chickens or turkeys for market, be glad. It should be no surprise that a chicken would get pretty ticked off when it's being picked up by the feet (sometimes two or three chickens in each hand) and stuffed into a cage. Although I tried to stuff my chickens into the cage as humanely as possible, it wasn't too long before enough of them had pecked my hands and helped me not to feel quite so guilty about the unpleasant and very unfriendly task I was performing. (And the turkeys could even peck you harder.)

Peter was originally from New Zealand. Although we were from different corners of the globe, he and I seemed to be sort of on similar spiritual journeys at this time in our lives. Like me, Peter was someone who at a younger age had been introduced to Jesus and who it seemed wanted to know Him or know about Him—better. Also like me, Peter was someone who at this chapter of his life was not opposed to complementing his spiritual journey with the addition of mind altering drugs. Except for the very rare toke, I never really saw any drug use at Nachshon. That was until one of the festive Brazilian members of the community let Peter and I know that he had a special tea. Actually, he had a dried plant from the desert that, if you made a tea out of it, would make you really high. "Now that's the ticket."

Not only did Peter and I take him up on the offer to enjoy a cup of tea, but we also ate the seeds used to brew it. (Our friend from Brazil said that this could make it "extra special.") Probably an hour or so after teatime, Peter decided to wander off in one direction, and I chose to go another. While walking along a pathway near my room, I came upon Avi Alon, the nice American gentleman who taught me how to repair kerosene heaters. We had just begun to exchange a few words when suddenly—*poof*—he disappeared. (Now that was different.) I continued down the pathway and ran into Pepe. Pepe was another one of the Brazilian members of the kibbutz. He was a guy that always had a smile on his face and who was always a pleasure to talk to. As we approached one another, Pepe raised his hand in greeting and smiled. Then suddenly—*poof*—he disappeared. (I had definitely never experienced anything like this before.) It actually became a little scary because I became unsure what was real and what was a hallucination. I ended up going back to my room and trying to sleep, which I did off and on (with some very weird accompanying dreams). At one point, I remember looking into the mirror and being a little freaked out at the size of my pupils. They were so huge it seemed that if I looked real close I would be able to see inside my head. (I knew I couldn't, but that was one of the many weird thoughts I was having.) As strange as my desert plant tea experience was, Peter's, I found out later, was even more bizarre. From what he told me and from what some people who witnessed his hallucinogenic experience reported, Peter had what could probably be called a bad trip.

Looking back, it's hard to believe that I was willing to brew up and drink a tea made from some dried desert plant, which I knew absolutely nothing about, except that it got you really high and that our friend from Brazil hadn't died from the effects when he tried it. Interestingly enough, I had just read about this plant. I did not, however, make the connection between what I'd read and what we were sipping at our tea party. Shortly before our desert plant experience, I had finished reading a couple of books. The first one, *The Drifters* by James Michener, told the stories of several young travelers in Europe and Africa. More than a few of my friends on kibbutz had read it, and the book seemed to be pretty much required reading for backpackers during the seventies. The second book, *The Teachings of Don Juan: A Yaqui Way of Knowledge* by Carlos Castaneda, was also circulating around with the volunteers. It told of the drug-induced lessons learned by Carlos while an apprentice to a Yaqui Indian shaman-sorcerer. (All in all, quite a strange read.) One of the drugs Carlos experienced during his apprenticeship was a plant called *datura*, or *yerba del diablo*, or devil's weed. Mr. Castaneda tells how while under this drug's influence he was turned into a crow and obtained the ability to fly. Wouldn't you know it, the dried desert seed pods that Peter and I made our cup of tea out of was in fact *yerba del diablo*. It wasn't until several years later that I learned our tea was indeed made from devil's weed. I also learned after the fact that high doses can be very poisonous and kill you. (Not one of my better choices in life.)

It was Peter who first heard about Moshav Ir Ovot. A *moshav* is a communal settlement much like a kibbutz, except that, as I understand it, the members of the community actually own more of their major possessions (things like their home for instance) as opposed to kibbutz, where all the major assets are owned by the community. Ir Ovot was a small settlement in the Arava region of the northeastern Negev. The community was started by Rabbi Simcha Peralmutter (or Sandy as we came to know him). Rumor was that Sandy, although an Orthodox Jew, was also a believer in Jesus. We also understood that Rabbi Sandy was the proud husband of two wives. (Ir Ovot was a community unlike any other in Israel to be sure.) We had heard that if Rabbi Sandy liked you, it would be possible to volunteer and participate with them making the "desert blossom as the rose" as prophesied in Isaiah 35:1, where it says, "The wilderness and the dry land shall be glad; and the desert shall rejoice, and blossom as the rose." If invited to stay in the community (and being that Ir Ovot operated a tomato farm), we would be participating with the desert blossoming as the tomato. Peter had gone on to Ir Ovot about a week before me and had been invited to stay. I too ended up becoming a volunteer in this very unique little garden in the desert. I never was able to really get a grasp on Rabbi Sandy's theological views despite attempting on a few occasions to sit down and talk to him specifically about his belief in Jesus. Our conversations always seemed to be diverted into some other direction. With what little I did learn, I would say that, yes, Rabbi Peralmutter was a believer in Jesus, or Yeshua. What that meant to him exactly, I never found out. And as to why Sandy felt that he should be blessed with two lovely significant others (at the same time), I never found an answer to that either.

Ir Orvot, although small, did seem to have a pretty robust little tomato farm going. Each day, we would spend several hours picking the tomatoes. And each and every day, Grandma (I believe she was Sandy's mother) would bring freshly baked chocolate cake and milk out to the fields for us to enjoy every day. It was awesome.

As interesting as it was to learn a little bit about tomato farming, it was even more impressive and even kind of inspiring to see the desert blossom like the rose and to actually be involved with the process. (The tomatoes grown at Ir Ovot by the way were really very delicious.) When not working, Peter and I would often find ourselves exploring the surrounding area. Living in the desert sometimes felt a little like something from another era or even like something from Bible times. Taking a walk and running into some friendly local camels for instance or visiting a nearby Bedouin tent and enjoying a cup of tea prepared on a little open fire was almost surreal. (It was wonderful.) When just hanging out in the community, I would often play a game called *shesh besh* (or backgammon) with Sandy's son. Although he was just a youngster, he almost always won. (I think now after forty years I'm going to have to learn to play that game again.) Although Ir Ovot didn't seem to receive a lot of guests (at least while I was there), we did one day have a visit from an Israeli soldier who was on sort of an unusual vacation. This young guy had apparently always wanted to take a trip across the desert on a camel. He and his trusty beast showed up one afternoon in search of water. Not only did they receive their water, but I'm almost positive that the young soldier also enjoyed a piece of Grandma's delicious chocolate cake before they hit the road (or rather the desert) again.

Journal entry (continued):

Saturday, 3/26/-

We went to Nuweiba and met Evert on the way in Eilat. It's been a good time for a couple days. Beautiful sunshine and a good place to run around naked. Also some beautiful coral and tropical fish.

Peter and I decided to take a little break from Ir Ovot, so after filling a bag with tomatoes for the road, we hitched a ride to Eilat. Eilat is a port town located on the northern tip of the Red Sea on the Gulf of Aqaba. While there, we met up with Evert, who was also a volunteer at Nachshon. Evert and his lovely sister Rita were originally from the Netherlands and had left their careers at home and come to volunteer in Israel. Evert was an optometrist by profession and was working in the glass factory at the kibbutz. From Eilat, the three of us caught a ride in the back of a truck, destination Nuweiba. In the '70s, Nuweiba (at least what I saw of it) pretty much just consisted of a dive shop, a lot of beach and blue water, and a kiosk where you could buy pita bread and hummus to go along with your bag of tomatoes. (Delicious.) Visitors to this beautiful little oasis seemed to pretty much be comprised of dive enthusiasts, travelers like myself, young Israeli soldiers on holiday, and a few old hippies. It was also a popular place for those who appreciated the freedom to run around naked. The soft sandy beaches, clear blue water, beautiful coral, and multicolored fish were all pretty spectacular. And truth be told, considering that swimwear was not required, I may have noticed one or two of the beautiful female beachcombers during our stay. (On a side note, Nuweiba is thought by some to be the site where Moses and the children of Israel crossed over into the Promised Land. If it was, I feel pretty privileged to have had the opportunity to sleep on the beach at such an historic location.) In 1976, we didn't have to cross a border to go to Nuweiba as the Sinai Peninsula was still under Israeli occupation. The peace treaty with Egypt would not be signed until 1979, and likewise, the subsequent withdrawal of Israel from the Sinai would not be completed until 1982.

For the last week, I've been back at the moshav with Peter. Yesterday Yosiy [one of the members of the settlement] *came back from a wedding in Be'er-Sheba and brought with him his very nice cousin Shlomit. She is very special, and we had some nice times talking. At the moment, I'm suffering from a million mosquito bites. It's been more than worth it though.* [I know the bit about mosquito bites is a little random, but it's what was in my journal.] *Tomorrow morning I'll get a ride in the truck to Tel Aviv. Hopefully I'll get to see Ronnie. After that, Peter and I will meet at the kibbutz.*

Sunday, 3/27/-

Today was fantastic. Came into Tel Aviv with Kenny and Bob. [Kenny and Bob were both members of Ir Ovot and were making a tomato delivery.] *After arriving, I was able to phone Ronnie, and we met on the beach. It was a very beautiful afternoon, and Ronnie is a very fantastic girl. There are so many really nice people that need to be remembered. God, You are so fantastic to give all the things that You do. I really feel happy about lots of things. Thanks so much.*

Monday, 4/4/-

Peter and I are now in Athens. It's really beautiful. We arrived yesterday on the plane. The last week on the kibbutz was fun. Peter and I spent most of our time catching chickens. Saturday night we celebrated Passover with a big meal and also managed to get a little messy. It was fun. On Wednesday, Ronnie called, so on Thursday we met in Tel Aviv.

She's really a lovely girl. The only reason I most hated to leave Israel was the people. There were so many nice ones. Hopefully, we'll meet again. Today I really could have kicked myself. Peter and I sold blood, and I got about $13, or 400 drachma. Well, we were going back to the train station and saw a man doing a game with cards. It looked like a game that you couldn't lose. [Right.] *Guess what, I lost. Another lesson learned. Don't gamble unless you've got enough money to lose.*

CHAPTER 10

Go West, Young Man

Both Peter and I had been thinking it was about time to leave Israel. Neither of us knew exactly where he was going, so we decided to go together. After flying from Tel Aviv to Athens, we took the opportunity to visit the Parthenon as well as the other ancient monuments that sit atop the Acropolis. (Pretty amazing to hang out at the steps of a structure that has been around for more than four hundred years before Jesus was born.) Peter had stayed in Athens before, so he was familiar with a cheap hostel where we could sleep on the rooftop. (They even had a friendly box turtle that lived up on the roof.) We both needed to save money, so there were no fancy Greek meals eaten by either of us while in Athens. There was, however, the most wonderful yogurt that on more than one occasion we enjoyed along with some delicious fresh baked bread. The yogurt almost seemed like it had a thin layer of cheese on top. (Even though Greek yogurt seems to be all the rage in the States these days, I have never since eaten anything quite like what we had in Greece.)

Somebody told us that one way to make a little money while in Athens was to sell blood. We also heard that when you did, you would be given a glass of orange juice. (Funny how motivating and how good that glass of orange juice sounded at the time.) We did sell blood but, wouldn't you know it, nary a glass of OJ to be had. (Guess we went to the wrong place.) Oh well, we were both about $13 richer for selling the blood. That is until we came upon what looked like a great way to increase our earnings—three-card Monte, although a con game that has been used to fleece foolish people like me for many hundreds of years (it apparently dates back to the fifteenth century and may even have been adapted from a shell game that was used to rip off unsuspecting "marks" or "patsys" or "suckers" in ancient Greece.) Around for hundreds of years and yet not something that either Peter or I had ever seen before. I'm quite sure that the guy handling the cards, along with his accomplices, saw the smoke from our hard-earned blood money burning a hole in our pockets from a block away. The point of the game is to guess which of three cards is the Queen. (Kind of like guessing which shell the pea is under.) The gentleman with the cards shows you all three, turns them over, mixes them up a little, and then picks them up one on top of the other. He then throws them down in a line, facedown. You (or in this case, me) simply has to pick the one believed to be the Queen. (That is, after betting on your pick.) The part that you don't know (or in this case, I didn't know) is that when the dealer is throwing cards down, he may or may not be throwing them down in order. You think he is throwing down the bottom, then middle, then top card, but he may be throwing down the card from the top when you just think it's the card from the bottom. The point is, try as hard as you like, you can never know for sure where the Queen is. And to make matters worse, he lets you witness a few rounds where someone actually does win the game. Unfortunately and unbeknownst to you (or in this case, unbeknownst to Peter and I), the guy you watched win the game is working together with Mr. Three-Card Monte man. When all was said and done, I lost my $13. And to make things worse, Peter got caught up in my enthusiasm to make some easy money and laid his earnings down as well. (And not even a glass of orange juice.) Dang it.

Journal entry (continued)

Monday, 4/4/-

Yesterday we went to the Acropolis and saw the Parthenon and all those good things. Athens is a very beautiful place. I'm very thankful to be here as well as everywhere else I've been in the last few months. Now Peter and I will try a little bit of travelling. Just exactly where, we'll have to see.

Wednesday, 4/13/-

Now sitting in the train station of Savona [former home of Christopher Columbus], *which is in Italy. (The pen is running out of ink.) Peter and I took the boat from the north of Greece to Bari. From there, we hitched and took a train to Rome. (I think I'll finish for now because no more ink.)*

Bari is located just about where the heel of Italy's boot meets the shoe. The landscape in that part of the country is absolutely beautiful to be sure. Trying to hitch a ride from there to Rome, however, would prove to be a little more of an adventure than we anticipated. Winding, narrow, mountainous roads can definitely be a unique and awesome sight. They can also be kind of scary when the driver of one of your rides thinks he is competing in a race. I remember Peter quietly saying to me, "This guy thinks he's Stirling Moss." (Mr. Moss was a former Formula One race car driver from England.) We ended up telling our gracious but crazy driver that he could let us out sooner than we had originally agreed upon. After being dropped off (and after thanking God that we were still alive), we decided to catch a train for the remainder of the trip to Rome.

Journal entry:

Friday, 4/15/-

The first night in Rome, we tried to stay in the train station but were moved out about 1:30 in the morning. We were then forced to pay a whole lot for a pension.

We ended up paying way more than we could afford for a guesthouse. Considering we had arrived in Rome the day before Easter, we were probably pretty fortunate to find anywhere to stay at all, especially at 1:30 in the morning.

> *The second night was great. We stayed in a big park (Villa Borghese). In the park, there is a little lake and on the lake a little house with a statue. It made a perfect hotel.*

In the midst of the busy metropolis of Rome lies the city's largest park, the Villa Borghese. On the shore of a little lake in the park sits the Temple of Aesculapius. It just so happens that there is room to lie down your sleeping bag next to the statue of good old Aesculapius. He is apparently the Roman god of medicine or healing, and he was kind enough to share his temple with Peter and me. We were a little surprised to wake up in the morning with people rowing around the lake in little boats. After quickly packing up and saying goodbye to Aesculapius, we spent the day exploring Rome. Having grown up in a Baptist church and with the exception of visiting a few Catholic churches that some of my friends went to, I really didn't know a lot about Catholicism. (Although there was the "friendly" priest in Ireland.) I was, however, very interested in visiting the Vatican. We actually "slightly" considered trying to visit on Easter Sunday but decided that was probably a bad, if not impossible, idea. The day after Easter, on the other hand, we were able to visit the Vatican without a huge crowd. I was half hoping that Pope Paul VI might be having a little downtime and perhaps we would bump into each other and maybe enjoy a cappuccino and a little conversation. (Hey, it could happen.) We didn't get to chat with the Pope, but we did visit the Sistine Chapel and get to see Michelangelo's *Creation of Adam*. Pretty cool.

> *Well, after another night in Rome, we hitched as far as Genoa. Then took a train to Savona. From there, we jumped on a train to Paris, and that's where we are now. It's really good to be here.*

On our way out of Rome, we thought it only natural that we should enjoy a plate of Italian spaghetti. We stopped into a little restaurant, and I must say the spaghetti was delicious. Also particularly tasty was the bowl full of fresh grated Parmesan cheese that was on the table. In addition to heaping it on our spaghetti, we may have—no, we *did* eat it by the spoonful. We may have even—no, we *did* eat the whole bowl. Having put our already licked spoons back in the bowl, we felt sort of obligated to eat it all. We didn't make it very far that first day when trying to hitchhike up the coast from Rome. After standing in the rain for quite some time without a ride, we decided to walk toward the beach and look for a place to set up the tent. We came to what looked like a private camp ground where you would likely be expected to pay. The site was surrounded by a high chain-link fence, but considering that it was getting late in the day and considering it was not a time of year when anybody else was camping, we thought it might be okay to climb over the fence and set up the tent for the night.

I think it might have been a little foggy that afternoon because we never did notice the big house that was just up the beach from where we were. We did become very aware of the house the next day, however, after being woken by the sounds of voices and barking dogs. Outside the tent was the proprietor of the camping ground along with perhaps his adult son and two quite large and quite excited dogs. By the tone of their voices and considering that the older gentleman was carrying a shotgun, it was pretty clear that they didn't appreciate our trespassing. They managed to communicate that we were indeed expected to pay for our cold, rainy campsite on the beach. The two men were using pretty loud voices, and the dogs were getting so excited that they started to nip at our legs. Although we were only able to exchange a few words in English, the younger of the two gentlemen did understand my suggestion that they take their excited dogs back to the house while Peter and I packed up our camp. We would then come to their home and settle up. Surprisingly, they agreed to this and left us standing at the tent as they walked back to the house. So here we were with a decision to make. Do we finish packing up and then walk to the house of the guy with the shotgun and two dogs that want to bite us, or do we finish packing up and quickly climb over the fence and run away? We went with run away. Fortunately, we were able to catch a ride at the highway without having to wait very long, and fortunately, the guys and their dogs must have decided that it wasn't worth chasing after us in the rain. That day, we made it as far as Genoa and, from there, caught a train to Savona and then on to Paris. Along the way, we passed by the town of Pisa, and although we didn't stop, we did at least look in the direction of the Leaning Tower.

Journal entry (continued):

Friday, 4/15/-

We are now sitting in Lopez's house. [Lopez was a cousin of Swaziek, the lovely bride whose wedding I attended in France. He had made the mistake of inviting me to visit if ever in the area. "If you invite Tim, he will come, and he might even bring a friend."] *Just washed some clothes and had a shower and am feeling really good. Yesterday when we arrived in Paris, we went to René's, but he had moved. Going to try and get in touch with him to get the 250 francs because I'm broke.*

Whenever imposing on friends or relatives and staying in their homes, I tried to help out with chores or contribute to the house fund or both. Some months prior while staying in Paris with René, in addition to contributing to the house fund, I also loaned him 250 francs (about $50) with the assurance that he would pay me back some day. I never really wanted or expected to get reimbursed for that little loan, and yet here I was—yes, wanting to pay René a visit—but also very much intending to ask for the money. We never did find out where René had moved to.

Journal entry:

Tuesday, 8/29/-

Well, it's been a while. Peter and I had a good time in Paris. Never did get in touch with René, but we did stay with Lopez and Anne. [Anne was sister to Lopez.] *We also saw Bridgette and Henry again.* [Friends from the Puck Fair in Killorglin.] *It was all great. We went to London from Paris, by boat and then train. We saw Sean for a couple of days, and to make a long story short, I came home. I'm not going to write a lot about what's happened between then and now, except that tonight I thought Nicholas was gone.* [Nicholas was my great cat that I thought had gone missing.] *Thank you so much, Lord, for an opportunity to feel so fantastic after having felt so bad. He was sleeping under the sink for about an hour and a half. Thanks so much.*

After making our way from Israel to London, Peter and I both had to figure out what was coming next. While in London, we dropped in on our old friend Sean, who had finished his working vacation on the kibbutz and returned to his job managing a pub. Sean was kind enough to invite us to crash at his place while we decided on future plans. Considering that my finances were getting seriously low, I determined that it might be time to return to the States. The last eleven months had been such an incredible experience, and although I was thinking about going home, I also knew that my traveling days were certainly not over. For now though, it would just mean returning to Washington and seeing where the road would lead from there. Peter had decided to remain in London for a while and look for a job in a pub. His plan was to then return to New Zealand but to make the trip via the USA. I said goodbye to Sean and to Peter and then jumped on a plane. Destination: Seattle, Washington. Turns out this would not be the last time that Peter and I would see each other.

33rd and South Sawyer

After returning to Washington State, I was very fortunate to be able to obtain a job working for my brother Mike. Brother Michael had retired from the modern home decor slash head shop industry, and together with his new business partner Larry, purchased the auction house from my folks. Mike and Larry had decided to phase out the auction side of the business and were concentrating on the sale of home furnishings. Because there were several apartments and condos being constructed at that time, they found themselves furnishing many of these new complexes. Much of my work revolved around driving truck, delivering, and setting up furniture. It was actually kind of a fun job. And everybody should learn how to navigate a big fully loaded furniture truck with very questionable brakes throughout the streets of Tacoma and the surrounding area. (I learned how to creatively downshift while also using the emergency brake in order to come to a stop.)

Before beginning the job with Michael, I first wanted to check out an opportunity that I understood might be available on the eastern side of the state. (An opportunity that I never even thought about until having picked grapes at the vendange.) Washington enjoys a diverse agricultural industry that among other crops includes apples, wheat, cherries, pears, and an ever-growing production of hops. And speaking of hops, wasn't it Benjamin Franklin who said, "Beer is proof that God loves us and wants us to be happy"? Even though there are lots of T-shirts out there (and I have one), that would lead you to believe that he did—he really didn't. Oh well, at any rate, Washington grows a whole lot of hops. It wasn't hops though that I was interested in at that time but rather cherries. It was cherry season in eastern Washington, and it seemed very reasonable that if I could find a job picking grapes in France, I should be able to find a job picking cherries in the state of Washington, where I grew up. (I was wrong. It turned out to be much more difficult than anticipated.) I hitchhiked over the Cascade mountain pass to Eastern Washington, and after a quick stop to visit with my brother Frank and his family (Frankie was a state patrolman living in the college town of Ellensburg at the time), I moved on to an area known for its cherry orchards. It wasn't until being told that there was no need for my mad fruit picking skills by about three orchard owners that one kindly orchardist (who probably felt sorry for me) did offer a place to pitch my tent, a ladder, and a picker's bucket to put the cherries in. There wasn't going to be much money being made, but the weather was beautiful, and the cherries were delicious. (I ate a lot of them.) There was even a crystal-clear irrigation ditch running through the orchard that provided a great place for a cool dip. That is until after a day or two when the owner advised me to be very careful about rattlesnakes and to be sure not to swim in the irrigation ditch because it contained pesticides (nice). Of course, I didn't receive that piece of information until after having already splashed around a couple times and soaked up a little organophosphate poison. Oh well, no harm done. (Although my hair all fell out and there was that nasty rash. Just kidding.)

The reason I had such a hard time finding a cherry-picking job was because there were literally "professional" pickers that had come from Mexico for the harvest. Why hire a novice like me when there were all kinds of folks (many who probably came back to the same orchards every year) to do the work—and do it very efficiently. Also, it turns out I had come a little late in the season, so there were only a few days of picking left at the orchard I was on. After finishing up, I didn't even bother trying to find another harvest job, especially considering how hard it was to find the one I had been given. Instead, I headed back to western Washington and began my career as a furniture deliverer.

As much as I needed a job, I also needed a place to live. Fortunately for me, in those days it was possible to find a fairly cheap place to rent without having to provide all kinds of references and financial information. (Perhaps it had something to do with the kind of place I was trying to rent. Rather than fairly cheap, "very cheap" would be more accurate.) Mom and Dad were extremely nice to let me stay in their spare room for a short time but with the understanding that I would soon be on my way. And hence, a new chapter of life in the house on 33rd and South Sawyer in Tacoma. What a great little house. It was easy to see how this had once been a very nice neighborhood. We even had a little corner store where you could pay way more for whatever you bought than you would somewhere (anywhere) else. I did occasionally buy some things there because I was pretty sure it was hard for them to make ends meet and because it was just very cool to have a little corner store. (I think they were robbed at least once, maybe twice while I lived there.) My excellent little house had an enclosed front porch, a small back porch, a couple fruit trees in the backyard, a claw-foot bathtub, and a picket fence. It was awesome. After painting the fence white and facing the front of the porch with cedar shakes, it was even more cool. I am sure there had once been several more places like mine in the hood, but they had been replaced with apartment houses. In the apartment house next door lived my friend Tyrone. Tyrone was a large black man who looked like he could have been a professional football player. He lived with his wife and little boy. Tyrone had recently been released from Walla Walla penitentiary for something to do with prostitution. Evidently he had been a pimp. Tyrone was a great neighbor. Each week he would borrow my trusty Schwinn bicycle to make his visits with a probation officer. In return, I always knew that he would be keeping an eye on my place when I was away. I seldom even locked my door. Tyrone and I did become friends. Once while paying a little visit and looking over some of my photographs of Europe, Tyrone pulled out a joint of what he called mint leaf. Although I didn't know what it was, I figured it was at least an herb of some kind. It really didn't matter what kind of herb it was because it turned out to be laced with a very horrible drug called PCP. PCP, or what's also known as angel dust, was the stuff that you read reports about of people jumping off roofs after taking it, thinking they could fly, or some other insane thing that bad stories are made of. I think it was after a couple tokes when Tyrone decided to divulge that the herb we were smoking may have contained a little something extra. I didn't smoke any more but had already had enough to become incredibly paranoid and to start obsessing about all the nasty things I thought might happen. Fortunately, the effects, although very weird, weren't quite as terrible as anticipated. Still, there was nothing angelic about angel dust.

My friend Tyrone's mom and dad were in the process of moving from one location to another, and because I was driving a pickup truck at the time, Tyrone asked if I could help them make the move. I remember driving with a truckload of household stuff along with Tyrone, his mom and dad and me all squished into the front of the truck. (Tyrone was a big guy, and his mom and dad were pretty full grown as well, so it was a tight squeeze.) Tyrone's dad opened up a little cardboard box that was filled with bottles of prescription cough syrup. He passed one around and said it was his "favorite brand." I didn't ask where he got it. Other than Tyrone and his wife, I didn't get to know too many of my neighbors. I did however get to know, at least a little, the very nice elderly Polish woman and her husband who lived across the street. I can imagine they had lived in that neighborhood for many years. We met after a UPS driver decided to leave a box on my front porch that actually belonged to them. It was surprising to me that my nice neighbor would be so completely astonished when I brought them over their package. Surprising and sad. There apparently hadn't been a lot of "love thy neighbor" happening in that neighborhood for a while.

So here I was, living in the little house on South Sawyer and working for Michael doing a job that I enjoyed. And to make things even better, there was Nicholas. Nicholas was a great rescue cat that somebody (I can't remember who it was now) asked me to take care of. He really was a great cat. Sometimes I didn't have official cat food at the house, so Nicholas would eat whatever I was having. He reminded me of the dog named Ash in Cognac, France, that liked to eat fruits and nuts. Among other things, Nicholas enjoyed lettuce and pineapple. All in all and practically speaking, life on South Sawyer was good. Good except for that place in my spirit that just wasn't being satisfied. I had come to find out that simply trying to do the "right things" under my own power wasn't going to fill the void. I was also pretty sure, however, that doing anything and everything I chose, whether I thought it was right or wrong, also certainly wasn't fulfilling my spiritual needs. I was confused. And so the journey continued.

The mid and later seventies brought with them two very powerful and undeniable phenomena—disco music and cocaine. I am happy to say that I was able to resist the siren's song of groups like KC and the Sunshine Band and the Bee Gees. Perhaps if I had been someone who enjoyed disco dancing, things would have been different. At the time though, I was one of those "disco sucks" kind of people. Unfortunately, I didn't manage to resist the call of cocaine. Particularly during the time I was working for Michael, cocaine was a very popular and (if you had the money to pay for it) available drug. Of the variety of drugs that I tried in my foolish youth, I believe that cocaine may have been the worst. With most recreational drugs, at least in my experience, you expected some kind of mind-altering effect from the substance you took. You knew though that what you were experiencing was not real life. (The mind was being altered.) Cocaine, on the other hand, had a subtle way of making you think that the hyper exaggerated confidence it was producing was the real you. Its effects included this very false confidence and the sense that you were way more on top of things than you really were. I'm guessing this would attribute to why so many people found themselves addicted to it. I saw more than a few people whose lives and whose family's lives were very profoundly and very negatively impacted by the abuse of cocaine. Fortunately, although I did use coke, I never had enough money to make it a regular part of my life. For that I am grateful. But never fear, I managed to mess up my head with plenty of other things. (Knowing that many people were and even today are huge fans of disco music, I really would like to take this opportunity to say something positive about it . . . I'm sorry, I just can't. Disco sucks.)

Probably because it's such a beautiful part of the world, many of my friends from school ended up remaining in the Pacific Northwest. One of those friends was my good buddy who, for anonymity's sake, we will call Roy. I guess we could call him Rinaldo, or Rizwan, or maybe Ruben. No, let's call him Roy. Roy was someone I had known and been friends with since junior high. We both worked for my dad back in the auction house days, and we were now both working for brother Michael at the furniture store. I can never forget the time (probably around our junior year in high school) when Roy and I were hanging out in the parking lot of the local Herfy's burger joint. With us was our good bud who also, for anonymity's sake, we will call Larry. When the three of us got together, it was frequently part of our agenda to smoke a little pot. Such was the case that day at Herfy's. I'm guessing the local police officer who also happened to be hanging at Herfy's must have seen the smoke coming from the windows of Roy's Volkswagen van. He walked up to the bus, which the three of us were now standing outside of, and asked, "So what's that funny smell?" Roy, who was someone who could always come up with a ready reply, simply said, "Dead fish." The officer then started looking around the front of Roy's van and noticed a little wooden club that was sticking out from under the front seat and asked, "So what's that for?" (I think just about every young lad that took woodshop in junior high made a little wooden club on the lathe as one of their projects. Some of the more resourceful even drilled out the center and filled it with lead. Many of those little clubs later ended up under the front seat of that young man's car.) Roy replied (and with a straight face mind you), "It's what we used to kill the fish." I'm not sure if the officer was amused or not, but at any rate, he decided not to pursue "that funny smell." Good old Roy.

Thinking back on the day at Herfy's with Roy, Larry, and the dead fish, I'm also reminded of the summer before our sophomore year of high school when Larry and I embarked on a pretty epic bicycle trip. (At least it was epic for two fifteen- or sixteen-year-old kids.) We strapped backpacks onto our Schwinn 10 speeds and headed out from our homes in Lakewood, Washington, across the Narrows Bridge, north up the Kitsap Peninsula, over the Hood Canal Bridge, and across the Olympic Peninsula to Port Angeles. Along the way, we stopped to spend the night at a campground outside the town of Sequim, where I got stung by a bee on the forehead. I remember being kind of scared when I looked into a mirror (and also remember Larry thinking it was really funny) when my forehead swelled up to Neanderthal man proportions. No worries, after a shot of Benadryl from a local doc and after a good night's sleep (which the shot of Benadryl guaranteed), all was back to normal. From Port Angeles (which was probably 110 miles or so from Lakewood), we took a boat to Victoria on Vancouver Island British Columbia and camped for a couple days. (I wasn't going to include this little story, but as they say, confession is good for the soul.) While on the island, my friend (who for anonymity's sake, we will call

Larry) and I had breakfast in a pancake restaurant. After finishing his food, my friend (who for anonymity's sake we will call Larry) excused himself to go to the bathroom. Surprise! He never came back. Larry had dined and dashed. So now I had to decide if I would make the same decision and slip out the back door like my friend did or would I simply pay for both of our meals. Sorry to say, I chose the low road. I excused myself to go to the bathroom. From Victoria, we rode to Sydney and, from there, took a ferry to Friday Harbor on San Juan Island. That night, we stayed with a cousin of mine who lived outside of Friday Harbor and even enjoyed some awesome fish and chips made with fresh cod that we caught right off the rocks. The next morning, Larry and I started our return trip home, taking the same route we had come. I'm thinking it must have been about a 275-mile bike ride, plus the boat sailings. (Pretty awesome trip for a couple young teenagers.) That last night on the way home, we pulled into a park near the Hood Canal Bridge. It was late, it was dark, it was rainy, and we weren't real excited about trying to set up the tent. Instead, we found that if you threw a plastic tarp down on the floor of the shower room, it made a pretty good place to sleep. We also found that if both of us held the door shut with our feet, the guy who wanted to take a shower in the middle of the night would finally go away.

We left early the next morning (thus avoiding having to pay for the night) and made the final fifty-plus-mile leg of our journey. Like I said, it was a pretty awesome trip for a couple young guys. Come to think of it, Larry and I experienced a few memorable escapades together. On one occasion, the two of us were invited to join our friend (who for anonymity's sake we will call Terry) on a very unique adventure. Terry, who I'm almost positive didn't actually possess a driver's license yet, would sometimes work for his uncle by driving a big septic truck and pumping out the portable latrines that were found at various public places where portable latrines needed to be pumped out. On this particular occasion, Terry was going out to the drag races where, because he was driving the truck and would supposedly be emptying the latrines, he would get in for free. The three of us went to the track and did get in for free and did get to watch both the drag races and motorcycle races. Lo and behold, we never did manage to pump out any latrines. It just so happened that we made this little trip on a day during what was called senior week at our high school. During that week, it was customary for seniors to find some unsuspecting sophomores and throw them off the bridge that spanned Steilacoom Lake. The three of us determined that rather than allow ourselves to be victims of senior week, we would instead take advantage of the fact that we were driving around in a giant poop truck with a hose that could be used not only to suck out latrines but also to spray doo-doo on seniors intent on throwing us off the bridge. We even cruised Herfy's in the truck, looking for any senior-weekers who might be so inclined. Fortunately, we never came across any. I'm not sure if we would have been bold enough to pull out the poop hose or not. (Probably not.)

And now as I'm thinking about some of the great friends I was privileged to know in high school. It would be a shame not to mention Carl and Jerry. It would also be a shame not to mention our little late-night art project. I really was fortunate in my youth and young adulthood to know some great people who became really good friends in school. One of those was Carl. Carl was the son of an Iranian mother and a Norwegian father. It was always a fun cultural experience to go to his house. And Carl owned a very cool 56 Chevy. Jerry was a guy who always seemed to have a smile on his face. You always felt like he was genuinely happy to see you. As a result, it was always a pleasure to see him.

I got to spend a little time with both Carl and Jerry in 2015 at our fortieth high school reunion. It truly was a pleasure to see both of those guys. Jerry looked like he had just walked out of the Old Testament with his long hair and long beard. And he was still smiling.

So one night Carl, Jerry, and I (come to think of it, and not wanting to leave anybody out, there may have been a guy named Steve accompanying us as well) felt incredibly motivated—nay, perhaps obligated—to do some painting and make some changes to a cigarette billboard. Actually, it was two identical back to back billboards advertising cigs. Looking out at you from the signs and trying to sell you on the idea of buying his brand of smokes was the image of a hip guy with black hair and a thick black mustache. It was uncanny how by just lengthening the billboard man's hair to shoulder length, giving him a little beard and adding a bit to the stash, he looked just like Frank Zappa. (Somebody had to do this.) Please know that I in no way condone the defacing of billboards, and very likely Frank Zappa would not have either. It was so classic though. But I digress—let us return to that time period when Roy and I were both working for my brother Mike. As already mentioned, this was becoming a confusing season in my life. Undoubtedly, some of that confusion was exacerbated by experimenting with drugs. On a few occasions, Roy and I chose to experiment together. Roy was living in a great little place just outside of Lakewood. One evening while relaxing at his lakeside abode, we thought it might be fun to drop acid. It just so happened that on this particular evening, Roy had also scheduled a visit from a Kirby vacuum cleaner salesperson to come out and give a demonstration. That poor girl. I'm pretty sure the Kirby company never instructed their salespeople on how to give a presentation to a couple guys tripping on acid. She was a really good sport though and didn't even mind whipping the cord around a little so we could watch the "tracers" that it produced. Very early that next morning, Roy and I went to a nearby park to catch the sun coming up. It truly was a glorious sunrise. Interestingly, I remember feeling bad because I wasn't experiencing this beautiful sunrise as it really was. Instead I was seeing it under the residual influence of a hit of acid from the night before; that bothered me. Go figure.

I am compelled to mention here that in those years of our youth when Roy and I were horsing around together; although we most likely didn't make any huge contributions to the human race, we did develop a lifelong friendship that I am very grateful for today. Between travels and marriages and families and life, we sort of lost touch with each other in the early eighties. We seldom if ever even spoke to each other for twenty years or so. Today, however, I consider Roy one of my closest compadres. We even manage to get together on occasion. I so appreciate that life still includes a few good old friends.

It wasn't a total surprise when my folks gave a call to let me know that they had been contacted by a young man from New Zealand who was in Seattle and who was looking for me. It was Peter. He had found a job in London as planned and worked there until the autumn. He then started his trip back home to New Zealand by way of the USA. While in New York, he saw a sign at the bus station which read, "From anywhere in America to anywhere in America $99.00." Peter went up to the counter and said, "I'll have one of those, from NYC to Vancouver

British Columbia." The clerk, in Peter's words, "got difficult and told me Vancouver BC was not in America." After about fifteen minutes of arguing about the USA, the American continents (North and South), and then finally with the intervention of a supervisor, Peter got his ticket. Three weeks later, he was calling from Seattle. The next day, he was staying at my place and also working along with me for my brother Mike. In addition to working for Michael, Peter and I were also offered a little weekend job from the manager of the grocery store where I had previously been employed. Our task was to clean out behind the trash compactor, which was located on the back side of the store. The compactor was a big machine that crushed all of the grocery store garbage and then pushed it into a big storage tank. When the container was full, a semi-truck would replace it with an empty one. The thing is, all kinds of rotting, extremely foul-smelling, and very slimy grocery store garbage would manage to fall between the outside wall of the store and the storage container. Our fun job was to slip around in the sludge between the wall and the tank and clean it up. If I remember correctly, there was no shortage of nasty little flying bugs behind the compactor as well. (Welcome to America, Peter.) Between working in chicken houses in Israel, and now this, Peter and I had participated in a couple pretty funky jobs. I think the compactor clean up did at least pay fairly well.

You'd think our experience with devil's weed while in Israel would have been enough to curb any future drug adventures for Peter and me. It didn't. In Western Washington and in the '70s, you could sometimes see people wandering around the local cow fields and looking as if they were searching for something. They were likely looking for the little mushrooms that could be found popping up among the cow pies. These psilocybin or magic mushrooms were of the hallucinogenic kind, and they happened to be growing at the same time Peter was visiting. I'm not sure if we ate them or made tea or what. I do remember going to the Point Defiance Zoo and having a conversation with the harbor seals. The seals started barking incessantly at us, and at the time (and in our mental state), Peter and I were both pretty sure that they knew we were high. (They were probably begging for herring.) Peter ended up spending a few weeks at my place and in that time had a chance to see a little bit of the Great Northwest, save up enough money to continue his journey home, and talk to harbor seals. The last time I saw Peter, brother Mike and I had dropped him off at a freeway onramp heading south on I-5 and wished him Godspeed.

With multiple travels and jobs and address changes between us, Peter and I managed to totally lose touch of each other for over thirty-five years. About three months ago, I was so completely surprised when the phone rang, and guess who was calling from New Zealand? What a great and unexpected telephone call. Peter had recently been reminiscing about his time in Israel and was motivated to find out if kibbutz Nachshon had a webpage. They do, and the site has a link where previous volunteers can post a little message. I had also found the kibbutz webpage about ten years ago and posted a message that included our home phone number. It was incredibly cool to have a chance to be reconnected with my old friend Peter.

In the summer of 1978 and while still living on South Sawyer, my parents presented me with an interesting proposition. Mom and Dad were people who liked to stay active. Now that they no longer owned the auction house something else was needed to occupy their time. To at least temporarily fill that void, they decided it might be fun to manage a little restaurant for a few months. Mom's sister June and her husband Glen lived on the northernmost tip of the Kitsap Peninsula in the waterfront village of Hansville. They had moved to the peninsula from Seattle in 1969 during the Boeing-triggered economic collapse after having purchased a salmon fishing resort that was located in Hansville's booming metropolis. (If you know Hansville, you know that there was no and is no booming metropolis.) After ten busy years of operating Forbes Landing, they were now in the process of selling the business.

It was during this transition period that my folks agreed to manage the restaurant. They planned to expand the hours by adding a dinner service and expand the menu by adding (among other things) some very tasty steak and seafood selections. Dad really was a great self-taught chef, and Mom was an awesome baker. She made the most wonderful breads and pies and incredible cinnamon rolls, all of which would be included on the menu. (I can almost smell the cinnamon rolls now that Mom would without fail bake for all of our family get-togethers.) Mom and Dad's proposition was to have me join them for this little restaurant adventure. Although working at the furniture store had been a fine job for several months and although the South Sawyer house had been a great place to live, I was starting to feel like a change of scenery might not be a bad idea. Also, the opportunity to work with my folks while at the same time living in a quaint little waterfront village for a while was a pretty nice thought.

A few months prior, I had taken out a car loan and purchased a very nice Volkswagen van that was all decked out for camping. With a loan to pay, I would have never been able to make the move with my folks, except that just prior to their offer, someone ran into me one morning on the way to work and the van was totaled. I was sorry to see the van go, but the wreck did get me out from under the loan. (I would, however, so love to have that van today.) After submitting my notice of resignation to Michael and after finding a replacement renter for the South Sawyer house (actually two coworkers from the furniture store took over occupancy), Nicholas and I set out for Hansville.

CHAPTER 12

Not the Author of Confusion

Over the years, our family had made several day trips to Forbes Landing for visits with June and Glen. As a young teen, I even had the opportunity to spend a summer with them, working as a dock boy. As dock boy, my jobs included everything from pumping gas out on the floating fuel dock to selling bait, to washing boats, to whatever needed to be done at a salmon fishing resort. One of the tasks included in my job description was to operate the boat launch. (I could hardly believe they let me do it.) Many people would bring their fishing boats to the resort, which then needed to be launched. The boats were lifted off their trailers with a sling system, hoisted up and placed on a big metal cart that sat on tracks on the dock. The cart was then sent down the tracks using a pulley system into the water below. With the potential for putting the slings in the wrong places and hoisting the boat up all catawampus, or sending the cart down the tracks too fast thus shooting the boat and its occupants into the water, or worse yet bringing it up too fast and shooting the boat off the cart and off the end of the dock, there was definitely the possibility of messing up, especially for a young punk kid. Thankfully, no boats were damaged, and no fishermen (or fisherwomen) were injured on those occasions when I was captain of the launch.

Happily, I was never once called upon to operate the boat launch while working along with Mom and Dad. My job consisted of doing a little bit of everything in the kitchen, from prep cook to clean-up. I managed to learn enough from my folks that when June and Glen did sell the business, the new owners asked me to stay on and take over supervision of the restaurant. This meant that I would also be cooking for the dinner service. For the most part, everything went okay with my new position, except I couldn't shake the feeling that they really needed someone with way more experience than me to fill these shoes. The recipes my folks had put together were all pretty easy to consistently prepare, so the food was always very good. (We didn't, however, have Mom's wonderful fresh baked breads and pies any more.) As kitchen manager, I really did want to do a good job and to perform my duties in a professional manner. (Most of the time.) There was, however, this one afternoon when John the day cook and I both decided it would be fun to eat a big chunk of hash. By the time evening rolled around (and the group of about ten members of a CB radio club showed up for their reservation), I was finding it a little harder (no a lot harder) to prepare their meals than I would have had we passed on the big chunk of hash. The reviews from the group were all good, but that would be the one and only time I got high while trying to cook for guests of the restaurant.

Initially, when I first started working with Mom and Dad, a camper belonging to Uncle Glen (the kind that sits on the back of a pickup) was made available for me to live in, and at the time, it was all I really needed. As adequate as it was, when the new owners later offered me one of the cabins on the beach to live in, I couldn't very well say no. (While still living in the camper, dear Nicholas tried to jet across the Hansville Highway at just the wrong time and was hit by a little truck. He never did get to enjoy the cabin on the beach. What a great cat he was.) With the exception of no longer having Nicholas, living in a cabin overlooking Puget Sound, where it wasn't out of the question to sometimes see a pod of killer whales swimming by, was a pretty sweet deal. One day we even had an elephant seal swim past right out in front of the restaurant. This was such a beautiful place that I felt kind of bad keeping it all to myself. In the spirit of sharing, I tried a few times to compose a just right letter to the lovely Miss Linda Ronstadt.

At that time, Linda Ronstadt was in my book the most talented and beautiful folk-rock musician around. It seemed only fair to me that, with her busy, stressful life, Linda should be given the opportunity to spend a relaxing little vacation at my place on the beach in wonderful Hansville. I never was able to come up with an invitation that I felt was worthy of putting in the mail, so lovely Miss Ronstadt most likely never did get to enjoy the Hansville experience. Sorry Linda.

Although the new owners of Forbes Landing were more than happy with the operation of the restaurant, my feeling that they really needed somebody with way more knowledge and experience than me to properly do the job never did go away. It wasn't so very long before I let my very kind employers know that although I would stay on until they could hire a replacement, my days at the Landing were coming to an end. Brother Mike's business had grown to the point where they were now furnishing some apartments in Anchorage, Alaska. He offered me a position to go up and assist a guy that was already there and who was organizing the project. A replacement was found at the Landing, and I started to prepare for the move north. Although Mom and Dad were very aware that I was on my way to Alaska, they for the second time presented me with an unexpected proposition. The folks were planning to spend two or three months down on the Baja Peninsula in Mexico and wanted me to stay in their house while away. As mentioned, I was all set up to head for Alaska (which my parents had known for quite some time), so this offer came as quite a surprise. Although Michael probably wasn't terribly happy with my decision, I did choose to forego Alaska and instead house-sit for Mom and Dad. Mike was still in need of some manpower at the furniture store in Lakewood, so although I wouldn't be helping out in Anchorage, I would at least have the opportunity to work for him locally.

While employed at the fishing resort, because I was fortunate enough to be provided with lodging as part of the deal, I was able to stash a little something into savings. Now, while house-sitting for Mom and Dad, I was also living rent free so expenses were pretty minimal, and I was again able to put a little bit in the bank. (Minimal except for what I was continuing to spend on recreational activities.) Part of the reason that I originally decided to take my parents up on their offer to work at the restaurant was that I thought getting away from the environment I was in (which included very easy access to recreational activities) might be good for my mental and spiritual health. Fact is, though, if a person is trying to fill a void in their life with things like mind-altering intoxicants or irresponsible, non-committed relationships, or whatever, they will likely be able to find access to those things regardless of where they live. I was. Unless a change were to occur, unless I were to change, life was likely going to continue just the way that it had for the greater part of my young adult life. Don't get me wrong, I had experienced an incredible life. And yet there was now an underlying confusion and a longing for something more that wasn't just going away on its own.

As a young man who grew up in what I think most people would call a Christian home, one of the things instilled in me was that the Bible was really and truly inspired by God; that it was genuinely a place where we could find direction from the Creator of the Universe. I believed that. Although the time I spent actually reading the Bible was pretty minimal and pretty sporadic at best, I did nonetheless read it. It was while house-sitting at the folks' place that I came across a scripture that caused me to start thinking a little more seriously about the direction I was going. In the book of 1 Corinthians, Paul writes about how things ought to function when believers are gathered together. He makes the comment "God is not the author of confusion but of peace" (14:33, KJV). More and more, I was finding myself becoming increasingly confused and certainly not experiencing this "peace" that comes from God.

Then it happened. I guess you could call it an epiphany. A friend and I had met up at a popular tavern in the bayside town of Gig Harbor. It was a favorite place for beer and rock and roll. On this particular night, I was standing at the bar, getting a drink, and suddenly, out of the blue, somebody pinched my butt. (Now what's this?) Standing next to me was a surprisingly friendly little lass with an intoxicated (not intoxicating—intoxicated) smile on her face and a twinkle in her eye. It was pretty clear this young lady was not looking for a meaningful relationship. She was, however, amenable to joining me for a couple beers, followed by a ride back to my folks' house. Throughout the course of our time together, my new friend made a comment that, while pretty unexpected under the circumstances, was also so incredibly timely, considering what was going on in my heart and my head. She said, "Ya know, I really shouldn't be here like this right now." Wow, little did she know that I was thinking exactly the same thing. In the days just prior to encountering the girl from Gig Harbor, I had been reading (again in 1 Corinthians) how an intimate sexual relationship is meant to be

127

so very much more than just the selfish, self-gratifying act that I had allowed it to be. After her comment, I was suddenly compelled to spill out all the things that had been going through my head and all the reasons why I also felt that what we were doing wasn't right. It turns out she was actually feeling troubled about our liaison not due to any particular spiritual promptings but because she had a boyfriend back home that she lived with.

Although our reasons were a little different, neither of us was feeling very wonderful and fulfilled. We made the twenty-five-or-so-mile drive back to Gig Harbor, where I dropped her off at her place (or perhaps her boyfriend's place), and that was the last time we ever saw each other. It was now very late at night (or more accurately very early in the morning). We had indulged in lots of smoke and drink. I was really tired and was now making a twenty-five-mile drive back home when I shouldn't have been driving at all. Thank You, God, there wasn't much traffic on the road for the journey home. And thank You, God, that during the trip, whilst driving the wrong direction on a freeway off-ramp (thinking I had entered the on-ramp), I didn't kill anybody.

What am I doing? What am I doing? *What in the hell am I doing?* Even in my blurred condition, it was crystal clear that this was not the way I wanted to live life anymore. As a child, I believe that I really did experience a genuine relationship with Jesus. Then as the years went by, some of the so-called "pleasures of this world" became more and more a part of my life and more and more a priority. There was that attempt during high school at making some changes, even to the point of promising God that I would. When all was said and done though, I couldn't, and truth be told probably wasn't ready to. Now I was ready. After finally making it home, I got down on the living room floor and began to have a heartfelt talk with the Almighty. Unlike four years prior when I was making promises and telling God about all the things I was going to do (or not do), this time no promises were being made. I had come to realize that if the changes I was longing for were really going to happen, He would have to be the one to do it. I think it was somebody associated with Alcoholics Anonymous that came up with the phrase "Let go and let God." I'm not sure if I was familiar with this phrase at the time or not, but in any case, it perfectly summed up what so very much needed to happen in my life. I can't remember ever really having a problem with the idea of Jesus being my Savior. I believed he was. I also believed that on many occasions since I was a child, He had shown Himself to be my friend. I hadn't, however, really ever grasped the concept of Jesus being my Lord. This would have meant submitting to His leading and actually trying to do His will. (I hadn't been and wasn't doing that.) Pretty much, I just did whatever I wanted to and hoped God would somehow and for some reason bless it, whether it was according to His good plan or not. I had asked Jesus into my life or heart or however you want to say it, at a young age, but over the years, it was like I progressively managed to limit Him to some little corner room of my heart's home. I hadn't really wanted Him residing in the whole house.

Now, in the wee hours of the morning, on the floor of my mom and dad's living room, through tears, I asked Jesus to please make Himself at home in my life, from the basement to the attic. I had tried doing things my own way and under my own power for enough years to realize that this was not the road I wanted to travel anymore. That morning, I asked the Lord of heaven and earth to please start showing me what His ways looked like and to give me the help and ability to actually try and follow Him, to continue on this journey in a direction that might even be pleasing to Him. Since those early morning hours, my life has never been the same.

I realize this whole "getting to know Jesus" thing I'm talking about all sounds pretty weird. It is very weird and pretty unbelievable. I also know that there's a whole world full of people out there who have experienced something very similar to what I have (the "getting to know Jesus" part, not necessarily the night of being loaded and driving the wrong way on a freeway off-ramp). Just last week was Easter Sunday. Although the festivities are recognized in many different ways by many different flavors of people from around the globe, of those folks who celebrated Easter and who also consider themselves Christians, many would probably agree on a few things. God chose to come to earth in the form of a human being. That human being was Jesus. This Jesus became a sacrifice for the sins of the world and was crucified on a cross. The crucified body of Jesus was laid in a tomb, and after three days, He rose from the dead and was alive again (hence Easter). He ascended into heaven and has made Himself available to us by His Holy Spirit.

He will give us a new life and actually live inside of us by His Spirit if we believe in Him. How insane is that? And yet now nearly forty years later, as much as I am capable of believing, I do believe those very things to be true. Rest assured, although life has never been the same since that morning, each day requires decisions, and I always have the opportunity of choosing to follow His lead or not. I can also choose to go my own stupid way (which I frequently have and still do). I believe it's what the Bible is referring to when it talks about the Spirit being at odds with the flesh and the flesh at odds with the Spirit. The wonderful thing is He is always there and will always give the power to follow His good way if I am willing. And even on those instances when I have gotten it wrong, sometimes very wrong, He has again and again graciously worked things out for good (in spite of me).

CHAPTER 13

Return to Israel

The weeks following my "epiphany" only served to confirm that a change in my heart and head really was taking place. Instead of feeling like I *couldn't* partake in mind-altering intoxicants because I *shouldn't* and then struggling not to, I found that I no longer needed to. I had been given the power to choose not to. Also, instead of looking at a young woman with sexual eyes, I started to see them as the beautiful creations that they are—daughters who are loved by their Father God. I also found myself with a desire like never before to read the Bible and try to better understand what was written and what I had, for as long as I could remember, considered to be true. Truth's like that spoken by Jesus when he said, "Abide in Me, and I in you. As the branch cannot bear fruit unless it abides in the vine, so neither can you unless you abide in Me. I am the vine, you are the branches; he who abides in Me and I in him, he bears much fruit, for apart from Me you can do nothing" (John 15:4–5, NASB).

I had been needing to learn that it simply wasn't possible to live the kind of life I had been longing for, on my own and apart from Him. In John 12: 24–25, where He said, "Listen carefully: Unless a grain of wheat is buried in the ground, dead to the world, it is never more than a grain of wheat. But if it is buried, it sprouts and reproduces itself many times over. In the same way, anyone who holds on to life just as it is destroys that life. But if you let it go, reckless in your love, you'll have it forever, real and eternal" (The Message). That's what this whole being born again thing was that I had heard about growing up. Although there was so much at that time that I didn't understand about living a life with Jesus (and quite frankly there's probably as much or more that I don't understand today), what I was "getting" for sure was that to believe in and have a real relationship with Jesus was way bigger than simply saying "I believe" and then working really hard to follow Him. (and then ultimately not being able to do it). Or saying "I believe" and then just doing anything and everything I wanted while naively thinking it would be pleasing to God. It meant trying to let go of my selfish, self-gratifying (self) and letting Jesus be the Lord that He is. To try to follow His direction while remembering that it was only by His grace and by the power that He gives that I would be able to follow Him at all. (And so the adventure continues.)

Sometime after Mom returned from her trip to Israel, she saw an article in the newspaper about an agricultural community in the north of the country not so very far from the Lebanese border. Although the settlement was much like a traditional moshav, it was at the same time very different. The members and residents of Nes Ammim were believers in Jesus and were all non-Jewish. She showed me the story and then tucked it away in a filing cabinet. Now, at a time when I was doing a lot of thinking and dreaming and praying about what the future might hold, I remembered the article. After some searching, I was able to dig it up from my folk's filing cabinet. The newspaper clipping told of a settlement located between Haifa and the border of Lebanon. This very unique Christian kibbutz was established in 1963 by a few individuals and families who, coming from Europe, were well acquainted with the atrocities of the Holocaust. The pioneers who founded the settlement wanted to show solidarity between Christians and Jews by living and working in Israel and contributing to its growth. By 1979 Nes Ammim had expanded into a vibrant communal village that, in addition to growing cotton and avocados, was also a major grower and exporter of roses.

Like other working agricultural communities in Israel, Nes Ammim needed volunteers to get all the work done. Their volunteer program (or work-study program) was a combination of working in a variety of jobs while also attending a number of lectures, along with taking trips throughout the country with the other volunteers. The program was designed to help explore the roots of the Christian faith within the Jewish context. (Jesus was after all, a Jew.)

Several months earlier, when Mom first showed me the article, the idea of returning to Israel to live and work in a Christian community was definitely not among my plans for the near or even the distant future (not at all). But now, after having gone through some pretty significant changes in my head and heart and after a couple weeks of thinking and praying and envisioning the whole possibility, it became undeniably clear that there was nowhere I wanted to go and nothing I wanted to do—more. This may have been the first time I ever genuinely and wholeheartedly prayed to ask God for some specific direction in life. Although I guess we can never be absolutely sure that what we're doing is in line with His great plan for our lives, I was more sure about returning to Israel and about knocking on the door of Nes Ammim than I had ever been about anything else prior.

My interpretation of the article about Nes Ammim may have been a little different than what the author was intending. Or maybe I just didn't see some of the fine points, like that part about volunteers needing to go through an application process and being selected into the program. I missed that. There was also the fact that Nes Ammim really wasn't looking for volunteers from America. Missed that too. What I did see was the part about a diverse community made up of "believers" from several different countries, living in the land where Jesus was born and where the volunteers were part of a program that would allow them to work and learn and hopefully get to know this Jesus better; that's what I saw. Now one might think that if a person were going to jump on a plane heading for Israel with the sole intent of living in a particular community, that person might have the forethought to first contact the community and make sure they were as excited about his coming as he was about going. (Nah, we got this. It's all good.)

Incredibly, when Mom and Dad returned from Mexico and heard all about my plans to hit the road, they didn't immediately tell me all the reasons why it was a bad idea. In fact, after having a chance to explain to them just what was motivating me and why, they were surprisingly encouraging and maybe a little excited about the idea. I even had a chance to tell my Dad about the "night out" that broke the camel's back so to speak and ultimately redirected the spiritual journey

I was on. That discussion with Dad was prompted by him asking the question and making the remark, "What happened to you while we were gone? You have changed." I knew that I had wanted to change and could only hope that what Dad saw was something real that was actually taking place inside. What an amazing and welcome confirmation it was to have my folks support me in a decision that I know for many parents would have been totally out of the question. They could have easily said, "Tim, you are twenty-one years old. You haven't gone to college, and you don't even know what sort of career you are planning to pursue. Come on, boy. Get your act together and reach for that American dream." They could have said something like this, but they didn't. It also surprised me when Mom and Dad somehow managed not to hear (or at least not to freak out) about the terrorist attack that had just taken place in the seaside city of Nahariya, just a few miles from Nes Ammim. I found myself half wondering if maybe God had shielded them from that little bit of world news so they wouldn't worry.

Having had the good fortune of living rent-free for several months and, as a result, being able to save up a fair little chunk of change, it was only a few weeks after my folks return that I was strapping on the backpack and returning to the land of Israel. In those days, there was no such thing as a cell phone or a GPS for the general public. What I knew for sure about the location of Nes Ammim was that it was just a little south of Nahariya.

Getting there was simply a matter of asking people the best way to do it. After a bus ride from the airport to Haifa and then another north on Highway 4 up the coast, the bus pulled over at my stop. The driver (who I had told my final destination) pointed to a road running next to an avocado orchard and stated, "Nes Ammim." I hadn't made it very far down this road when a car coming in the opposite direction pulled over next to me and a guy with a big smile stuck his head out the passenger window, asking in English and with an American accent where I was going. The gentleman asking the question would along with his wife become two of my very dearest friends.

Lev (the passenger in the car) and his lovely wife, Hava, were originally from the States but had been living in Israel for several years. They were, at that time, the only American members of Nes Ammim. I told both Lev and Bob (Bob being the driver of the vehicle and who I think was originally from Switzerland) that I was someone who had come to Israel, believing that I should be living and working in their fair village. Both Lev and Bob were probably thinking, *Oh great, another one of those "God told me to come here" people.* The thing is, I really did feel like God was involved with my coming to Nes Ammim. Lev got out and headed over to the bus stop that I had just come from. Bob invited me to jump in and, after turning the car around, gave me a lift to the village. He brought me to the office of a surprisingly young-looking English guy named Jim, who I'm guessing held the position of administrator of the community. Whatever his official title, Jim was the guy who needed to decide if I would be given the opportunity to stick around for a while or not.

Typically, the only volunteers in Nes Ammim were those who had gone through the application and selection process. I had intentionally chosen not to contact Nes Ammim before landing on their front door. The truth is, I felt very strongly that I shouldn't contact them first. Jim told me that had I written and inquired about the possibility of being a volunteer, I would have been told that they didn't currently have ties with any churches in America and hence no program to receive volunteers from America. He ended up inviting me to stay long enough to be interviewed by a small team of community members who I guess were called upon at times such as this. The little committee ultimately decided that I would be welcome to remain as a volunteer and also participate in the work-study program. Did God have anything to do with my coming to this unique Christian community in the north of Israel or with things working out so that I would be invited to stay? I've always thought He did.

The village was made up of a diverse mix of members and volunteers from Holland, Germany, Switzerland, Sweden, and Canada. There was also Lev and Hava, the only American members in the community, and one other American volunteer named Rolf. Rolf was from New York, but I believe he had lived several years in and perhaps was even born in Norway. Rolf was a thoughtful, philosophical kind of guy who had recently graduated from a Bible school in the States and then come to live and work in Israel. Like me, he was one of the chosen few who had been invited to stay at Nes Ammim without having gone through the "system." Rolf became sort of a spiritual big brother to me, and although we haven't seen each other for over thirty years (and actually haven't even exchanged letters for a few years) I consider him one of my closest lifelong friends. I don't know how Rolf managed to travel with so many books, but he had an incredible library in Israel and ended up passing along a number of his books to me. This included some classics like *The Pursuit of God* by A. W. Tozer, *The Cost of Discipleship* by Dietrich Bonhoeffer, *The Normal Christian Faith* by Watchman Nee, *Rees Howells Intercessor* by Norman Grubb, and *Mere Christianity* by C. S. Lewis (and those are just a few of the ones that I can remember). What a wonderful, unbelievable gift for a young guy wanting and trying to get to know Jesus better, to be able to live and work in a Christian community where there were several other people on a spiritual journey not so unlike my own while at the same time being able to see the land that the Bible I was reading was actually talking about. And then on top of all that, to be able to read some classic books along the way. Oh, have I mentioned that about a half hour on a bicycle, I could be at a beautiful beach on the Mediterranean—it was very good.

In addition to spending a little free time at the beach, I would also occasionally hike through some nearby old growth olive groves and up into the nearby hills. One day, I headed off with the goal of visiting an old castle ruin that some of the other volunteers had told me about. I knew what general direction it was in, just not exactly how to get there. After a few hours of wandering around the hot Israeli hillsides and finishing off a boda bag of water, I managed to develop a nasty migraine headache (the kind that messes up your ability to see). I was grateful to come across a little shelter that somebody had made by stacking rocks together and for the shade it provided. After hanging out there for a half hour or forty-five minutes, my vision started returning to normal. Unfortunately, I never did find the castle ruins (at least not on this trip). On the way home though, I was fortunate enough to wander into a little community that at the time was made up of an American guy named Danny, his Israeli wife, Irit, and their two sweet kids, Carmel and Adam. Also living in community Clil was another American guy named Raphael along with his Israeli wife, Devora. These honest-to-goodness pioneers were just in the beginning stages of building their little piece of heaven on earth in the foothills of

Western Galilee. At this particular phase of development, they were all living in tents. Danny and Irit provided me with a much-needed drink of water and also filled up my wine skin before I made the trek back to Nes Ammim. This would not be my only visit to community Clil as we all became very good friends, and I ended up visiting them often. Little Adam was about a year old, and Carmel, although only three, tried to teach me some Hebrew. She took her teaching pretty seriously and made sure to speak up when I pronounced something wrong (which I did a lot), sometimes rolling her eyes.

My friendship with the people of community Clil really was too good to keep to myself. I introduced them to some of the other folks from Nes Ammim, and a group of us even ended up helping Danny and Irit to build their home. They had managed to obtain a little wooden cabin that I believe had previously been some kind of military housing in one of the Scandinavian countries during WWII (I just can't remember which one). The walls and roof were already assembled in sections and just needed to be put together on a cement foundation. Skilled construction guy that I was (not), I managed to stab Danny in the leg with a shovel while mixing cement for the floor. It still makes me cringe to think about it. Lucky for our friends at Clil, several members of the little building team actually knew what they were doing, so Danny and Irit ended up with a sweet little wood cottage.

I have mentioned that Jerusalem was one of my very favorite places in the whole world. That only became more true during the return trip to Israel. While living at Nes Ammim, I would make the 110-or-so-mile journey to the City of Peace as often as possible. In addition to walking the narrow, colorful streets of the Old City souk in the Arab Quarter, another one of my favorite places to visit in Jerusalem was the Garden Tomb. Many believe that this is the actual tomb belonging to Joseph of Arimathea, where Jesus was laid after the crucifixion. Many also believe, however, that the church of the Holy Sepulcher is the location of the tomb where Jesus's body was placed. I think that ownership of this site (the sepulcher) is shared by the Greek Orthodox, Armenian Orthodox, and Roman Catholic churches. Also on the scene are the Coptic, Ethiopian, and Syriac Orthodox churches with each denomination carefully guarding their designated section. Rumor had it that on occasion, fists would start to fly during arguments over who was in charge of what. While visiting the Holy Sepulcher church, I was assured by one of the several gentlemen in long robes (not sure just which orthodox he was) that this was indeed the "genuine" location of the tomb. This same gentleman also offered to say a prayer for me, but if I remember correctly, this service was only available for a nominal fee. In contrast, when visiting the Garden Tomb, the first thing you notice is how simple it is. There is a garden, and there is a tomb. If you ask one of the caretakers if this is "the place," they may likely tell you not only that they don't know for sure but also that it doesn't matter. They will also probably remind you of the words spoken by the angel and found in Matthew 28:6, where it says, "He is not here, for he has risen." The fact that Jesus is risen and no longer in any tomb is more important to them than where the tomb is located. Although I have no idea if either the Garden Tomb or the Church of the Holy Sepulcher is the actual location of the site where Jesus was laid, it would be very easy to believe that the garden is the actual place. The whole vibe is just so genuinely good. And I don't think anybody there would ever offer to pray for you and then ask to be paid in return.

As much as I liked visiting the old city souk and the Garden Tomb, I also had a few more regular stops when in Jerusalem. Funny thing how they all had to do with food. (A young guy does need to eat after all.) I don't know if any of these places still exist, but at that time, there was a little baker's shop just inside of Damascus gate known as the Green Door. (Wouldn't you know it, the door was green.)

Inside this ancient old city bakery was an Arab guy baking breads in a clay oven. In addition to bread, he would also use his dough to make you an awesome little pizza, but not just any pizza. He would typically place some cheese and a raw egg or two into the middle of the dough before baking it and that in itself was delicious. The savvy pizza eater, however, knew that if you made a stop in the market and bought a few veggies prior to seeing Mr. Pizza Man, he would cut up and add those veggies to your personal pizza. (Delightful—and you might even notice a hint of smoky flavor from the cig hanging out of good Mr. Green Door's mouth.)

Another one of the several gates of the Old City is Herod's. Not far from Herod's gate was another favorite spot for delicious food called Uncle Mustache's. You could always count on Uncle Mustache for a great plate of roasted chicken and rice. But seeing how man does not live on savory food alone, it was also necessary to find a few extraordinary locations that offered something sweet. I was never disappointed by the sugared Turkish-style coffee and baklava (or other yummy baked goodies) that could always be found in the old city souk. Sometimes, though, I or the people I was with would be craving a little something different. On those instances, we would head outside of the old city walls and over to a tea shop called Tea and Pie, Don't Pass Me Bye. In addition to tea and coffee, you could also get a piece of awesome homemade pie. It kind of reminded me of some places back home, and after all, there's nothing quite like a great piece of pie. It's a little embarrassing, but my wife will tell you that although I can't seem to remember people's names, I can always remember what, where, and when I ate something, no matter how many years ago it's been. Just the glutton in me, I guess.

The members and volunteers of Nes Ammim were comprised of a colorful mix of religious backgrounds and denominations. Everything from Dutch Reformed to Catholic to Lutheran to the oddball like me who grew up Baptist. We met together as a church community on Saturday morning for a pretty traditional sort of service (with the exception of everybody being in shorts and sandals). It was Israel, and it was hot. I can't deny that one of my favorite parts of that gathering was when we enjoyed coffee and freshly baked cake after the service. (There's that glutton in me again, and the lovely European ladies of Nes Ammim always made a delicious coffee cake.) It was on Saturday afternoons that I probably experienced some of the most memorable "church" that I ever had and perhaps ever have since. Lev and Hava were friends to a dear elderly English couple who lived just north of the community. On Saturday afternoons, these lovely people would open up their house to a group of folks (including Lev and Hava) who were all wanting to try and get to know Jesus better. Lev and Hava were kind enough to invite some Nes Ammimers that they thought might be interested in participating, and I was fortunate to be one of those. Although we never officially referred to it as one, I guess you would call this little gathering a home church. Stanley was a retired English naval officer, a pastor, and also the most knowledgeable and engaging Bible scholar that I have ever known. Between Stanley's wonderful way of bringing the Bible to life, along with his lovely wife Ethel's incredible English piccalilli that she always made available for our Saturday evening meals together, it was a beautiful thing. (If you have never eaten homemade English piccalilli, I can only hope you have the opportunity to try some. It's good.)

Our Saturday gathering at Stanley and Ethel's often made me feel like I was experiencing something out of the book of Acts, where believers would come together from house to house for fellowship. And we were in Israel no less. Not that I thought being in Israel had some kind of extra added spiritual significance. (Well, maybe a little.) There was, however, no place on earth I would have rather been.

Carol and I just received a letter last week from Hava. On February 6, 2017, at ninety-nine and a half years old, it was time for dear Stanley to remove his earth suit and take flight to eternity. In the words of Hava, "Until the end his light for the Lord was shining! He was still clear in his mind and remembered the young people who he and Ethel ministered to along the way." I will forever be grateful for the privilege of knowing this man who made such an impression on my life. I believe he was a classic example of what it looks like to "be real." To live out what he claimed to believe.

One of the afternoons at Stanley and Ethel's house took place just after their return from a few weeks holiday in Great Britain. Earlier the same day of the meeting, I had been hanging out with a Canadian volunteer named Paul. We were talking about some of the great music being made by people who were motivated by their relationship with Jesus—artists and groups like Larry Norman, Love Song, Honeytree, Keith Green, 2nd Chapter of Acts, Andrae Crouch, Randy Stonehill, Barry McGuire, and others. Paul mentioned how he wished he had brought a tape from his home in Canada, which had songs by a guy named Don Francisco. The one tune in particular he wanted me to hear was called "He's Alive." It was a song about the life and resurrection of Jesus as told by the disciple Peter. Well, that evening during the get together (Paul was there too), Stanley pulled out a cassette tape that he and Ethel had recorded on a little portable recorder while at a home group meeting in England. He wanted us to hear this great song that apparently a guy was playing at the meeting. It was a song about the life and resurrection of Jesus as told by Peter, and the guy singing it was

Don Francisco. Did I believe we had just experienced a "God thing"? Absolutely.

Another very special time of "church" that I was fortunate enough to experience while in Israel and will forever remember was a little prayer group that a few of us met together with when in the old city. I can't recall how we heard about it or who from Nes Ammim was originally invited, but this unique little ecumenical group of folks (which sometimes included a nun or two) met together in an upstairs apartment located on the Via Dolorosa. You know the place, the street in the old city of Jerusalem that Jesus walked on the way to His crucifixion. I felt pretty privileged to be there.

My work at Nes Ammim mostly revolved around the glass houses where the roses were grown. At one point, I was part of a little group known as the D Team that prepared the D glass house for planting. Everything from digging the beds to laying the drip irrigation lines to filling the beds in with tuff, a small volcanic rock used for hydroponic growing (no dirt necessary). The D Team included my good buddy Rolf along with a couple Dutch volunteers who also became my friends. We did make a pretty good team. Another one of my compadres in the community was a big Canadian guy named Jan. Jan was a construction worker by trade and is probably the reason that Danny and Irit's little cottage came out as nice as it did. For a while, Jan and I were responsible for using a tractor with a forklift attachment to load the large and surprisingly heavy boxes of roses into a big truck for transport. This would be my first experience with using a forklift. Hopefully, not too many roses were damaged when I may have a time or two poked the forks through a box.

At Nes Ammim, we celebrated both Jewish and Christian holidays and also sometimes just had parties for fun. On occasion, we had costume parties. I think it was at one of those "just for fun" costume parties that Jan put on a poodle dress as if he were going to a sock hop and came as my date. I went as a fifties greaser. (No disrespect intended and not that Jan wasn't a good-looking guy, but he wasn't a very pretty date. Maybe it was the mutton chops.) Before going into the party, we thought it would be fun to first try and master how to do a back-to-back flip so we could awe everybody on the dance floor. We locked arms, and I bent over forward while Jan tried to flip backward over my head, landing on his feet. I'm not sure where we went wrong, but while Jan was still upside down with his feet in the air, he fell off my back and landed on his head. We were doing this on a cement floor. Needless to say, Jan and I didn't impress anybody with our fancy fifties-style dance moves, and I'm not sure, but he may have suffered a concussion. It wasn't a very fun date. In addition to loading the boxes of roses, Jan and I were also tasked with replacing cracked or broken panes of glass on the glass houses. Sometimes while working with sheets of glass on the roof, you could find yourself in a precarious position with the potential for losing your footing and falling through. The roof was probably about ten feet high at its lowest and maybe fifteen or twenty at the peak. (Far enough to hurt a bit when you hit the ground if you fell through.) Thankfully, on that occasion when I lost my footing on the roof, it was only my arm that broke through the glass. It was interesting to say the least being able to check out what the muscle inside my arm looked like. I still have a good-sized scar just below the left bicep to remind me to be grateful for not having experienced more damage.

My friend Jan was also among the little group of folks that met at Stanley and Ethel's on Saturday evening. At one point during our time together, we were looking at the topic of baptism. Six of us who were participating in this particular study (to include Jan and me) came away with a sincere desire to be baptized. Actually, I think all of us were choosing to be rebaptized. I had been dunked as a young boy but honestly didn't really know what I was doing or why. The five others had likewise been baptized before but as infants having come from a reformed background. For all of us, I think we just wanted to make a tangible statement and demonstrate that we really believed in Jesus and truly believed that He had given us a new life. I am well aware that people have different opinions about what baptism is and about what it should look like. (Such was the case at Nes Ammim, and not everybody agreed with what we were choosing to do.) The six of us were simply trying to be obedient to the Scripture as we understood it and do what we thought we should. In the end and despite the controversy that was ultimately generated, it was a great day for each of us when on April 12, 1980, we all took the plunge in the Jordan River.

When looking for a little solitude, the underground bomb shelter at Nes Ammim was sometimes the place I would go. During one of those visits to the shelter, I was reading the Bible and talking to God. Although I knew it probably wasn't the recommended way to try to communicate with the Creator of the universe, I found myself asking God if He would please give me a special message. Something just for me and something that on the surface seemed like a reasonable request. I would close my eyes, open the Bible, put my finger on the page, open my eyes, and voila, whatever verse I was pointing at would be my special word from God, just for me. That at least was my hope. After opening my eyes and eagerly gazing upon the text beneath my finger, it seemed pretty obvious that this wasn't the special word from God that I was looking for. The verses were something along the lines of "The sons of Japheth were Gomer, Magog, Javan, Tubal, Meshech, and Tiras. And the sons of Gomer were Ashkenaz, Diphath, and Togarmah. And the sons of Javan were Elishah, Tarshish, Kittim, and Rodanim." And so on and so forth. If there was a special message there just for me, I wasn't seeing it. Oh well, no harm done. I turned to another place in the Bible, this time just to do some reading. When I did, it was like a verse jumped out at me from the page, as if the print were highlighted. The words were from James 4:3, and it wasn't a verse I was familiar with. It read as follows, "You ask and do not receive because you ask with wrong motives, so that you may spend it on your pleasures" (NASB). I was actually reading a King James Bible, and it read like this "Ye ask, and receive not, because ye ask amiss, that ye may consume it upon your lusts." Yikes. So I'm asking God for a special word that was "just for me." Not a word that would be good or helpful or anything for anybody else, but "just for me." I flip to a scripture that seems pretty obviously not to be an answer to my prayer. God didn't give me what I asked for. Then suddenly I'm unexpectedly given exactly what I was asking for and not only is it words on a page that are speaking to my head, but I feel like it's God speaking directly to the needs of my heart.

I could then and still can easily believe that this was a very specific answer to my prayer. As already mentioned, this probably wasn't considered the recommended way to hear from God. For me, I guess it was kind of like, "Why not ask and see what happens?" Turns out that night in the bomb shelter wouldn't be the only time I played Bible roulette with God. During my stay at Nes Ammim, there was a time when I suddenly found myself feeling incredibly weak—I mean really, really weak. I had honestly never felt so tired. As it turned out, I had some-how managed to pick up what was evidently hepatitis A. I was never sure where I got it, and nobody else in the community experienced anything similar. Whatever the case, I was given a nice little bungalow to stay in for several days during a pseudo quarantine. During this mandatory vacation, I was praying for my friend David's dad who was at that time a hostage in Iran. (David was the high school buddy that I lived together with in the school bus during our senior year, along with Bart, GJ, and Smokey—good doggies.) His dad, Colonel Thomas Schaefer, was the US military attaché and ranking US military officer at the embassy in Tehran when fifty-two Americans were taken hos-tage on November 4, 1979. While praying for the safety and release of Dave's dad and the other hostages, I once again asked God for a special word. This time though I wasn't asking for something "just for me" but rather a word that would be encouraging for Dave and his family. Like during the visit to the bomb shelter, I closed my eyes, opened the Bible, put my finger to the page, and when I opened my eyes, this is what I was pointing at: "And suddenly there came a great earthquake, so that the foundations of the prison house were shaken; and immediately all the doors were opened, and everyone's chains were unfastened" (Acts 16:26, NASB).

Now I realize it may be a stretch to think this verse was actually the special word I was praying for. (It wasn't until several months later that the hostages were released, and there was no earthquake involved.) At the time though, I was pretty encouraged by what I read and genu-inely thought it could be, enough that I wrote David about it in a letter. (Dave might have thought I was a little over the top with all the Jesus stuff.) As far as the verse goes, it doesn't really matter if it was a special word just for that moment or not. I do know that several years later, Dave's dad was quoted as saying, "My bottom line was that my faith in God and belief in the power of prayer got me through it all." Colonel Schaefer was by the way a hostage for 444 days, and 150 of those were spent in solitary confinement.

One day, while a group of us were taking a little break from the glass houses, somebody pulled out a cassette tape they had received in the mail and put it into a tape deck for us to hear. It was a newly released album from Bob Dylan called "Slow Train Coming." This was so cool. Bob Dylan, a good Jewish boy, was singing all these great lyrics that were so obviously motivated by the Bible. Songs about his new-found faith and even about Jesus in particular. Hearing the songs being sung by one of the most influential musicians of my lifetime, who was also Jewish, at a time in life when I was trying to get to know Jesus better, and hearing them while living in Israel, somehow just made it all the more cool. Occasionally, if we were in Jerusalem on a weekend, a few of us would go to the Baptist House (a church in the city) for a morning service. During one of those services, the little kids all came out singing "Man Gave Names to All the Animals" one of the songs on the *Slow Train Coming* album. I wonder if Bob ever knew that one of his songs was being sung by the children at a church in Jerusalem.

A couple years after the release of *Slow Train*, Bob Dylan released an album called *Shot of Love*. This was the third of three albums Mr. Robert Zimmerman (aka Bob Dylan) put out that openly talked about his faith. Not everybody was real happy with the type of music Bob was doing during that period. They didn't want to hear about Jesus; they wanted to hear "Lay Lady Lay." I think Mr. Dylan received a lot of criticism over those years and can imagine it was pretty difficult. It seemed to me that you could really hear the trouble that Bob was feeling in the title song "Shot of Love." For several years after that album was released, I thought about sending Mr. Dylan a letter of encouragement (a shot of love so to speak). It probably ended up taking at least a decade before I finally put pen to paper and got a letter in the mail addressed to Bob. I never heard back from him, and most likely, he never even saw it. Oh well. The fact remains; we could all use a shot of love.

After fourteen months of living in Nes Ammim, it started becoming time to figure out what would be happening next. I thought a lot about pursuing the possibility of changing from a volunteer to a permanent resident of the community. Living in the Holy Land had definitely been one of the most significant chapters of my life. I couldn't help but to seriously think about staying longer. At the same time though, and as grateful as I was for this incredible gift of living and working in Israel, I also found myself thinking about a possibility that had never ever been something I'd genuinely considered before. Having grown up during the Vietnam War, I had pretty much decided that military service was not going to be part of my life. In fact, prior to the end of the draft in 1973, I was someone who would have told you they would go to Canada rather than ever being drafted. That's really how I felt. Now, while asking God what the future might be holding for me, I wasn't just considering the possibility of serving in the military. Surprisingly, I was developing a heartfelt desire to do it and specifically to serve in the medical field.

After much thought and prayer, I did ultimately choose to leave the land of Israel and head for home—not however until after enjoying one more wonderful trip into the middle and southern parts of the country. Lev and Hava had decided to celebrate their anniversary (not sure how many years it was) by loading up the community VW transporter pickup with camping gear and an additional four friends to celebrate with them. I was so very fortunate to be one of the four invited to come along for the ride. (Four volunteers and a nice little dog named Muchie.) It was great to have one more chance to travel into the Sinai Peninsula and once again enjoy the beautiful coastal beaches. (No running around naked this time.) We camped on the beach of Dahab located on the southern end of the Gulf of Aqaba before the gulf reaches the Red Sea. At that time, Dahab appeared to be little more than a few Bedouin families residing in this desert oasis. One little group of Bedouins who had their tent set up quite near to our campsite even provided us (for a minimal fee) with some delicious thin bread they had prepared over a fire on the lid of a steel drum. I was sad one morning to see that our neighbors had packed up and moved away without a sound and also sad that the night before they had managed to steal some of our gear while we were sleeping—literally right out from under our heads. Oh well, it wasn't anything we couldn't live without, and hopefully they found their take useful.

In addition to camping on a beautiful beach, the trip also included throwing our sleeping bags down at the foot of Masada. Masada is an ancient mountaintop bastion, which was the site of the Jewish Zealot's last stand against the Romans after the fall of Jerusalem in AD 70. Located in southeastern Israel, Masada sits atop a rock plateau, overlooking the Dead Sea. After camping out for the night (and being eaten alive by mosquitoes or some other nasty little flying bug), we got up early the next morning and took the hike up what's called the "snake path" to the top. From there, we could look around the ancient ruins of what had once been a desert fortress built by Herod the Great. I think it must have been the same day that we also visited and took a dip in the Dead Sea. It's a pretty unique experience to float around on top of the mineral rich waters of this salty sea with its shores at over 1,400 feet below sea level, making it the earth's lowest elevation on land. The water makes a person so buoyant that I saw a guy having his picture taken reading a newspaper while floating around. It was pretty fun playing in the medicinal mud baths as well.

Our tour of the country included a visit to the Flour Caves, where you could wander around the unique underground passages created by water erosion of the soft limestone. When you came out, you really did need to brush off the limestone "flour" that gets all over your clothes. We also made a stop at Qumran to visit one of the several caves where what we have come to know as the Dead Sea Scrolls were found. In 1947 a Bedouin shepherd discovered the first of these parchment and papyrus scrolls inside of some clay jars. I believe the dates when these documents were written ranges from the first century BC to the first century AD. The Dead Sea Scrolls are apparently the oldest surviving manuscripts of the Bible that exist today.

CHAPTER 14

Neither Jew nor Greek— or Colonel or Private

It just so happened that at the same time I was making plans to leave Israel and head for home, my parents were making plans to visit England and Ireland and spend a little time with our wonderful relatives. Mom and Dad were kind enough to suggest that I join them for the trip, so instead of flying directly to the States, I met up with my folks in London and once again had a chance to impose upon our incredible cousins in both England and the Emerald Isle. Needless to say, we had a wonderful, wonderful time. While riding on the boat from Scotland to Northern Ireland, I had the great pleasure of meeting a lovely girl from Belfast who had been on holiday in England. Geri was a school teacher and also among a very unique group of people living in Northern Ireland. One of her parents was Catholic, and the other a Protestant. (That was definitely not something you saw very often in Ireland, especially in those days.)

Before departing the boat and saying goodbye, Geri invited me to visit her family home in Belfast, where she lived with her siblings. Sadly, Geri's mother had passed away some time prior, and her father was residing in a nursing home. I did take Geri up on her offer and spent a great day with her as my guide in Belfast, followed by a couple days in the family home along with her and her brothers and sisters. I was also able to accompany Geri to the nursing home and meet her father. What a huge honor to meet this man; in spite of the turmoil and danger that he and his wife surely faced, they didn't let the political and religious craziness and troubles of the time dictate the outcome of their life together. I would have loved to also been able to meet Geri's courageous mother.

While visiting this great family, I was tasked to go out into the vegetable garden and dig up some potatoes for dinner. I'm a bit embarrassed to say that Geri had to give me a little lesson in how to properly go about it. (Need to be careful not to bruise or cut the tubers, don't you know.) Getting to meet Geri and her family was a real privilege and a wonderful addition to my time in the country. Although we exchanged some letters for a few months, Geri and I never did manage to see each other again.

After having enjoyed a wonderful time with our relatives in England and Ireland, my folks and I flew back to the States together. I let Mom and Dad know about my plans to enlist in the military, to work in the medical field specifically, and to join the army in particular. Surprisingly, even though Dad had such a distinguished military history, he wasn't all that excited about my plans—probably because I was fairly certain about joining the army as opposed to any of the other branches of the service. He made me promise to first at least speak with an Air Force recruiter before making any decisions. It just so happened that one of the guys at the church I had grown up in was a recruiter for the Air Force. We sat down together to discuss the possibilities, and wouldn't you know it, his recommendation to me, if indeed I was interested in the medical field, was to pursue an MOS (military occupation specialty) in the army called 91C. The 91 Charlie job category was simply a combat field medic with some extra training in the hospital setting. After a designated amount of time working as a "short Charlie," there was potentially the possibility of being chosen for and attending the "long Charlie" program. Completion of this course would classify you as a patient care specialist and also provide the opportunity to receive a civilian practical nursing license after graduation and after passing the state nursing examination. This all sounded like the direction I was wanting to go, so it wasn't very long before I was sitting down in the army recruiter's office and taking the required enlistment tests. After the test scores were in, the recruiter started telling me about all the great jobs I would qualify for—helicopter mechanic, this thing, that thing, all kinds of things, but no medical thing. I asked him what the deal was, and he explained that because I divulged having used recreational drugs on my paperwork, I would not be eligible for the 91C program or any job categories that might include working with medications. Bummer. He then went on to say that it wasn't so much whether or not I had "used drugs" but if I had "bought drugs."

He also said we could even change that answer on my paperwork if necessary. Considering I really felt that joining the military was what I was supposed to be doing and truly hoped that perhaps there was even some divine direction behind my thinking, lying on the documentation about having bought drugs or not really wasn't part of my plan. Yes, I had bought drugs. I let the recruiter know that I wouldn't need to be changing anything but would be happy to write up a letter explaining my youthful experience with "pharmaceuticals" and also the reasons I had come to realize why that was such a physically and mentally and spiritually unhealthy way to live. As well as the reasons why I had chosen a new way. I submitted the letter to my recruiter who said he would let me know in a few days what the powers that be had to say. I did hear back a few days later, and he informed me that I would be welcome to attend the 91C medical program and that the army was chalking up my history with herbal and other mind-altering substances to "experience."

Fort Leonard Wood Missouri—what a lovely place to attend basic training in the winter. Not really, but having since been to Missouri in the summer, I realize that would have probably been worse. Upon arriving on the post late at night, we were escorted to some old wooden barracks. When you entered the barracks doors, there were two large barrels, which I believe were meant to provide you with one last chance to get rid of any contraband on your person by throwing it into a barrel with no questions asked. I later wondered if one young recruit didn't perhaps have a little stash on his person and choose to swallow it rather than throw it into the barrel. We were informed that because the barracks were made out of wood, we needed to have a "fire watch." Someone had to be up walking around the building all night, making sure it didn't burn down. I'm guessing the point of this was to make sure that nobody got much sleep. So one person would make sure that the building didn't burn down for an hour or two and then wake up the next person whose job it was to make sure that the building didn't burn down. (I never found out why there was any danger whatsoever of the building catching on fire.) I was awake in my bunk, thinking about and talking to God about this potentially very foolish thing I had done by joining the army. I watched as the fire watch on duty walked up to and shook the oncoming fire watch who was asleep in a top bunk and who just happened to be the young man I believe had chosen to swallow his stash. The boy in the top bunk suddenly sat up, started screaming at the top of his lungs, fell to the floor and half crawled half ran out of the building, still screaming. We never saw this fellow again. Oh my, what have I done? This would be the first of many times over the next few years when I needed to remind myself that I chose to do this army thing. Actually, I needed to remind myself several times just during basic training.

One day while standing in formation, a big southern drill sergeant stood in front of me with his drill sergeant hat touching the brim of my hat and asked the following: "Gates, you used to be a flower child, didn't you?" I wasn't sure if I had heard him correctly and responded with "Excuse me, Drill Sergeant." (Because the prescription for my eyeglasses was apparently a little harder to fill than those of some of the other recruits, I was the only person in my company that hadn't been required to wear a pair of ugly black horn-rimmed army-issue glasses. I was still wearing my wire-rimmed frames. Perhaps the sergeant thought they were a little too hippyish.) He then said, "You know, the ever-flowing waves of peace."

Although I never qualified as a flower child, the wannabe hippie in me replied, "Yes, Drill Sergeant."

Mr. Drill Sergeant then shouted in my face, "Well, now you're a warrior!" (I think he even got a little spit in my eye as he shouted.)

Actually, this particular drill sergeant had a pretty good sense of humor. On one occasion, he called me out of formation for something I had apparently done that ticked him off and ordered me to give him fifty or however many push-ups. I think he must have reconsidered whether I had really done anything that warranted having to do a bunch of push-ups in front of the whole company because he got down on the ground in front of me and, with a smile on his face, joined me in the exercise. He was one of the few drill instructors that actually may have enjoyed his job a little. We had some that obviously didn't. They were the ones that tried to make basic training as miserable for you as it was for them.

One of the things that made basic a little more enjoyable for me was being asked to call cadence while we were marching. So I was the guy who yells out a song to keep everybody in time, and they in turn shout it back to you. This job followed me from basic training to the field medic program I later attended in San Antonio, Texas. It was kind of fun to be able to sing anything I wanted to. While at Fort Sam Houston, I even had our platoon singing Psalm 133:3 in Hebrew. It sounded kind of cool, and when I explained the translation "Behold how good and how pleasant it is for brethren to dwell together in unity," most everybody was willing to shout it out. There was one guy, however, who let me know that he was "an American" and didn't want to be singing anything in another language. I asked him where his grandparents came from and turns out he was a mix of Norwegian and some other European heritage. I pointed out that unless he was an American Indian, he was a mutt just like most of the rest of us. I think he finally got over it.

From San Antonio, I was assigned to work in the hospital at West Point for a few months as part of the short 91C program. What a great assignment. I arrived in Manhattan late at night wearing my class-A dress uniform but mistakenly got off the bus prematurely at a little stop outside of the center of town. It was late, it was dark, and I was pretty lost. I set my suitcase and duffel bag down just long enough to try and read the bus schedule and figure out how to get into the city center. While reading the schedule, a guy (who I didn't even know was there) surprised me when he came up and said, "Man, don't ever put your bags down like that. Someone will rip you off." Fortunately, he wasn't looking to rip me off. In addition to giving me some very valuable advice, he also showed me on the schedule the bus that I would need to catch. So here I was, late at night in Manhattan, wearing my class-A army uniform, carrying all my gear and looking about as out of place as I could get. A few young guys came up, and I asked them if they knew of a good cheap place to stay for the night. One of them responded, "With a woman or without." I wasn't sure if he was joking or not. Another one of the guys suggested a location on Lexington

Avenue, which turned out to be a house that was apparently founded in the early 1900s to be a "home away from home" for military personnel and at an affordable price. What a wonderful place—a beautiful big old house just a short walk from where I was, with a clean comfortable bed and even a reading room with lots of books. I ended up staying for a couple days before heading north to the new assignment at Keller Army Hospital West Point.

About fifty miles north of New York City overlooking the Hudson River sits West Point Military Academy. It's here that the Army provides a select few up and coming military officers with their college education. It was also here that I had the pleasure of spending the next few months working in the hospital as part of my medical training. It was a very interesting environment to be in as a twenty-three-year-old private E1 among a group of military cadets many, if not most of which were younger than me. My hospital uniform consisted of white shirt and pants with no identifying rank due to only being an E1. Having several cadets confused about whether to salute, call me sir, or just what was kind of fun. On several occasions, I told them to just call me Tim.

As a person who had been blessed with some of the flattest and most unusual-looking feet that God ever saw fit to form and fashion, I had always used some kind of orthotic arch support in my shoes. Since childhood, I wore just about everything from plastic to thin metal to leather. (Knowing people who were denied entry to the military because of their feet, it was pretty miraculous the physician who performed my military physical ever okayed me to join. My feet really are pretty weird.) While at West Point, I decided to pay a visit to the podiatrist (foot doctor) to see about having a new pair of inserts made.

Captain Yanklowitz was very interested in the fact that I had recently been living in Israel. The good doctor was also very interested in the fact that I was a Christian. Although he was Jewish, Barney had recently come to know Jesus as his Messiah. What an unexpected surprise and pleasure to become good friends with Captain Yanklowitz over the months that followed. It just so happened that Barney had recently been attending a weekly home Bible study with some of the academy military faculty. I could hardly believe it when I found myself joining Dr. Barney for these studies and sitting in the living rooms of some West Point officers and their wives, with officers ranging in rank from captain to colonel. (Keep in mind, just a short time before this, I was getting screamed at and doing push-ups in basic training.) It's amazing how liberating it felt while at my first visit to the study I was addressing one of the officers (who happened to be a colonel) as sir and he responded with "Hey, call me Andy." It honestly seemed as if I was experiencing what's written in Galatians 3:28, where it reads, "There is neither Jew nor Greek, there is neither slave nor free man, there is neither male nor female; for you are all one in Christ Jesus" (NASB), except in this case I could include "neither Colonel or Private." (It was very cool.) In addition to making me a part of the Bible study group, Barney also introduced me to his friends David and Jane. Dave and Jane lived in the beautiful little town of Cornwall on Hudson. Like Barney, they were Jewish, and also like Barney, they were both believers in Jesus. I had the great pleasure of becoming very good friends with Dave and Jane. I was also incredibly fortunate to be able to enjoy the wonderful hospitality of their home as well as to join them on several occasions to the church where they fellowshipped. Life was good.

One other thing that happened while at West Point definitely worth mentioning was the opportunity to attend a genuine Bob Hope USO show celebrating his birthday. Joining Bob for the party was his wife Dolores, George C. Scott, Mickey Rooney, then Vice President George Bush, Marie Osmond, Brooke Shields, Sugar Ray Leonard, Glen Campbell, Mary Martin, and the *42nd Street* dancers from the Broadway show *42nd Street*. How cool is that? Now I realize that many of those names may not belong to people that everybody recognizes. Some younger folks today probably don't even know who Bob Hope was. Mr. Hope was an actor who during World War II started bringing groups of celebrities (which always included some pretty girls) around the globe to entertain the troops. Wherever military members were located—Korea, Vietnam, the Persian Gulf, or wherever—Bob and his team would travel in and put on a great show. I was feeling pretty honored to be able to witness one of his shows and also to be able to help celebrate his birthday. (I think he was in his late seventies at the time.)

From West Point, I was assigned to a medic position for a tank battalion in Erlangen, Germany. Erlangen is a beautiful little college town located in Bavaria. Before starting the new job as a tanker medic, I had a few weeks' vacation, which allowed me to spend some time at my folks' place in Washington. It also allowed for a quick stop in the north of Minnesota to attend the wedding of my dear friends Logan and Elsje. Elsje, who was originally from Holland, had been a volunteer at Nes Ammim during the same time I was. Logan and I had also met in Israel, but at a conference of primarily Jewish believers that was taking place in the village of Rosh Pina. Rosh Pina is located on the northeastern slopes of Mt. Canaan overlooking the Hula Valley and the Golan. The village name translates to "head of the corner" and comes from Psalm 118:22, where it reads, "The stone which the builders refused is become the head stone of the corner" (KJV). According to the book of Acts in chapter 4 verse 2 and according to the apostle Peter, Jesus is that cornerstone. The main speaker at the conference was a Messianic Jewish gentleman named Art Kats, who had authored a book about his faith journey entitled *Ben Israel* and who was quite popular among some of the believing Jews in Israel. Logan had come along with Art, his wife Inger, and a few additional folks who lived together in a community of believers in Laporte, Minnesota.

Community Ben Israel was founded by Mr. Katz in the mid '70s as a learning center and as a place where believers (several of them Jewish) could live and share life together, using the example of the first followers of Jesus as recorded in the book of Acts. Although Logan may have originally intended to return to the States after the conference, he instead decided to stay in Israel for a while and was able to find work on a kibbutz not far from Nes Ammim. He became good friends with many of us in the community to include Elsje—and the rest is history. It was such a wonderful surprise to receive an invitation for Logan and Elsje's wedding, which was taking place at the Ben Israel community in Minnesota. Also, the timing was perfect as I was actually able to join them for their wonderful day. After the wedding and after a stop at Mom and Dad's, it was "Deutschland, here I come."

For the next eighteen months, when not providing medical support to members of the second of the eighty-first tank battalion, I was making every effort to enjoy as much of Germany as I could. I hadn't been in the country very long before purchasing a bicycle, which I used to explore the surrounding countryside as often as possible. Erlangen, being a college town, was also a community with a large population of young adult students, many of which weren't terribly happy about having an American military base in their lovely little town. Although there were those of an older generation who had some recollection of what had taken place in the country under Hitler and who were grateful for America's intervention after the war, there were also quite a few young people who saw Americans as simply warmongers, and the soldiers at Ferris Barracks as an extension of the American war machine. As much as I tried to stay under the radar when out and about town and tried to use what little German I had learned whenever possible, there was still the rare cafe that refused me service, assuming I was an American soldier.

Fortunately, this was the exception and by no means the rule. There were loads of very nice people living in and around Erlangen who intentionally wanted to get to know Americans better. A small group of those folks were members of a club called Kontakt. Kontakt was organized to allow US soldiers and residents of the local community an opportunity to get to know and socialize with each other and to gain a little better understanding of one another's culture. It was also a great place to work on your German language skills. By participating in the Kontakt Club, I gained some great friendships, some of which have remained until this day. One friend is a high school teacher who has stayed with us here in the States a few times over the years. He and his wife were also kind enough to have our youngest child as a guest in their home in Germany while he was traveling around Europe a couple years ago.

Sometimes during training exercises when we were out in the field, it was my job to drive the jeep for our company physician's assistant. Depending on where we were training, I would sometimes get up early in the morning and take the jeep into whatever village was near to pop into the *backerei / konditorei* (bakery / pastry shop) and the *metzgerei* (butcher shop) and pick up some wonderful fresh goodies for the medical platoon. Not that C-rations can't be made to taste pretty good (especially if you have the ability to heat up your unidentified meat in a can). There's nothing though like fresh German breads and cheeses and meats and pastries.

I was a pretty popular guy after making those little early morning trips. Although there were definitely benefits to being the medical platoons designated jeep driver, it could also be kind of a pain. The company would periodically go out to the field for several days so the tanks could qualify with their big guns and make sure they could hit their targets. In addition to providing support during these exercises, the medical platoon would use this time for some additional training. Our platoon sergeant was a weathered, combat seasoned, crusty E-7 who could be pretty scary-looking first thing in the morning. (His nickname was Nosferatu, which I believe translates to vampire.) He had undoubtedly been through more as a military medic than I could even imagine and really did have some hard-earned knowledge and experience. At this point in his career, however, closing down the NCO club along with one or two of his old soldier cronies may have become the most important part of the training day. Fortunately, he had a few very capable senior NCOs who were more than able to manage and train our platoon. Unfortunately, it meant the jeep driver (me) would have to drop the good sergeant and his buddies off and then pick them up, sometimes late at night when I would have much rather been on my cot sleeping. Truth be told, the club was probably off limits during the exercises, and I finally told Sergeant Nosferatu that unless he gave me a direct order I couldn't make these late-night trips anymore. Gratefully, he and his friends found a new mode of transportation.

In addition to functioning as a medic for the tank company, I also had the opportunity to spend a few months working at the Army hospital in Nürnberg. I was provided housing next door to the hospital for about half that time, but prior to a room opening up, I needed to commute each morning on the train from Erlangen to Nürnberg. Kind of like back at West Point when the cadets weren't sure from the white uniform with no identifying rank (because I didn't have any) whether I was even a member of the military, I would remove my rank and hat for the train ride (wearing whites) and was able to make the trip incognito. It was nice just to feel like a regular guy.

Before completing an eighteen-month tour of duty in Germany, I was advised by our warrant officer / physician assistant that I would be representing the medical company along with a couple other guys in a week-long testing process where US and NATO combat medical personnel (both enlisted and commissioned officers) attempt to obtain the coveted EFMB. The EFM what? Until then I had never even heard of an EFMB or Expert Field Medical Badge. Turns out receipt of this special skills badge was kind of a big deal for those who wanted to demonstrate their knowledge and skills as a combat medic. Personally, I was more than happy to just do my job and leave it at that. After finding out about the extent of written and physical testing that a person needed to complete in order to receive the prize, I wholeheartedly tried to talk the PA out of sending me. No dice, his mind was made up. In the end, I was kind of glad that he did make me go because somehow, much to my surprise and only by the grace of God, I managed to get through the required events and receive the badge. One of the most challenging components of the test at least for me (more than the timed twelve-mile road march with a standard fighting load and more than any of the many combat medical tasks) was the night navigation course. I considered it a genuine miracle when in the middle of the night my team member and I were able to make our way through the woods with just a map, a compass, and little red penlight, finding several predesignated locations. Neither of us could believe it when we ended up at our final checkpoint within the time given. (I really did consider it a miracle.)

Knowing that time with the second of the eighty-first tank battalion was limited and would only last for a year and a half, I tried to be proactive about where my next assignment would be. Several months before the tour ended, I started submitting requests to be stationed at a location that would be interesting to visit while also somewhere I had never been. Turkey was my first choice, but that was denied. I then tried for Korea, which also got nixed. Finally, I requested to just stay in Germany, which seemed like a good plan as the Army wouldn't need to go to all the trouble of sending me across the globe. When the orders came in, they were not to stay in Germany. Instead, I would not only be returning to the States but to Washington State in particular. I ended up as a field medic with the fourth of the twenty-third infantry battalion at Fort Lewis, just a few miles from where I had grown up.

I can't deny that I'm pretty grateful for having served in the military during a relatively peaceful period of time. Other than Grenada in 1983 and with the exception of the sort of things that special forces–type units may have been involved with (that I didn't even know were taking place), it was a fairly uneventful few years militarily speaking. Several of the soldiers I served with and came to know while in the tank and infantry battalion were, however, familiar with a very different kind of Army. They had also served in Vietnam. I couldn't even imagine the horrors of what some of those guys had experienced. Truth is, I felt guilty having had it so easy. Not that we didn't sometimes participate in some pretty intense training—we did, particularly with the infantry battalion. Still it was just training, nothing more than training.

Soldiers who have served since the time that I was in the military have not had the good fortune of concentrating their efforts on training. With the Gulf War, Somali civil war, intervention in Haiti, Bosnia, Kosovo, Afghanistan, Iraq, Libya, and who knows what will be happening tomorrow, times have been anything but peaceful. Although a little guilty, I can't help but also feel grateful for being able to serve during the unusually quiet period that I did.

As a medic for the infantry battalion, I spent a short time with headquarters medical platoon, but it wasn't long before being assigned to the Scouts. Those are the guys with expertise in reconnaissance and surveillance. I don't think Scouts are traditionally tasked with "engaging the enemy" but rather are responsible for collecting information about their positions and activities and relaying that information back to command. This was not always the case with our Scout platoon. These guys loved to be in the thick of things, and on more than a few occasions, I found myself on the back of a jeep manning a .50-caliber machine gun. No question about it, the boy in me had a pretty good time firing things up from the rear end of a machine gun. (For training purposes only, mind you.) Talk about playing army. On one occasion during night maneuvers, we drove to a designated landing zone out on the military reservation. We then waited until the giant Chinook helicopters were hovering overhead and proceeded to hook our jeeps up to them with a sling system. The Chinooks flew off with jeeps swinging beneath to a location where we later arrived after having been picked up and flown over in a Black Hawk helicopter. Once there, we jumped off the Black Hawk, ran to our jeeps, which were being lowered to the ground, unhooked them, climbed in, and away we went. I wasn't sure but had to wonder if our Black Hawk pilot wasn't trying to see whose stomach he could turn over during the ride. I remember thinking to myself, *Don't throw up, don't throw up.* It was a close one, but I didn't.

Although working as a medic for a combat unit was anything but boring and probably allowed me to be in the best physical shape of my life, I couldn't help but get excited when Uncle Sam surprised me with the orders that I'd hoped for since enlisting. I had been selected to participate in the long 91 Charlie patient care specialist program. This would mean transferring to Fitzsimmons Army Medical Center (just outside of Denver) and attending the intensive ten-month nursing course. So what do ya know? Maybe there was a reason for not getting to go to Turkey or Korea or to stay in Germany. The Army was actually giving me what I had originally signed up for.

CHAPTER 15

Will You Marry Me?
On Saturday?

Because I didn't own a car after returning to the States from Germany, I needed to find a vehicle to get around in. Something that was dependable and cheap. It just so happened that my brother Mike had followed in Dad's footsteps and was now in the car business. He gave me a great deal on a '69 Olds 88. What a wonderful car. Even with a zillion miles on the odometer, she ran beautifully. After receiving orders for school, I packed up the Olds, and we hit the road. Destination: Fitzsimmons Army Medical Center, Aurora, Colorado. I took a couple days to get there, stopping at a park or two along the way and sleeping in the back of the car at night. Except for my clothes and a few essentials, which included a Schwinn Super Sport 10 speed (the one I'd ridden on the awesome bike trip several years prior), a cassette player, and box full of cassette tapes, I travelled pretty light. Unfortunately, the tapes were sitting up above the back seat of the car next to the window, and as the weather was hot and sunny, a few of them melted along the way.

I still listen to some of the tapes that weren't melted today. More often though, I'll just throw on one of our old albums from the '70s. So glad I didn't decide to bring my albums to Colorado and end up melting those too. The Oldsmobile made the trip like she was right off the showroom floor.

I had never been to the Rocky Mountain State prior to the Army deciding to make Fitzsimmons Medical Center my home. What a great place to be invited to live. Wonderful camping, wonderful skiing, great bike trails (which I took advantage of as often as possible), lots of sunshine—all and all, I couldn't have asked for a better location to be going to school. If that wasn't enough, I also made some great friendships while there, one in particular that would change my life forever.

Beginning with a Baptist church in Tacoma and including all kinds of colors and flavors of fellowships in a variety of places, some on different continents, some traditional, some not traditional at all, I had truly grown to love the dysfunctional family called the church. Getting together with other folks (in some form or fashion) who were also trying to get closer with Jesus had become a very real and very important part of my life. After arriving in Aurora, I wanted to find a place with some of "those kind of people." In my efforts to find such a place, I looked in the phonebook. We used to do that. The name of one church in particular seemed to stand out to me. (I really wasn't looking for a specific denomination or flavor.) For some reason, Gateway seemed like as good a place as any to at least pay a visit, and it wasn't located too many miles from our student housing. Gateway Christian Church turned out to be not just a nice place to visit but also the fellowship where I found myself getting together with other believers for the entire time I was stationed in Colorado. It wasn't the perfect church, but I'd never been to one that was. In fact, some wise person had once told me, "If you ever find the perfect church, don't go there. You'll only screw it up." True words.

So Gateway had a group of single adults that were about my age. I became close friends with a number of those folks, and sometimes we would do fun things together as a group. Among the group was a beautiful blue-eyed girl named Carol. (I think I even remember the very first time seeing Carol standing there in church after a Sunday service with those blue eyes.) I'd be lying if I said that at twenty-six or twenty-seven years old I wasn't sometimes thinking about whether or not I would meet that special someone who would spend her life together with me. I was. I had known Carol for a few months and done some things together with her and the group, but it wasn't until just before the end of the nursing program that I finally asked her out on a date. Our evening started by visiting a wonderful elderly woman who lived in Denver and who had been introduced to both Carol and me by a mutual friend. Hannah Shwayder Berry was a delightful Jewish lady in her late '80s who had lived in Denver since the days of silent movies. According to Hannah, she had in fact played the piano for a silent movie theater in Denver's red light district when she was a young girl. Another one of Hannah's claims to fame was that two of her brothers had started the Samsonite luggage company. We learned from Hannah that the company had originally been named after the Samson of the Bible. We also learned a little something about one of Hannah's brothers and his dislike for borscht. During our visit, Hannah let us know that she had just made some beet borscht and was kind enough to offer us a taste. I love beets and gladly accepted a little bowl full of the delicious red soup. Carol, on the other hand, is not a beet lover and graciously declined the offer. Hannah thought for a few moments and then in a matter-of-fact voice proclaimed, "My brother didn't like borscht. He's dead now." She was such a kick. After our visit with dear Hannah, it was time to bring Carol out for dinner. Mataam Fez is an amazing Moroccan restaurant located in East Denver. For a guy who was trying to impress a young lady on their first date (which I was), this was definitely the ticket. The inside of the restaurant is (or at least was) draped with tapestries, giving the allusion that you are inside a tent. Guests sit on pillows on the floor, and the incredibly delicious and authentic Moroccan meal is eaten without the use of silverware. (You get to lick your fingers.) And let us not forget the lovely belly dancers. It really was one of the most delicious and most memorable meals I have ever enjoyed, and best of all, there was this beautiful blue-eyed girl named Carol.

The Army's 91C nursing program was probably unlike any other practical nursing program anywhere. In addition to rotations through every potential work area in the hospital, the school was also designed to prepare its students' for the possibility of having to work in a combat field setting. We had to complete a surgical rotation, which I'm pretty sure would raise the voices of animal rights advocates today. I regret that some animals lost their lives as a result of the labs, and although I never had to perform a splenectomy on any human-type people in the field, I do believe that the training was very valuable. Our program provided the opportunity to observe several surgeries, but this particular lab allowed the possibility to actually perform a surgery. It was incredibly stressful and incredibly humbling for me to actually put my hands inside a living creature and to realize that it was giving its life so that I and the other member of my team could learn. Could learn and experience something that we hoped to never need to use. Probably the most dreaded rotations of the nursing course were the med passes. That's when you were responsible for providing a medical floor full of patients with all their morning medications. This also meant you needed to be intimately familiar with all the medications that you would be passing. This required you (or at least me) to be up all night before a med pass trying to learn every possible thing you could about the drugs you were giving and would likely be quizzed on. During the med pass, one of your instructors would be standing next to you, observing the way you handled yourself with your patients and also asking random questions about the medications. During one of my passes and after having been up all night studying, I was in the room of and giving morning medications to an ornery old fellow who was obviously very sick. With my instructor looking over my shoulder, the old guy mumbled something to me under his breath. I hoped I had heard him wrong, but to be sure (with my instructor looking over my shoulder), I asked him, "Excuse me, sir?" He then loudly and clearly repeated (with my instructor Captain Tate still looking over my shoulder), "Your breath smells like hell." (Isn't that special? And with Captain Tate standing right next to me and hearing every word.)

Now I realize that I had been up all night, but I had brushed my teeth and really don't think that my breath smelled like hell. I did, however, apologize to the grumpy old geezer and let him know that I would be sure to take care of it. Captain Tate was kind enough to also give me a breath mint. I heard the next day my old friend had passed away that very night. I could only hope I didn't kill him with my breath.

School was quickly coming to an end, and I had received orders to go from Denver to Walson Army Hospital in New Jersey. Having enjoyed a few more very nice dates with Carol, it was clear to me that I wasn't ready to just say goodbye to someone that I wasn't ready to just say goodbye to. It seemed that a better plan might be to invite Carol to join me in Washington State for a week or so, giving her a chance to see the Great Northwest and giving us a chance to spend more time together and get to know each other better. She could stay at my parents' house so essentially it would be a free trip to the Evergreen State. How could she resist that? I was very happy that Carol was agreeable to the idea and also happy that she was able to take a week off from her work as a typesetter for Denver suburban newspapers. I too had a couple weeks off before having to report to the new assignment in New Jersey, so it could potentially work out very nicely. I really did feel as if Carol might very possibly be that just right person for me and was hoping I could possibly be that just right person for her. I sat down with Mr. Poll (Carol's dad) to assure him that my intentions were honorable and to let him know that Carol would be staying with my mom and dad and would have a very nice guest room in their home. I also spoke to him openly about my feelings for his daughter. I sort of asked him if he would be totally opposed to the idea of me (if it were God's will, of course) perhaps marrying his daughter. Lo and behold, he wasn't opposed and even went so far as to give me his blessing. Looking back and considering that Carol and I really didn't know each other that well, it was a pretty bold thing to ask her dad if I could marry her. I was definitely a man on a mission. Before leaving on our trip I even asked the wonderful group of elderly ladies at the church to be praying about Carol and me and about her visit to Washington, reminding them that "you just never know what could happen." Carol by the way wasn't actually aware of the thoughts and emotions that were swirling around in my head and heart or about my talking to her dad or to the powerful praying grannies. I think she was pretty much just looking forward to a fun-filled free vacation in the Seattle area. (Little did she know.)

The unsuspecting Carol and I did have a great time. Although we only had a week, Carol was able to explore the city of Seattle (including colorful Pike Place Market), spend a day playing on one of Washington's beautiful ocean beaches (where we enjoyed some kite flying,) see some of my favorite places where I grew up, get to know my folks, and get to know me. She hit it off with my mom and dad right off the bat. It was sort of a fun coincidence that Carol shared the same birthday as my dad. We discovered another surprising coincidence when Dad was telling Carol about some old friends he and Mom had who lived and worked in Denver. It just so happened that Ivan, a retired Air Force major that had served together with my dad, was now a manager at the newspaper where Carol worked. He may have even been involved with originally hiring her. What were the odds of that?

So here we were. It was Wednesday, and Carol was due to head for home the next day. As crazy as it seemed, I had come to believe that she really was the one for me. I was also pretty sure that trying to maintain a long-distance relationship with me living in New Jersey and her in Colorado wasn't something I wanted to do. If a long-distance relationship wasn't an option, the only other thing to do was ask her to marry me, so I did. Actually, I think what I asked was more like, "Would you like to serve God together and join me on this adventure called life?" Poor Carol, talk about an awkward and stressful situation. Carol didn't say yes; what she did say was that she'd pray and think and consider this crazy proposition and let me know in the morning. Our only problem was that Carol was supposed to be back to work on Friday. If she did say yes, her job would need to provide a little extra time off. Instead of returning home on a Thursday, we would want to change her ticket for Sunday, which is when I was scheduled to fly back to Denver. Not only was Carol expected to be back to work, but on top of that, I don't think she even had any additional vacation days. This is where the "coincidence" of my dad being a dear friend with one of Carol's managers turned out to be a very nice thing. Dad gave his old buddy Ivan a call and worked out the details, providing Carol with the extra days. I'm not sure how much sleep Carol got that night. I know that I didn't get a lot. The next morning, it was time to find out what the future would hold. Carol lovingly told me that she thought it would be best if she flew home that day as scheduled. Although I had wholeheartedly hoped she would say yes, I was also willing to accept that her decision was as it should be. Now having said that, I wasn't quite ready and willing to lose all hope, so I responded to her (sort of half-jokingly and with a smile) by saying, "Okay, we will get you to the airport today in time for your flight. Or . . . we could go to the courthouse this morning and get a marriage license and be married on Saturday."

At this point, I can imagine Carol was pretty convinced that I was totally and completely nuts. Her response, however, made me think that she was equally as crazy. She said, "Well, I guess we could go there and see what it looks like and see what happens." What? What was that? Was that a yes? I do believe that was a yes. To be sure I understood what Carol was saying, I first let her know that "no, we won't be going to the courthouse to see what happens." I then went on to ask her the question that had been asked the day before, but this time actually speaking the words "Will you marry me?" I couldn't believe it when she said, "Yes."

This is not, by the way, a method I would recommend anybody else use to get married. Looking back now, it really was a very risky thing to do. Fortunately for me, I found a girl unlike any other. Carol had little idea what she was getting herself into when she agreed to marry me. Now thirty-three years, three children, two sons in law and one grandchild later, I'm so glad that she decided to join me on this crazy journey. Has God been involved every single day, helping us not to totally blow it and screw up the life together we've been given? I am thoroughly convinced He has. Could we have made it this far without His supernatural help? Not a chance.

We did go to the courthouse that morning and did get our marriage license, joined by my brother Michael, who served as our witness. What we didn't know was that Washington State required a three-day waiting period from the time you get your license until the time of the wedding. (Are you kidding me?) Three days meant we would have to wait until Sunday. Waiting the extra day would have been a little hard to pull off, considering we were going to be flying out late Sunday morning. Now I can't say for sure that God was working behind the scenes to help us out with our logistical problem, but by some miraculous stroke of the pen, we didn't have to wait the full three days. Let's just say the person in charge of our paperwork was very kind. After getting our marriage license, we thought it might be a good time to give Carol's mom and dad a call and let them know that if they would like to join us for the ceremony they would be needing to purchase some tickets—quick. Of course, Carol's folks wanted to join their little girl for her special day, so on Friday we drove to the airport and picked up Mr. and Mrs. Poll as well as Carol's younger brother Tim. I was still calling close friends on the phone until about midnight Friday night to invite them to the wedding, which was being held in Mom and Dad's living room. Our guests brought potluck, Mom baked all kinds of wonderful homemade bread, and on Saturday, April 28, 1984, I was married to my beautiful blue-eyed soul friend. Thank God Mom filled the house with the smell of her homemade bread, or otherwise Carol may have decided to bail at the last minute. I've heard her tell people, "I was thinking about sneaking off but would have felt too guilty after Tim's mom did all that baking."

P H O T O S

Always a fashion animal

The Gates Bros.

St. Patty's Day with
the Cousins

Pat, me and the
1940 LaSalle

Prancer and Pug

Frankie demonstrating brotherly police brutality

Lovely Willy Holland 1975

Copenhagen Denmark 1975

Wonderful Homestay Family Denmark 1975

Moscow Russia 1975

Prague Chekoslovakia 1975

Family and Friends Congresburry England 1975

Our campsite in St. Briavels 1976

Cousin May at Bridgenorth 1976

James, Berry and Rod The Lake District 1976

Where Grandma Bessie
Grew Up
Oatlands N. Ireland 1976

Dear Family in N. Ireland
1976

Conner Pass
(Dingle Peninsula) 1976

Giants Causeway N. Ireland
1976

Catching the boat from
S. Ireland to France 1976

The Wedding in Brittany
1976

Maryvonne's Good Kitty
Adolphine -
The Vendange 1976

The Vendange
(Grape picking)
Near Rauzan France 1976

Mr. Buzanga & Friends
Near Cognac France 1976

With Katherine at Versailles
1976

Jericho Israel
1976

Mount Hermon
Golan Heights 1977

Working in The
Kibbutz Gardens 1977

Sean and Mom
Kibbutz Nachshon
1977

Garden Tomb
Jerusalem 1977

Jerusalem with
Uncle Jack 1977

The Negev
1977

Nuweiba with Evert
1977

The camel the soldier
rode in on. 1977

Near Ir Ovot
(Tomatoe Farm) 1977

Campfire at Kibbutz
1977

Punkie at Nachshon
1977

Sitting at the Parthenon
1977

Our hotel in the
Villa Borghese Rome 1977
(Thank you Aesculapius)

At the Vatican with Peter
1977

Nes Ammim Israel 1979
(Glass House)

The D-Team
Nes Ammim Israel 1979

Mutchie - Nes Ammim
1979

Work crew at Danny & Irit's
Community Clil 1979

Nahariya Israel
1979

Baptism - Jordan River
1980

Hot date with Jan
1980

My sweet Hebrew teacher
"Carmel"
1980

Dahab - Sinai Peninsula
1980

Galilee Baptism 1980

Erlangen Germany
1981

Headquarters Medical Platoon
2/81 Armor
Germany 1982

My little corner of
Ferris Barracks 1982
(6 man room)

Nurnberg Army Hospital
1982

Good German beer from the
Keg 1982

The Great Group from
Gateway
(Where I met Carol)

Dear Hannah and our friend
Christine 1984

Camping in the Rockies
1983

Skiing in the Rockies
1984   (Carol)

Carol enjoying her 1984
vacation in Washington
(Little did She know)

While in Seattle 1984
(Carol was still clueless)

April 28 1984
We Did!!!

A reception from the
Wonderful Family and Friends
in Colorado

Our Wedding Day

CHAPTER 16

Roaches in New Jersey

Once Carol and I actually had our marriage license in hand, we did call the airline and change her flight from Thursday to Sunday. After the wedding and after a very quick Saturday night honeymoon at a lovely little waterfront cabin on the Hood Canal, it was Sunday, and it was time to fly. Upon our return to Denver, we had about a week to get Carol moved out of her apartment, load up her Datsun B210, my trusty Oldsmobile and a little U-Haul trailer filled with all our stuff, get her finished up at the job with the newspaper (she didn't even have a chance to give them a two week notice), and start our road trip to New Jersey. We also had just enough time for our wonderful friends and family in the Denver area to surprise us with a little reception.

Sixteen hundred miles on the road with house plants sticking out the windows of Carol's car, one blow out on the U-Haul, and a few days of communicating car to car by walkie-talkie, we made it to Fort Dix, New Jersey. I had been assigned to work as a nurse in the six-bed cardiac care / medical intensive care unit at Walson Army Hospital. This critical care unit was definitely the best and most interesting place to work in the whole hospital. The thing is, when the sergeant in charge of placing new nurses in their new jobs asked me where I would most like to work, I replied, "Anywhere other than the intensive care." Truth is, as a new nurse, I was intimidated by the idea of taking care of the complex and critical patients. Turns out I ended up being so glad that the good sergeant wasn't swayed by my fears and chose to assign me to the one place I didn't want to go.

Fort Dix was a training post that had been around probably from at least WWI and perhaps longer than that. As a result, the family housing for a low-ranking NCO like myself (I was promoted from specialist fourth class to sergeant E-5 shortly after arriving at Fort Dix) was anything but modern. It would probably be fair to say that the brick row house style six-plex we were provided to live in was pretty old. Don't get me wrong, I like old. Today old can sometimes even be called rustic or vintage. (In the case of our housing, it was just old.) Because of the old construction, there were no firewalls in the attic between the units. This might not be a problem unless of course you had a fire. Or unless you had an infestation of roaches. (My Lord, I had never seen so many roaches.) With the exception of a few giant cockroaches in Hawaii when I was a little kid and we went to visit my Uncle Bill and Aunt Nancy, I hadn't really seen any. That all changed at Fort Dix. We sprayed. We powdered. We bombed. We did it all. The problem though is that no matter what you did to get rid of these nasty little creatures, if all the occupants of the building weren't trying to control the problem, the bugs would just travel next door via the attic for a little holiday. When the fog cleared, they would come back home. It's a good thing that Carol and I weren't trying to start a family while living in the brick row house haven for roaches. With all the pesticides we used, it probably wasn't a safe place for us, much less for a baby. We would place roach hotels in all our cupboards, and within no time at all, the little boxes would be full. Additional guests of the hotels would just crawl in one side and out the other, walking over the carcasses of their friends and family. We knew we were in big trouble when Carol pulled out a can of killer foam and blasted an amazingly bold little roach that was walking across our living room floor in the middle of the day. (Some people will tell you that roaches just come out at night—not so, not in New Jersey.) This little fellow crawled out from under the pile of foamy poison and just kept on trucking as if nothing had happened. (He might have flipped us off.) It was a little like something out of the twilight zone. Kinda scary.

Before marrying me, Carol never really had much to do with the military. Her introduction to military life started with marrying a military guy in three days from proposal to marriage. Then immediately drive across country with her new military husband, two cars and all her worldly possessions in a little U-Haul, move into old military hous-ing, and have a bad roach problem as a special bonus. I'm so glad she decided to hang in there as opposed to packing up and moving back to Colorado, which did cross her mind, seriously. Instead, Carol chose to learn the military way how to *improvise*, *adapt*, and *overcome*.

I loved our little house. After some paint and wallpaper and flow-ers growing in the garden, it was a wonderful place. We just needed to get rid of those nasty roaches. I really appreciate that my lovely wife has got some grit. Not knowing that it was against army regulations to circulate a petition, Carol and another military wife who lived in our neighborhood (and who had the same bug problem that we did) went door to door throughout the housing complex, circulating a peti-tion and getting signatures from all the folks being plagued by roaches. The petition, although not officially legal to circulate, made its way to the desk of the general of Fort Dix. It wasn't so very long before an exterminating company came out and fumigated the whole housing area from top to bottom. They went through our building, spraying their pesticide from one end to the other. When the guy came out of the last apartment and took off his face mask and respirator, he, with eyes as big as saucers, said, "I have never seen anything like that." All the roaches that didn't die along the way ended up in that last unit. I looked through the kitchen window and was gagged to see what I saw. The floor and countertops and tabletop were all black because they were covered with dead and dying roaches. It was nasty. The moral of this story, however, is that because of Carol and the other concerned and involved military wife, we had the roach problem taken care of.

Oh, and there was also the time before the neighborhood-wide fumigation when Carol brought a bag full of dead roaches to a quar-terly community meeting. I don't think the baggy made its way to the general, but it did get into the hands of the executive officer of the post (who was a full bird colonel and who was also attending). At another meeting, Carol brought a carefully composed letter describing how we had performed the nasty task of catching and killing a huge rat that had been living in our home. On several occasions, we had caught a glimpse of this thing but didn't really know just how huge it was. One evening, we decided to go out to dinner, but before leaving, I baited a big rat trap and left it on the kitchen floor. When we returned and opened the front door, it was the weirdest thing because you could clearly hear what sounded like a heartbeat going at about three hundred times a minute. I went into the kitchen to find a monster rat caught in the trap. Both rat and trap started flipping over and over on the floor, and yes, it was the rat's heartbeat that we were hearing. I won't tell you here the method I used to put Mr. Rat out of his misery, but I know they heard all about it at the meeting. We weren't sure if the general of Fort Dix appreciated Carol's enthusiastic participation in the community or if he was just glad to see her go, but shortly before we left New Jersey, she received a letter of appreciation (worthy of framing) signed by the good general himself. Carol was underwhelmed.

My bride did grow to love our first little home together once the roaches (and the rat) were gone. Fort Dix was a perfect location from which to travel into Pennsylvania or into New York. We made several trips to both. The East Coast is so incredibly rich in culture, tradition, and history, and we tried to travel whenever possible. It was always a lot of fun to go into Old Philadelphia (the City of Brotherly Love) or to Lancaster County (home of the Mennonites) and also to travel into Manhattan for a weekend. While in New York City, because I was a service member, we could take advantage of the USO, which provided all kinds of wonderful and much appreciated perks. Goodies ranging from early morning coffee and pastries to free tickets for off-Broadway plays. (We had a chance to see *The Country Girl* with Hal Holbrook.)

During one of our trips to New York, we traveled up near Woodstock and stayed with my old buddy Rolf and his wife Ineke. (Rolf had met his lovely Dutch wife-to-be Ineke while living at Nes Ammim. They were later married and spent some time living near Rolf's parent's home in New York.) I was also able to show Carol around West Point and to introduce her to my dear friends Dave and Jane at Cornwall on Hudson. Our two years living in New Jersey really were a wonderful time. Carol found a job near the post with a little publishing company, which in addition to volunteering in the office for the post chaplain (in conjunction with her enthusiastic community involvement) kept Carol pretty busy and helped to soften any homesickness she may have been feeling for Colorado.

As our time at Fort Dix along with my military enlistment was quickly approaching a conclusion, Carol and I had both determined that a long-term career in the military was not our plan for the future. As a result, I was not intending to reenlist. Having worked in the critical care unit, along with doing some time in the emergency room both at Walson Hospital and Nurnberg hospital in Germany, I discovered that I had an undeniable interest in and desire to continue working within emergent / intensive care medicine. My vision, however, was not to work in the hospital setting but instead to pursue paramedic school.

While still living in New Jersey, I started checking out and contacting different medic programs in Washington State, which is where Carol and I were planning to go once I was out of the Army. Although my superiors had been made very aware that I was not intending to reenlist, they nonetheless advised me that I had been slotted to attend a several weeklong leadership course that was necessary for promotion. After completing and even doing pretty well in the majority of the course (a couple other soldiers and I had been vying back and forth for the number-one position), I was notified that my father had experienced a major heart attack and was receiving treatment in the cardiac care unit. I contacted and spoke with one of the physicians caring for Dad and learned that his prognosis was uncomfortably uncertain. We decided that I should request to withdraw from the leadership course so Carol and I could get to Washington as quickly as possible. Although I had no burning desire or intentions of redoing the course, I could if I chose to. Carol and I did make it to Washington within a couple days of hearing about my dad. We stayed for a week or so and until we felt confident that he was doing well and best we could tell he was going to be okay. Dad did recover from the heart attack, but it would turn out that there was another medical problem nobody knew about, which would soon be revealing its ugly head.

As the months went by, I became more and more intent on attending paramedic school and had in fact applied for the program being held at Central Washington University in Ellensburg. As is so often the case, it sometimes really does matter who you know. Central Washington's Paramedic Program had been established by and was directed by Ms. Dorothy Purser. In addition to being professor of physical education at the college, Dorothy was also a pioneer of paramedic education not just at CWU but throughout Washington State. It just so happened that Dorothy was also a friend of my brother Frank (who was a state patrolman in Ellensburg) and had also taught my niece Dawn Marie how to swim. (Rumor has it that Dorothy's swim class teaching method was to start by throwing you in the pool. After getting to know Dorothy, I could believe it.) Although some written testing and a couple interviews were necessary to be invited to CWU's paramedic course, I'm pretty sure that it didn't hurt for me to have my brother Frank putting in a good word (probably on several occasions) to the director of the program.

Just a few months prior to my military discharge date, Carol and I received the horrible news that Dad was once again in the hospital. This time, however, it was not for his heart but due to an aggressive lung cancer that had rapidly metastasized to his brain. We were advised that under circumstances like these and because I was quite near to my discharge date, I could request an early release from the Army. This would mean leaving the assignment at Fort Dix in order to be home with Dad and finishing up whatever little bit of enlistment time I had with a reserve unit back in Washington. We chose to take advantage of this option and started making arrangements to go. As much as I would have loved to hang on to the wonderful old Oldsmobile, she was beginning to get pretty tired and probably wouldn't have made the trip across country. My faithful Olds 88 had been one of the best cars ever but would now become the possession of a local mechanic we had come to know and who I felt fairly confident would take good care of her. This time, instead of dragging a U-Haul trailer, we just let the Army take care of shipping our stuff for us. We loaded up Carol's little Datsun with our essentials, said thank-you and goodbye to Fort Dix and to New Jersey, and set out for Washington. Within just weeks after our return to Washington State, Dad passed away.

My father truly was one of the very best and finest people I have ever known. As much as I hate the fact that Carol and I weren't given more time with him on this earth, I even more regret that our three children never got to know their grandpa and to experience and appreciate what a wonderful grandfather he would have been to them. I have mentioned that Dad seldom went to church while we were growing up and that he used to say he "didn't want to be a hypocrite." It wasn't until several years later after Dad and I had both gone through some changes that I may have understood a little better what he meant. In my case, I needed to learn that it wasn't a cause-and-effect sort of thing where the good things I did or the bad things I didn't do would incontrovertibly dictate the kind of relationship I would be able to have with Jesus or not. Rather, it was totally because of His love and grace for me and for the world that I was able to have a relationship with Him at all. It wasn't about what I did but about what He had done. Likewise, I think Dad may have had a similar sort of "works" mentality that led him to believe that neither he nor many of the people in "the church" were worthy. He didn't want to pretend that he was.

During one of our conversations after I had returned from Israel for the second time, Dad commented that he just couldn't see how someone like Hitler, for instance, could ever go to heaven, whether he was truly sorry and truly asked forgiveness for the things he had done or not. The idea of that kind of unconditional love and grace from God was just too big to grasp. Considering that Dad had experienced World War II and some of its horrors firsthand, I can see why this would be a very difficult concept. Probably due to all the years of seeing and enjoying the kind of supernatural, unconditional love that Mom displayed, I believe that Dad's heart genuinely went through a change on this. I believe that he really did come to understand that the love and life that Jesus gives is an undeserved gift and isn't dependent on what we do or don't do. For the last few years of Dad's life, he was often accompanying my mom to church and enjoying time together with all those other dysfunctional members of God's family. Ones like me.

CHAPTER 17

Anywhere but Yakima

After laying Dad to rest, Carol and I stayed with my mom for a few months and until we received the news that I had been accepted into the paramedic program. With the exception of attending military schools and then a few college courses that were offered at Fort Dix, this would be my first actual experience with "college life." I had spent my post high school years pursuing travel and then the army so this was going to be a very new and exciting adventure for both Carol and I. Ellensburg is a windy little college town in Eastern Washington with a bit of a western flare. (The annual rodeo is always a popular event.) The town actually sits right about in the center of Washington State and was apparently at one time being considered as a site for the capital. Several very cool historic old buildings built in the late 1800s can be seen around the city. (If ever visiting Ellensburg, you really must say hello to *The Bull* sculpture, which sits on a park bench in the middle of town. Keep in mind that he is anatomically correct, so you might not want the kids peeking under the hat on his lap.) It was a special bonus for us to have my brother Frank and his family living just a few minutes' drive from our campus housing. Having family nearby really was a wonderful gift when living in a new place, which reminds me that while living in New Jersey we were very blessed to have Carol's aunt Audrey just a forty-five-minute drive away. She made sure to invite us over for many a "home-cooked by your auntie" meal and to make us feel welcome during our stay on the East Coast. During the school year at Central, we lived in a sweet little duplex, which was within walking distance of my classes and also just a short walk into town. On those days, when not in the classroom, I would often be away, performing clinical time and working in an area hospital or at one of several different emergency medical services. These included a number of fire departments and private or hospital based EMS agencies located throughout the state. On these occasions, Carol would frequently walk into town and visit one of our very favorite places, the Valley Café. There she would enjoy a cup of coffee, a thick slice of delicious garlic cheese toast, and a chance to sit back and read the newspaper or a book. Ahhhhh, the simple pleasures. (I also managed to enjoy my fair share of good coffee and awesome homemade cheese toast at the Valley. And back then it was cheap.)

When performing clinical rotations in the participating hospitals, students would often carpool together. One of our rotations took place in the operating room where we learned the art of performing endo-tracheal intubations. (That's where you insert a breathing tube into a sedated patient's airway and then breathe for them. This is frequently executed prior to surgical procedures by the anesthesiologist or nurse anesthetist but is also performed by medics in emergency situations when patients are unable to breathe for themselves.) On this particular day, I was the one doing the driving from Ellensburg to a hospital in Yakima, where a couple other guys and myself were hoping to perform several of the intubations. Rather than make the thirty-five-or-so-mile drive on the Interstate, I chose to travel via the canyon road which ran along the Yakima River. It was about half the distance, and although you couldn't travel at highway speeds, you could still make the trip in pretty good time. Unfortunately, I wasn't satisfied with pretty good and tried to make the trip in great time. The state trooper that pulled me over wasn't willing to be swayed, even after I mentioned that my big brother Frank was a fellow trooper. He responded with, "Frank, sure I know Frank. We were roommates at the academy," as he handed me my ticket.

I'm pretty sure it wasn't my hellashish breath that opened the door to the hereafter for the old gent back at Fitzsimmons during nursing school. (I really don't think my breath was all that bad on the morning of the med pass.) I may, however, have been responsible for nearly killing somebody during our rotation at the hospital in Yakima because of a little different form of bodily bouquet. Growing up the youngest of four boys and in a house that (with the exception of Mom) was all boys, it wasn't uncommon for us to make a joke out of something as crude as a stinky fart. (Sorry, Mom.) Fart humor was an undeniable source of many a good laugh in our house, and even Dad was willing to participate on occasion. (Oh man, could he participate.) Well, during our intubation rotation, when we weren't actually preparing for or performing an intubation, we would wait around in the hallway, which connected the operating rooms. A fellow student named Evan and I were at different ends of the hall, waiting when much to my embarrassment I let loose with a silent but unbelievably deadly gasser. Rather than remain in the area and incriminate myself, I slipped into a nearby empty room and closed the door. At that very moment, one of the surgeons came walking down the hall, having to pass directly through the cloud. From behind the door, I could hear a loud, distressed voice blurting out, "My gaaaaaaawd, what did you eat!" He was directing his question to my buddy Evan, who was obviously the gaseous culprit considering he was the only person in the hall. Poor Evan. I think he tried to deny any connection to the crime, but the evidence was pretty clearly against him. As terrible as it sounds, I didn't come to Evan's aid and confess my guilt. In fact, it took several minutes before I could stop laughing and even come out of the room. (It was a terrible thing to do, I know.)

CWU's paramedic program had agreements with several advanced life support services, which included a hospital-based system in Monroe; private companies in Wenatchee, Yakima and Vancouver; and fire departments in Lakewood, Ellensburg, and Richland. I spent many, many hours and responded to countless emergency calls during internships with each of these locations. In an effort to cut down on the hundreds of miles I was driving to obtain the mandatory ambulance ride time, I started concentrating my efforts on scheduling with Yakima Medic 1. It was relatively close to Ellensburg, and the call volume was surprisingly high. Yakima proved to be an excellent place to finish up the ambulance time I needed and also to experience a great variety of medical emergencies. Of all the places I had an opportunity to precept with, Yakima Medic 1 definitely provided the best student experience of any of them.

After graduation from the paramedic program, it was time to start concentrating my efforts on finding a job. I applied for Medic 1 (along with several other organizations), but truth be told, Yakima was not a first choice. It was in fact the last place that Carol and I wanted to live. Although responding to drug-related (especially heroin) emergencies and a relatively high number of violent trauma 911 calls is interesting and something that a newly graduated paramedic can appreciate, living in a town that offers a high volume of those kinds of calls wasn't what Carol and I had in mind. We had to laugh a little whenever driving on the freeway and seeing the sign that read, "Welcome to Yakima, the Palm Springs of Washington." Yakima may have been Washington's Palm Springs, but it was also at that time known as a hub from which heroin was distributed throughout the state. (Not the kind of place either of us had always dreamed of raising a family.) We had been talking to God about what was in store for our future and even tried to negotiate a little with a prayer that was something like, "Lord, we will go anywhere, but please not Yakima."

Surprise, surprise! Who should be the only organization to have an immediate vacancy and to offer me a position but Yakima Medic 1. Funny how circumstances have a way of sometimes helping you figure out what steps need to be taken next. And interestingly, after actually receiving the job offer (though it be in a place where we didn't think we wanted to live), both Carol and I had a total change of heart and were able to see Yakima as a new and exciting adventure. We didn't particularly want to live there, however, and managed to find a place just outside of Yakima proper in the nearby bedroom community of Selah. Carol and I were drawn to the quiet agricultural town of Selah because of its welcoming vibe, and (although it wasn't the Palm Springs of Washington) it seemed like the kind of place where we could make a safe, happy home. We were also intrigued by the name Selah, which I believe is a Native American word that means something like "still or smooth water." It's also a word that you find several times in the Psalms and as we understood it meant to "stop, pause, and meditate." Pausing for a while in this sleepy little community where we could walk into town for groceries if we chose and even walk to church on Sundays turned out to be a great chapter in our lives. (And I never saw a roach the whole time we were there.)

Employment as a paramedic (at least at that time in Washington State) could range from a very lucrative position with a fire department, a job with a private ambulance company (which often wasn't terribly rewarding financially), or something in between. Working for Medic 1 gave me the opportunity to experience the private ambulance end of the spectrum, and although the job wouldn't allow us to put much in the bank, it was an experience I wouldn't have traded for anything. The job of paramedic, I would have to say (with perhaps the exception of working in the kibbutz gardens in Israel or maybe helping out with the Union Gospel Mission in Yakima which Carol and I had a chance to do), was about as fulfilling as any job I could have imagined. It was humbling and at the same time a huge privilege to perform a job where you were being asked to participate in what might be one of the most significant times of a person's life. (By *asked* I mean to have a loud obnoxious alarm go off at any time of the day or night to let you know there was a situation requiring your assistance. A situation requiring your assistance *right now*.) Calls could range from the birth of a newborn baby to a person overdosed on heroin who had stopped breathing, to a giant car crash where multiple lives might be lost, to just about any bizarre thing you could imagine. (I won't go into detail.) Whatever the nature of the call, it was the job of EMS personnel to do everything they could to help in the very most appropriate way they knew how. Sometimes the outcomes were wonderful, but regrettably, sometimes you just couldn't do enough. Fortunately, at the end of the day (actually at the end of the twenty-four-hour shift) and when all was said and done, the happy endings far outnumbered the sad.

Back while living in New York and stationed at West Point and during one of several trips into the city, I had the great fortune of getting together with my old friend Pete. Pete and his buddy Dave had traveled together to Israel and ended up as volunteers on a kibbutz near to Nes Ammim. Peter tells the story of how when he was a bicycle courier zooming around the streets of Manhattan he experienced a pretty nasty crash on his bike. I don't think there were any injuries that ultimately sent him to the hospital, but I know he did get beat up pretty bad. While still picking himself up off the pavement, Peter noticed a little paper booklet lying next to him on the ground. Turns out it was a little booklet that talked about getting to know Jesus. Pete didn't tell me exactly what it said, but whatever it was, it was just what he was waiting to hear. The bicycle crash happened at a time in Peter's life when he was seriously being moved to seriously consider what Jesus was all about. Both he and Dave ended up on spiritual journeys together, and both were motivated to come and spend some time in Israel. The two of them became friends with many of us at Nes Ammim. They also became regular attendees of our little group, which met at Stanley and Ethel's. Peter and Dave were just two examples of the many wonderful people I was so incredibly fortunate to meet while in Israel. People, many of which were wanting to get to know Jesus better. And here we were, all of us being given a chance to travel this road together at the same time and at the same place. It was a gigantic gift. Dave and Peter had returned to the States, and Pete was now living in Manhattan.

On the way to wherever we had decided to meet up, I found myself stopping to talk with a gentleman who I think had just spent the night sleeping on the sidewalk. I wish that I could clearly remember his whole history but unfortunately cannot. His name was Bob, and while we were getting to know each other, it seemed to me that maybe Bob would benefit from having a Bible to read. From our conversation, I was given the impression that he might even like that very much. We said goodbye, and I headed off to meet Pete but first ducked into a bookstore and picked up a Bible with the intention of running it back to my new friend. I wrote a little inscription in the front cover and addressed it to *Bob*. Wouldn't you know it, when I did get back to where Bob had been, he was nowhere to be found. Dang it, and I was even thinking this was something that perhaps was being orchestrated by the Holy Spirit. Oh well, had to at least give it a try. The Bible went into my pack, and I was off to meet Pete. It was great to see my old friend.

After walking around the Big Apple, Peter and I took a seat next to the East River. We did some reminiscing about how cool it had been to live in Israel and then began to pray together. We probably prayed about a lot of things, but it was when we started asking Father God to please let us be involved with something that was important to Him that a cool surprise happened. A lot of car horns started blowing from the highway behind us. Looking through the chain-link fence, we could see they were blowing at a guy stumbling along the road right next to what I remember (I think) being several lanes of traffic. Pete and I ran up and yelled at the guy to come over to the fence. He stumbled over, looked at us, and in a slurred voice said, "Wow, thanks, you guys. I was praying for help." Our new friend *Bob* (no, not the same Bob from that morning but Bob nonetheless) was living at the Salvation Army in New York's Bowery. Due to Bob's altered condition, we never really did learn his whole story. What we did know was that he was someone who had a huge battle going on with drugs and alcohol. He was at this moment in life losing the battle in a big way and had decided that the best place for him was to be stumbling around next to traffic on a busy highway. We helped Bob over the fence and, after finding out where he lived, hailed a cab and took a little ride to the Bowery. I had taken a cab or two in Manhattan before but never one like this. It was the stuff that stories about crazy cab drivers in New York City are made of. (I think we prayed not to get in an accident for most of the trip.) I'll have to admit though, in addition to being a totally insane driver, he was pretty fearless and got us to our destination quicker than expected. Gratefully, we did make it to the Bowery, and after giving Bob the Bible I had picked up earlier in the day (which already had his name in it and which he was very grateful to receive), we tucked him in at the Salvation Army. (I came to believe that the Bible, which had originally been purchased with someone totally different in mind, really was meant just for Bowery Bob and that perhaps a little prompting by the Holy Spirit really had taken place that day.) After saying goodbye to our new friend, Pete and I dropped into the Bowery Mission and joined them for dinner. That evening, the mission was serving soup and bread, which turned out to be really good. You'd have probably spent big bucks at a restaurant in the city for that same soup and bread. I think this was the first time I ever considered how very right it seemed to have places like the Mission or the Salvation Army—places where you could be all messed up and not really deserving anything from anybody but still get some help (and help that was even being given in love).

This may have also been the day it occurred to me that if Jesus really was the Lord of the Universe and the Savior of the world, then He was Lord and Savior for everybody—the guy wearing an Armani suit and working out of a view office in a New York skyscraper, the guy living on the street, or the guy like me. We were all loved by Jesus, and we all needed the life He gives in just the same way. After experiencing the vibe of the Mission and the Salvation Army in New York, I knew that somehow, somewhere I was going to be involved with rescue missions.

Yakima was incredibly fortunate to have within its fair city walls a wonderful place called the Union Gospel Mission. After getting established with the new job at Medic 1 and after settling into our new home in Selah, I decided it was time to pay them a visit. UGM of Yakima was established in the mid-1930s as a place to serve those in need during the Great Depression. By the late '80s, they had expanded into an overnight shelter and rehabilitation program for men, a family shelter, a food bank, a part-time dental clinic, and a place where hungry folks were given hot nutritious meals. They also operated a summer youth camp located in the woods of the Wenatchee National Forest. There, disadvantaged kids could experience a wonderful camping adventure and also learn about the love of God. Whether driving a pickup around town to collect donations, using a forklift to move pallets of bailed clothing that had been donated but were over and above what could be used locally, delivering firewood in a big dump truck up to the youth camp along with a mission resident named Corky, facilitating one of the Mission chapel services and sharing a little good news about Jesus, or just hanging out with some of the fellas in the recovery program, being involved with the mission was one of the very best experiences of my life.

Carol also found herself catching the wave and discovering how great it was to participate with the work they were doing. In the same way that Peter and I felt like we were being given a chance to participate in something that was close to God's heart on the day we helped Bob over the highway fence and joined him for a cab ride to the Bowery, I always felt like I was being given a special gift by helping at the mission. It just seemed like something that was making Jesus happy. Carol and I both had a great time working with the kids up at one of the Lost Creek summer camps, and we both also enjoyed helping out by coordinating a team from the little church we attended in Selah. Once a month, we brought a group to the Mission to provide the evening chapel service and then serve dinner to the guests. We were privileged to help out at

UGM for about two years, and toward the end of that time, I even found myself wondering what it might be like to join them as part of their full-time staff if a position were to open up. I never got past the wondering phase though as no opportunities became available, at least not just then, and when they did, we were already embarking on a new adventure. By this time in our marriage, Carol and I had purchased a little house in Selah (I think we paid about $36,000 for that sweet little house) and our family had grown by one with the birth of our first child Hannah. Even wee little Hannah managed to bring lots of joy to many of the folks at the Mission when we allowed them just to hold our sweet little baby girl.

So here we were, living in our little old house next to the elementary school in Selah, within walking distance of the church we were going to. I was working in a fun and fulfilling job (despite the fact that it didn't pay much). We were enjoying the opportunity to volunteer with the mission, and we had a beautiful new little baby daughter. Who could ask for more? I guess the short answer would have to be—me.

As a member of the emergency medical services scene in Washington State, it was just about impossible not to develop friendships with lots of EMS-type people. For me, it started with those folks from medic school that I studied with and struggled together with, hoping to graduate as a competent and capable medic. From there, after securing a job, you might very possibly end up working together with other medics who had years of knowledge and experience and who could pass on invaluable insights that were never learned in school. (I know I did.) Then there were those folks that would come together each year for annual EMS conferences. It just so happened Yakima (the Palm Springs of Washington) was in the 1980s a favorite location for the state's biggest conference. A whole lot of networking went on at the annual EMS gatherings, and it was during one of these that a former graduate and guest lecturer of the medic program I attended started telling me about a very progressive hospital-based EMS agency that she was a part of. They were looking for someone who would be a good fit with their team, and she seemed to think that I might be that kind of person. I was familiar with their program as it was one of the agencies I had ridden with as a student while in school. Medic 10 was known for the excellent care they provided and for the experienced and competent medics they employed. Truth be told, the idea of being a member of their team in addition to potentially increasing my salary by a pretty significant chunk was not such a terribly hard idea to entertain. The problem was, the job was located on the west side of the state, and making this change would mean uprooting Carol and Hannah (and our great doggy Beauregard) from our home in Eastern Washington. So what were we to do, continue to "stop, pause, and meditate" in our sweet little house in Selah in a community that Carol had grown to dearly love or justify a giant life shakeup and move our family to a new location on the other side of the state under the auspices of it being a "great opportunity" and a "good career move"?

CHAPTER 18

Making the Move

Whether or not to pursue this career change was really the first major decision I had to make as a husband and a father. As a single guy, making big life-changing decisions was a much, much easier thing to do and, for the most part, only affected me. Now, I had made a promise to someone, assuring them that they would be loved and taken care of (along with any little ones we may be blessed with) for the rest of their lives. Married life had been relatively easy up to this point because Carol and I had pretty much been in agreement with whatever we were doing and whatever life decisions we were making. Not so this go-round.

My dear Carol came from a little farming community in Minnesota with a population of about one thousand. In 1968 at age twelve, her dad was transferred from his job as a property guard for Vice President Hubert Humphrey to a position as a property guard for the newly elected President Richard Nixon. One day, she was in rural Minnesota surrounded by corn and cows, and the next she was living in Dade County Florida during one of our nation's most tumultuous times. With the assassination of Dr. Martin Luther King, the assassination of Bobby Kennedy, race riots in many major cities, mandatory busing with many schools (an effort not always embraced by all of the students being forced to travel away from their neighborhoods), Carol, much like Dorothy from *The Wizard of Oz*, found that she was not in Kansas (or Minnesota) anymore. Unlike the Coca-Cola TV ad that came out a couple years later where a large, diverse group of smiling people with flowered shirts sang "in perfect harmony," all was not "apple trees and honeybees and snow-white turtledoves." (Although there was Woodstock and it did produce some pretty cool music.) In Minnesota, where my wife grew up, *busing* meant that you got to ride on a bus to school. At her new home in Florida, it meant that she was the only white kid on an all-black school bus in junior high. For Carol, the times they "really were a-changin'."

I feel the need to mention here that our daughter Hannah is married to a great young man who is a wonderful husband and a wonderful father to their son and our beautiful grandson, Kalib. It just so happens that our son-in-law is black. We love RJ very much and are incredibly blessed to have him as a member of our family. It wouldn't matter if he were purple. Actually, purple would probably be a little weird and hard to get used to, but the point is, ethnicity or color isn't an issue for either Carol or me. Having said that, life for Carol as a young girl in a racially charged environment in the late '60s, where she was afraid to ride the school bus and always sat right behind the bus driver, was a scary and very difficult time. She never wanted to move from her comfortable home in Minnesota but never had a choice. Although it didn't occur to me at the time, I now believe that, having experienced that unwanted and difficult move as a young girl, Carol found my proposition to leave our comfortable home in Selah, all that more of a painful idea.

We prayed, we talked, we prayed, we argued, we cried, we prayed some more. We made a list with all the positives and negatives that such a change might have on our family. After weeks of trying to figure things out and after Carol reluctantly agreed to go along with whatever I ultimately chose to do, I did apply for the position and was offered the job. It probably took about two months to both find a buyer for our little house and to locate an affordable home in the Seattle area that wouldn't be too huge of a commute to my new place of employment. During those two months, I started working at the new job and had to travel about 150 miles each way over a mountain pass in the winter. I was working twenty-four-hour shifts and only ten of them a month, so although the drive wasn't always real fun (especially when the pass was covered in snow), it was still possible to do. There were a couple of occasions when all the passes were closed and I had to take an alternate route along the Columbia River, which meant travelling over 350 miles just to get to work. Fortunately, that only happened twice before we made the move to our new home.

If you have ever heard that real estate in the Seattle area is expensive, that's because it is, and it was in 1990 when we were looking for a house. Not just expensive but for us, untouchable. It got to the point where we were forced to start looking at some alternative options. One of the last places I ever expected to live again was the wonderful little town of Hansville, the place where my aunt and uncle owned and operated the fishing resort. After they sold the resort, June and Glen started a construction company and began to build houses in the Hansville area. In our desperation of not being able to find something we could afford that was fairly close to the new job, we gave June and Glen a call. It just so happened they had a little three-bedroom house, which had been a rental but was now on the market, and they were willing to make us a really great deal. Living in Hansville would mean that in order to get to the job I would need to drive about twenty minutes to a ferry, take a thirty-minute boat ride across Puget Sound, followed by an additional thirty-minute drive to work. Compared to traveling 150 miles from Selah to Monroe, that was a piece of cake. And for me, it was kind of a dream come true because we would be able to live in beautiful Hansville. (I'm pretty sure Linda Ronstadt really would have loved it there in the '70s.) For Carol, although she was agreeable to the idea, "dream come true" might not have been quite how she was thinking about the whole thing. As the mom of a fourteen-month-old, moving to this rural little village on the northernmost tip of the Kitsap Peninsula, where she would be a stranger in a strange land, was a little like moving to another planet. In fact, on the day we visited Hansville and did a tour of what would be our new little castle in paradise, she sat down on the front porch, looked around, and threw up. I could only hope that things would get better.

Things definitely did get better, and although it took a while, Carol grew to love our home in Hansville. In the five years we lived there, lots of things happened—the birth of our second daughter Abigail, the birth of our son Philip, and a new position as a paramedic firefighter in the town of Kingston for a fire department that provided emergency services where we lived. No question about it, I was a very blessed and a very fortunate guy. We remained in our little Hansville house for another year or so after starting the new job and then decided that it might be nice for the kids to each have a bedroom of their own. Although we weren't able to locate anything in Hansville, we did find an affordable house with the extra bedroom we were looking for in a great neighborhood that wasn't too far away. (I later came to find out it was 12.5 miles from home to the fire station when commuting to work by bike.) We rented out the Hansville house for a while but then decided on selling it to a nice young couple who had recently been blessed with a newborn baby boy. Since we were given such a great deal from Aunt June and Uncle Glen on the house, we thought it seemed only right to pass that on to the new buyers and pay it forward with the agreement that they would do the same if and when they sold. Last I heard, the young couple (who ended up doing very well as owner operators of a local business) built a big beautiful home and moved out of the little Hansville house. I hope they remembered our agreement and chose to pass on the blessing.

Unfortunately, not so very long after making our move to the new house, I found myself dealing with what was a very advanced case of arthritis in the left hip. Arthritis had been diagnosed a couple years earlier, and we knew that something would have to be done someday but never expected it to be so soon. As it turned out, I ended up needing and receiving a hip replacement at only thirty-nine years of age. I was actually the youngest person my surgeon had ever performed a hip replacement on up to that point.

Just a week after the hip surgery, our whole family had their world shaken when unexpectedly Mom ended up in the hospital needing an operation for her heart.

Our dear mother passed away in the cardiac care unit just a day after the surgery. I think my brothers and I we were all so stunned and numb from losing Mom that we were a little hasty when we decided not to have an autopsy done. We all determined that whatever the reason for Mom's death, there was nothing anyone could do about it now, so why even pursue the issue. Although that was true and knowing why Mom died wasn't going to bring her back, I later determined that it would have been pretty important for the doctors, surgeons, and nurses to know just what may have happened, and truth was, I really did want to know. Regardless of that, Mom has been more missed than

I can possibly say. I do so hope heaven turns out to be at least a little something like I think it will (and that I'll actually get to be there). I am longing to spend time with Mom and Dad again. Also, I love the idea that someday (after they've lived long and fruitful lives here on earth) my kids will have a chance to get to know and spend time with their grandma and grandpa.

Being employed by the fire department was without question one of the greatest gifts I had ever been given. Great people, great job, and all kinds of job satisfaction. Happily, the hip healed up fairly quickly, and it wasn't too long before I was back to work. It was actually after getting the new hip that I started making the 12.5-mile bike trip from our home to the fire station as part of my rehabilitation. Fortunately for other riders, the county finally widened the shoulders of the road where I used to travel. Every commute was kind of a crap shoot as to whether a truck with big mirrors was going to take your head off or not. At one point, I decided to get fancy and buy a new special set of pedals for the bike which would clip onto the new fancy bike shoes that I also purchased. This way, not only did you have the ability to push while pedaling but also pull up because your feet were securely stuck to the pedals. It was a nice concept and worked out quite well, except for the couple times when it was icy and I found myself pedaling fever-ishly but not going anywhere because of the ice. I couldn't free myself from the pedals and was unable to put my feet on the ground. My only option was to just fall over. This happened once in our driveway, which wasn't so bad, but it also happened while riding along a busy road. Admittedly, it was a little embarrassing to fall over sideways with traffic traveling by. Probably within a week of the highway fall, I replaced the very cool and very modern little clip in pedals with the biggest old-style ones I could find. I then brought the very cool and very modern bike shoes, along with the pedals to the Goodwill. Please know that although I did attempt to step it up a little as a bicycle commuter and give the fancy pedals and shoes a try, I never did feel the need to go with the stretchy bicycle wear. As a wise person once told me, "Spandex is a privilege, not a right."

Something that followed us from Eastern Washington to our new location on the west side of the mountains was an ongoing desire to be involved with city missions. The church we were attending had a close connection to a mission in Seattle as its director and his family went to that same church. They were looking for someone to coordinate a group of folks to go over each month on the ferry and provide a chapel service for the mission guests and then help serve them dinner. Seeing how this was one of the ways Carol and I had participated in Yakima, it seemed like a nice fit and a good way to help out. This time we were able to bring not just baby Hannah, but all three of our kids to the mission with us. It was a chance for them to serve others and also to see firsthand that there were folks out there who weren't nearly as fortunate as them.

In addition to a desire to be involved with city missions, I had also often wondered if our family might ever have the opportunity to participate with missions in an international setting. My love for travel and to experience cultures other than my own was still very much alive. Living, serving, and learning in another country was something I thought would be really good for our whole family. If I thought that Carol was unenthused when I suggested that we move from Selah to Western Washington, I would come to learn what "unenthused" really looked like when I pushed the idea of moving our family to another country.

CHAPTER 19

C'mon, Honey, Can't We Live in Vietnam?

As mentioned earlier, Carol and I were a little unconventional (to say the least) when we chose to get married after only a three-day engagement. In the short time we had been getting to know each other prior to marriage, although we both learned a lot, there was definitely some missing information yet to be discovered. For instance, Carol knew that I had spent a few years living and working in other countries. From that little bit of info, she deduced (and hoped) that I was done with that phase of life and would now just want to settle down in the good old US of A. I knew that Carol had also traveled in Europe during her younger years. From that little bit of info, I deduced (and hoped) that like me, Carol was such a lover of other cultures she would naturally want to give herself and our kids the opportunity to grow and learn by living and serving in another country. We were both a little mistaken.

At least to some extent, part of what motivated me to pursue becoming a paramedic was the idea that it might be a skill that could be useful and desirable outside of the United States. It just so happened that the Seattle area (where we lived) was home to the headquarters of a few organizations involved with medical and humanitarian missions serving all over the world. One of these organizations in particular was in the process of expanding a program in Vietnam, which provided vocational training for disabled young people whose lives had been impacted by the long-term effects of Agent Orange. The project was headquartered out of Da Nang, Vietnam's third largest city located on the country's eastern seacoast. After communicating back and forth by email with both the director and manager of the program, I was led to believe that working with this project was not at all out of the question and could in fact actually be a reality for our family. It could have been that Carol didn't think I would pursue the whole idea of moving our home to another country quite as intensely as I did, or perhaps she didn't think that an international aid organization would be quite so interested in having our family serve on their team. Whatever the case, the organization was interested, and here we were, Carol and I needing to make a decision about whether this was something we were able to seriously pursue or not. Although the two of us had been talking and praying together throughout this process, we hadn't come to a place of agreement about what we thought God had in store for our future. Truth be told, inside I probably wasn't so much asking for God's will but rather that His will would be for us to go. And I'm pretty sure that Carol's prayer from the depths of her heart was that God's will would *not* be for us to go. For me, it was pretty clear; we should be living and working in Vietnam. For Carol it was also pretty clear; she was very, very happy living and raising our children in the Great Northwest and, at least during this particular season of life, wasn't at all convinced that we should be living and working in Vietnam. What we did agree upon was that a decision this huge needed to be as thoughtful as we could make it and one that neither of us would regret. As a result and in order to be as well informed as we could, Carol, Hannah, Abbie, Philip, and I found ourselves spending about three weeks traveling throughout the land of Vietnam and also meeting together with the country director of the project which we had been considering.

What an amazing, amazing experience. It was difficult to imagine that this unbelievable land, so rich in sights and sounds and tastes and smells and wonderfully hospitable people, was the same place I had spent most of my childhood and teenage years hearing such horrible reports about on the news. The same place that saw a war lasting about two decades and that was responsible for the loss of anywhere from 1.3 to perhaps as many as 3.9 million lives (depending on what statistics you look at). This was even harder to imagine when, on more than one occasion, the staff at some of the hotels we stayed at would laughingly chase our kids around in order to give them a big hug. We originally flew into Saigon (Ho Chi Minh City) and from there visited Cu Chi (and the Cu Chi tunnels), the Mekong Delta, Da Nang, Hoi An, Hue, Hanoi, Ha Long Bay, and completed our trip back in Saigon. I'll never forget the beautiful French influenced city of Hoi An located just south of Da Nang. While there, we made friends with a young couple who owned and operated a tailor shop and who had a little boy about the same age as our youngest. While Carol and I were talking with them about having a few pieces of clothing made, we managed to lose track of Philip, who had been outside having a pretend sword fight with their son. We couldn't find him because he was upstairs in the house above the shop where his new friend and family lived. Our kids were all keeping journals during the trip, and we later saw that Philip's entry from that day included a drawing of him and his little buddy having a pillow fight while they were upstairs. (It was so classic.) We were constantly being awed by the wonderful surprises that Vietnam had to show us, whether it be the amazing stalactites and stalagmites inside the cave of a towering rocky island in Ha Long Bay or a cruise down the Perfume River with a stop at the magnificent ancient capital of Hue. Or a visit to a small island while on a boat ride down the Mekong River, where our kids could hike through the jungle, ending up in a little village where we drank tea and enjoyed the sounds of traditional Vietnamese folk music. (It was strange, but the music somehow made me think of blue grass from back home. The lovely young lady doing the singing actually reminded me of Emmylou Harris.) While on the island, the kids were excited about getting to meet and hold a very large boa constrictor. Carol, on the other hand, chose to pass on a chance to wear a big friendly snake around her shoulders. During our time in Hanoi, we spent a day with the director of the Aid organization I had been communicating with, along with his wife. We were able to learn some more specifics about the project as well as a little bit about what it was like to live in Vietnam as an American. We truly did have an unforgettable and magnificent trip and, by its end, were much better prepared to make a more educated and intelligent decision about living and working in Southeast Asia, or not.

CHAPTER 20

Carol Tried to Kill Me

We went, we saw, we had an unforgettable time, we came home. We were then able to decide together that although working with the program in Vietnam would have been a very worthwhile and valuable thing to do, it was not what we really and truly felt God was calling us to do as a family at that time in life.

"It's better to have a partner than go it alone. Share the work, share the wealth. And if one falls down, the other helps, But if there's no one to help, tough. Two in a bed warm each other. Alone, you shiver all night. By yourself you're unprotected. With a friend you can face the worst. Can you round up a third? A three-stranded rope isn't easily snapped" (Ecclesiastes 4:9–12, The Message). That's a scripture I had often heard growing up and one that Carol and I asked to have read at our wedding. Nice words and a great concept about the benefits of two people going it together. A concept I never really understood though until I started sharing life with Carol. If I had been a single guy when an opportunity to work in Vietnam presented itself, there is just about no question that I would have jumped on it. As it turned out, I didn't have to make that decision alone, and when all was said and done, the decision that we made turned out to be for the best.

Carol is my wife, my partner, my very best friend, the mother of my children, and yes, I'll say it with all joy, my lover. Without question, and although married life is so much bigger than making love, I'd be lying if I didn't say that it really is one of the best parts. I have had to learn though that at least in my marriage, much like the wearing of spandex, physical intimacy is a privilege and not a right. Not too many months after our return from Vietnam, while thoroughly enjoying an intimate and privileged moment with my dear wife, I developed a horrible (and I do mean horrible) pain in my back. I was hoping that it was just a pulled or torn muscle of some kind, but as it continued to get worse and as I started to turn pale and began sweating bullets, we had to conclude that *maybe* something else was going on. As a paramedic, I was aware of some of the nasty things that could possibly be the cause of what I was experiencing but preferred to just keep thinking and hoping it was a torn muscle. I finally had to ask Carol to give me a ride to a nearby hospital. We gave our dear friend and neighbor Lori a call, and she came up to stay with the kids. (Although I was a paramedic and a firm believer that people should always call 911 if experiencing an emergency, I personally would have never called for an ambulance unless I couldn't get to the car.) I did make it out to our van although had to kind of hang over the back seat during the ride in an effort to ease the pain. With Carol driving, we arrived at the emergency department and were able to get into a room pretty quickly. Shortly after telling the ER nurse that as a child I sometimes heard medical folks talking to my parents about a condition called Marfan syndrome and as the back pain started to creep around into my chest, the ER doc decided to perform a CT scan.

In a nutshell, Marfan syndrome is a genetic disorder that effects a person's connective tissue. People with Marfan's usually present with a few specific characteristics, which among other things include being tall and slender, sometimes double-jointed, and having flat feet. These were all special gifts that I had been given. Whether or not I might have Marfan's was sometimes a topic of discussion while growing up. Probably the biggest and most nasty complication of the syndrome is the potential to develop an aortic aneurysm or dissection. Well, wouldn't you know it, when the good doctor returned with the results of my scan, his eyes were as big as (maybe even bigger than) the roach exterminator man's eyes in New Jersey. My ascending aorta, the big vessel that comes up out of the heart to deliver blood to the whole body, had a diameter of six centimeters. (A normal ascending aorta for a guy my age would have been about 2.5 centimeters.) That's an aneurysm. The layers of the descending aorta (that same vessel which makes a loop and then heads down to provide blood to all the organs and lower part of the body) had split apart on the inside. That's a dissection. (Bummer.) It wasn't long before they had me on a helicopter flying to the University of Washington Medical Center. After about a week in the hospital followed by a few weeks of keeping my blood pressure really low at home to prevent either the aneurysm or dissection from getting worse, a remarkable surgeon and his team opened up my chest and gave me a new mechanical aortic heart valve and also wrapped the ascending aorta (I think with Dacron) to prevent it from rupturing. They chose to leave the descending aorta alone in the hope that by keeping my blood pressure really low it would remain stable enough not to have to do further surgery. This would probably be a good place to mention that had Carol and I been in the process of making a move to Vietnam when this whole aortic thing happened or perhaps even in Vietnam when the aneurysm and dissection occurred, our future would have undoubtedly been very different. I may not have even been around to write this now. Obviously, Carol didn't really try to kill me, but it's kind of fun to say that she did. Not to be morbid and although it's a very selfish thought, if I were going to die, I can't think of a nicer way to go. Of course, I wouldn't ever want to put Carol through something like that. All the same, just sayin'.

CHAPTER 21

Kurdistan

I had been working as a paramedic with the fire department for about six years on the evening that my wife and I were so rudely interrupted by the episode of horrific back pain and by the nasty medical issues that were causing it. During that sixth year, my boss had started giving me the opportunity to perform some of the tasks a medical officer would normally be performing and to represent the department at some of the meetings a M.O. would routinely be attending. Our assistant fire chief had for several years (in addition to his chief duties) also been functioning as medical officer. There had been some discussion about filling the position with one of the department's paramedic firefighters, and we had unofficially even discussed the possibility of me perhaps one day being placed in that role. Unfortunately, after the surgery I was informed that functioning as a paramedic firefighter would no longer be an option. My surgeon had issued a fifty-pound lifting restriction, and as any paramedic or firefighter will tell you, there is no way to safely and effectively perform either of those jobs with a fifty-pound lifting restriction.

During my recovery period, it was determined by administration and by the board of commissioners that it was time to fill the medical officer position with someone other than the chief, and surprisingly, it was also decided that I would be a good fit for the job, despite the fifty-pound lifting restriction. *Wow, rest assured, I realized then and still do today what an unbelievable gift I was being offered. Did I think that I was receiving an underserved blessing from the fire department and from God?*

Absolutely and without question. As wonderful an opportunity as this was, at my core I knew it was going to be a big stretch to put on a white shirt and make the shift from being a patient care provider to performing primarily administrative tasks. That first year as medical officer, I still tried to function as a medic on rare occasion so as to maintain some patient contact. This meant though that we needed to be sure to have enough bodies available on the scene to do any often necessary heavy lifting. It was "possible" to function this way, but I never did feel comfortable with having to rely on someone else to perform the lifting that every medic should be able to perform.

About a year after the original surgery, while at a routine follow-up visit with the surgeon and after having the first of many annual CT scans, the doc gave me the news that my descending aorta had gotten bigger in diameter and a second surgery would need to be performed. (Bummer.) This go-round they would be wrapping (I think with Dacron) about four inches of the big artery that flows blood from the heart down. It would be much like the procedure performed on the ascending aorta, except without the extra added bonus of having to put in a heart valve. Another thing that would be a little different about the second surgery was that instead of going in through the chest, they needed to go in from behind. This meant removing a rib from my back in order to gain access. I asked to keep the rib as a souvenir after surgery, thinking it would be fun to engrave it with something from Genesis and give it to Carol. Something from chapter 2, where it talks about God taking a rib from Adam and using it to make Eve. Dang, the hospital wasn't willing to let me have it.

Looking back, I can imagine that Carol was probably about this time wondering why in the world she ever made the mistake of marrying the strange army guy from Washington after only a three-day engagement. Three kids, a hip replacement, a big heart surgery, and now another big heart surgery later, she was again having to figure out how to take care of the kids and at the same time travel to and from Seattle to spend time with me in the ICU. And all this nonsense being generated from a guy who she thought was really healthy when she married him. I thought I was really healthy. Thank You, God, for the wonderful friends and neighbors who helped her out during this time.

Carol tells the story of one of those days in the ICU when I must have been pretty heavily medicated. Apparently, while sitting up in bed, I closed my eyes, pinched my thumb and index finger together, placed them to my lips, and took a long slow drag as if enjoying a toke. I have absolutely no recollection of this event, but it does go to show how some old habits die pretty hard. Having been a military guy, a fire service guy, and a dad with young kids, smoking pot wasn't in my vocabulary, at all. It would have been well over twenty years since I partook in herbal medicine. And yet surprise, surprise, over two decades later, here I was thinking I'm taking a hit in the intensive care.

Although Washington State is considered by some to be the most liberal state in all of the United States and although, along with Colorado, was one of the first two states to legalize marijuana, I don't believe you will find any of the intensive care units providing joints to their patients. On the other hand, it is Washington.

Just like with the first surgery, recovery ultimately went quite well, and I was back to work before too terribly long. Back to work also meant getting back into the groove of attending meetings (lots of meetings). Although there were meetings (maybe several of them) that had you wondering if everybody's time and effort couldn't be better spent doing something else, there were thankfully some that actually made a valuable contribution and difference in our county's emergency medical system. In addition to having the pleasure of attending lots of meetings, I was also tasked with coordinating and teaching our fire academy's emergency medical technician course. Students included members of our own department's resident program, residents from other area departments, and some students who came to us via the local community college. It was fun to see these mostly young adults learn new information and master new skills. Particularly gratifying to me was working with the students who really did have a heart to take care of their patients, which, come to think of it, was most of them. Part of my little spiel with each new class was a reminder that they would be in the business of providing patient care and that in order to provide "patient care," you'd first have to actually give a rip about the patient. It would also be really, really good to actually "care." If you didn't care, perhaps the field of emergency medical service wasn't the best choice for a career. So here I was, staying busy doing lots of stuff—talking about, teaching about, planning about, and going to meetings about the business of taking care of patients. The problem was I was just about never actually doing it. Just about never, except for on those forthcoming occasions when I was given the wonderful gift of participating with a medical relief team. A few years after coming on with the fire department, I had applied to volunteer with a faith-based NGO, or nongovernment agency, which had its headquarters outside of Portland, Oregon, and which provided medical and disaster relief all over the globe.

When Carol and I decided that Vietnam was not the direction we were going to take, I did find myself wondering if and when serving in an international setting might ever be a reality. Just when I was starting to think it probably wasn't going to happen any time soon (particularly after having had the heart surgeries), hello, I get an invitation to travel to, of all places, Iraq. On this particular team, we wouldn't actually be performing hands-on patient care but rather would be sent to evaluate the nursing programs being taught in the north of the country and specifically in the three major Kurdish cities of the region (Erbil, Sulaymaniyah, and Dohuk). Any specific areas of medical care we identified as ones that could use some continuing education would be considered for future teams to come and teach on. The trip was taking place just about two months after the United States made its invasion on Iraq and on Saddam Hussein. I should probably mention here that I was one of those very skeptical people concerning whether or not an invasion of Iraq should have ever taken place. It was pretty clear Mr. Hussein was a horribly bad fellow responsible for several years of terrible atrocities, which included among other things the use of chemicals to annihilate untold thousands of Kurdish villagers in the north of the country; that was a given. As to whether or not he was actually harboring chemical weapons at the time of the US invasion, that was another story. Although a wholehearted supporter of the men and women who serve as members of our military, I was not in support of invading Iraq at that time. I was very much in support, however, of an opportunity to help some of the people of Iraq in any way we could.

Journal entry:

05/28/03

> *Wow, Father, I can hardly believe that I'm here. Arrived in Portland for a 3:00 PM briefing with NWMT. We are scheduled to fly on in the morning. Destination: San Francisco, CA. From there we go to Frankfurt and spend the night. Hopefully, Gerhard and Roland will come to visit at the hotel.* [Gerhard and Roland were old friends from the Kontakt Club I was a part of while stationed in Germany. We had all kept in touch over the years, and I let them know I would be in Frankfurt for a night and would love to get together.] *Lord, I truly don't deserve to be here. Please help me to be an asset to this team. We have two docs, Bob and Dick; one RN, Marie; and myself. (This is so awesome!) Called Carol and the kids a little bit ago. Please, Lord, take great care of them and let them know your presence. I think this is the longest that I have ever been away from Carol. She really is a wonderful woman.*

Over the years, I had been given the huge privilege of being able to take some vacations with my family. Usually, these little getaways lasted a few days or at the longest a couple weeks (except for the trip to Vietnam, which was three weeks). The trip to Iraq would require being away from Carol and the kids for just over three weeks. Somehow, when I received the invitation to go, there was enough paid time off available to actually pull it off. I hadn't yet returned to full duty after the second surgery, so there weren't any pressing MO tasks that wouldn't wait or that couldn't be taken care of by another department member. I would be functioning more as a nurse than a paramedic, so the fifty-pound lifting restriction wasn't going to be an issue. Dear Carol had agreed to hold down the fort and take care of the kids by herself while I was away (albeit a little apprehensively), so when all was said and done, much to my surprise, I got to go.

Journal entry:

05/31/-, 10:40, Frankfurt Airport.

Hello, Lord. Well, here we are at the airport. Yesterday was wonderful. Gerhard and Roland came and met me at the hotel. We took a ride to the Taunus Mountains (hills) and went up to the highest one (Feldberg). You get a view of Frankfurt from there. We then went out to dinner in the town of Königstein. What a cool place. Old-style cobblestone streets and a castle on the hill. (I think it might have actually been an old fortress where a castle had once stood.) We had dinner outside on the street, and it was awesome. I couldn't have asked for anything better. Ruladen [a wonderful braised beef roll stuffed with goodies like bacon and onions and mustard and pickle—yummy], *red cabbage, potato dumplings, and hefeweizen.* [There was no way I was going to eat this amazing German meal without a good German beer.] *Some folks going to a rehearsal for a castle festival walked by in costume. It was a blast.*

What a wonderful highlight to the trip having Gerhard and Roland take the time to pay me a visit during our layover and also to treat me to this amazing dinner. It was way above and beyond what I could have imagined to be sitting with my old friends and enjoying a delicious meal in the village of Königstein, where from our cobblestone street table we could gaze up at the old castle fortress on the hill. Oh, and then the people in Old World costume came strolling by, just in case we were lacking atmosphere. It was so great.

From Frankfurt, we flew into the city of Diyarbakir located in the southeastern Republic of Turkey. Diyarbakir, unofficially considered the capital of Turkish Kurdistan, is also known for its massive medieval walls that surround the city. At ten to twelve meters in height, three to five meters wide, and nearly six kilometers in length, the fortification is second only to the Great Wall of China in size. After a night in Diyarbakir, we travelled by van to the border town of Silopi from where (after a several hour process) we made the crossing into Iraq.

Journal entry:

06/03/

Father God, I really cannot believe that You allowed me to be a part of this team. Thank You very much. We started the day by visiting with the Minister of Health of Kurdistan Mr. Jamal Abduil Manaed, who has his office in Erbil. We then traveled to Dohuk, where we met with the Director of Dohuk School of Medicine, Dr. Farhad. From there we went to the Director of Health in Dohuk. Tomorrow we will go to the teaching hospital for an orientation with the director of the hospital and a tour of the different departments.

06/05/-

We have now been in Dohuk for three days and have met everyone from the Director of the School of Nursing, the Director of Health, Director of Azadi, Director of the Emergency Hospital, the Nursing Director of the Technical School (a wonderful woman that reminds you of Mother Teresa), and the Planning Manager for the Dohuk Department of Health to name a few.

I can't remember exactly what it was about the Director of the Technical School that made me think of Mother Teresa. It may have been a combination of her obvious and genuine concern for others along with the little twinkle in her eyes. While in Northern Iraq, our group first met with the appropriate medical powers that be in Dohuk, Sulaymaniyah, and Erbil. After making all the required introductions, we visited several hospitals and medical schools in those same cities with the goal of putting together a list of medical topics, which small teaching teams could develop curriculum for and then later return to the country to teach. Although I never did see the final report, I know that some of the needs we identified included topics as simple as basic life support, CPR, and basic infection control to more complex areas, such as advanced cardiac life support, advanced trauma life support and burn care. I wasn't one of those privileged to later join one of the teaching teams, however, I believe that several small groups did come and provide some much needed continuing education. Our trip to Iraq was I believe, valuable, and did ultimately help to facilitate better medicine and nursing care in the cities which we visited.

In addition to lending a helping hand, I had hoped that after spending some time in the country, I might be able to determine with a little more clarity if our military invasion of Iraq really was a good and necessary decision - or not. Like many people, I was very confused about the reports we were hearing at home of Hussein having a huge stockpile of hidden chemical weapons. He had of course already proved his willingness to possess and use this kind of weaponry in the past, but the evidence being presented proving that he still had anything hidden away was from my perspective, pretty weak at best. It just so happened that our in country contact and guide while traveling from city to city (we'll call him Dale) was the same person who had been tasked with coordinating and building a number of chemical shelters in the northern Kurdish areas of the country. According to him, everybody he was associated with was for the most part convinced that Hussein did not have a stock pile of chemical and or biological weapons. Also, according to our guide, for Hussein to confirm one way or the other if he did or didn't have these weapons at his disposal (as opposed to keeping the world guessing and giving the impression that he was in control) would cause him to "lose face" and appear weak (something the megalomaniac dictator of an Arab nation is probably not in the habit of doing). Although pretty sure that Saddam Hussein was not harboring weapons of mass destruction, our guide also realized that he was a crazy man and that building shelters "just in case" was a very reasonable thing to do. Another issue that was for me kind of a ridiculous proposition was the idea that after "liberating" the nation of Iraq from its insane leader, those holding power would for some reason be interested in developing a Western democratic form of government. Why would a land which had functioned under a very tribal form of government for thousands of years now choose to do things "our way." In addition to the struggle that exists between Sunnis and Shiites, Iraq is also home to powerful tribal Sheikhs who probably have little to no interest in changing the way they rule or in losing any of the power and position they possess. And it's not like the different factions of Kurds were asking for a democratic form of government. Their differences had even led to a civil war in the mid-1990s between the PDK (Kurdistan Democratic Party) and the PUK (Patriotic Union of Kurdistan.) And there was also the PKK (Workers Party) to add to the mix. The point is, at least to my simple way of thinking, the people of Iraq were not going to suddenly change a century's old way of governing.

Journal entry:

06/15, 7:45 PM

Well, it's now Sunday the 15th, and I am back in Erbil. Due to leave for the border in the morning. Felt kind of punk today, but thank you, Lord, seems to be getting better. I must write this while I'm thinking about it. Carol, an Australian who works for the State Department had a large amount of money stolen from her home by the house cleaner. In order to write it off, she needs to file a police report. The father of the girl said that if Carol does file a report, he would kill his daughter in front of her. Kind of a dilemma. Not sure how it's going to work out. I think [Dale] will write a letter for her so it can be documented and at the same time the family won't be ashamed. A very different culture. So different that I won-

der if the US attempt to establish a Western form of government could ever work. I wonder if George didn't bite off a little more than the US can chew.

After completing our assignment in Iraq, I said goodbye to the team and traveled independently by car back to the Turkish border and then on to Istanbul and finally home. Before leaving the country though, I had the chance to spend a couple nights at our guide's home in Erbil. It was while staying with Dale that I was invited to dinner at his friend's house, who worked for the State Department and who told us the story about her housekeeper. "Losing face" it would appear was not just a major issue for Saddam Hussein but also for the father of Carol's housekeeper. Hearing the story only further convinced me that a tribal form of government with an overriding culture of honor over shame (at all costs) was not going to easily or even ever be willing or able to conform to Western democracy.

Before closing this chapter on Kurdistan, I want to mention that during the course of our travels in the north of Iraq, we would sometimes need to drive through the city of Mosul. Although Mosul wasn't at that time a city under siege, it was a place that our guide knew would be best to avoid and to travel through only if absolutely necessary and then very quickly without stopping. It was after finding out that I would be going to Iraq and then making an effort to research and gain a little more knowledge about the country that I discovered a surprising fact about Mosul. Most everybody has heard the story of Jonah and the big fish. You know the one; a guy named Jonah is told by God to go to the city of Nineveh and make it clear to its inhabitants that He (God) was not at all pleased about their wicked ways. Instead of doing what God had told him to do, Jonah decides not to get involved and instead goes to the port of Joppa, where he finds passage on a ship to Tarshish. (There seems to be some debate as to exactly where the city of Tarshish was located in the time of Jonah, but whatever the case, it was nowhere near Nineveh and not at all in the direction Jonah had been told to go. Simply put, he was running away.)

Well, during the voyage, they were hit by a huge storm, which starts to break up the ship. After some investigating by the captain and the sailors on board, it comes out that Jonah was running from God and is very likely the reason for their woes. They all agree that the best thing to do is to throw Jonah overboard in hopes that this will quiet the storm. Immediately after giving him the old heave-ho, the storm stops its raging, and the ship, along with its occupants, are spared. All spared except for Jonah, who finds himself bobbing around in the middle of the sea. This is where the fish comes in. A really big one swallows Jonah up, and it's inside the big fish's belly that Jonah makes his home for the next three days and nights along with whatever nasty things you would find in the stomach of a fish big enough to swallow you up. Horribly "slimy" comes to mind. Jonah's stay at hotel big fish did provide him with an opportunity to seriously contemplate life as well as to have a really good prayer time with the God he had been trying to run away from. Apparently, Jonah wasn't very easy to digest because after the three days he got puked up onto a beach. So much for running away from God. Jonah received another word from on high but this time was instructed not just to let the people of Nineveh know that the Lord of the Universe was pretty ticked about their evil and violent ways but also that in forty days all of its inhabitants were going to be overthrown.

This time around, Jonah was a little more amiable to doing what God asked him to do, and after a three-day walk to Nineveh, he proclaimed God's message all over the city. You would think that Jonah would have been pleased when the king and all the people heeded his words and everybody fasted and prayed, asking God to help them to turn from their wicked ways. (It wasn't just all of the people that fasted, prayed, and covered themselves with sackcloth and ashes, but not even the animals were given food, and they too received a sackcloth covering.)

It really ticked Jonah off that God listened to the prayers of the people, changed His mind, and decided not to wipe them out. Turns out the reason Jonah didn't want to go to Tarshish in the first place was because he had a feeling that God would be loving and forgive the people if they repented. I won't go into details here, but the biblical account ends with God teaching Jonah a lesson about love and forgiveness. The book of Jonah tells the whole story. It's only four chapters long and found between Obadiah and Micah. The point of mentioning this is that the city Nineveh is in fact the city of Mosul today. (Pretty cool, I'd say.)

Iraq is so incredibly full of wonderful historical sites. You may recall when early in the US involvement of Iraq an American military convoy was ambushed when they had entered the Iraqi occupied town of Nasiriyah. Several soldiers were killed or wounded, and then several were taken into captivity as prisoners of war. It was headline news when one of the wounded captives was rescued by Special Forces from Saddam Hussein Hospital in the town of Nasiriyah, where she was being held. It just so happens that Nasiriyah is located very near to what was known as the city of Ur. That's the place Abraham originally came from when he was told to leave his home and set out for the Promised Land. (Kind of a significant place.)

Other well-known historical sites located in Iraq include Babylon, where, as the story goes, ancient Mesopotamians tried to build a giant tower reaching into heaven. Apparently, they were hoping their efforts to build what we have come to know as the Tower of Babel would impress God and show Him how resourceful they were. Instead of being impressed, the chief architect of the cosmos decided to put a stop to their project by confusing the people's speech and causing them to speak in several languages rather than the one tongue they had all been using. Construction was shut down due to folks no longer being able to understand each other. Although historians differ as to its location, Babylon may also have been the place where one of the Seven Wonders of the Ancient World (the Hanging Gardens) once stood. I was very surprised to learn that the capital of Kurdistan, Erbil, where we spent a great deal of our time in Iraq, is considered to be the oldest continuously inhabited city in the world. Outside of Erbil's Citadel, or Qalat, which sits in the heart of and at the city's highest elevation, you can find a very unpretentious hand-painted sign that gives a brief history and makes the claim of being an inhabited community since 7,000 BC.

The day we visited the Citadel, there was a car parked in front of the sign, making it difficult to read and photograph. At the suggestion of Dale, we stealthily pulled the sign up out of the ground, moved it over to a place where it could be easily read, took a couple photos, and then returned it to its happy home. (Probably a good thing no one else was around when we tampered with the official sign at the oldest continuously inhabited city in the world.)

My return trip home was for the most part uneventful, except maybe for the delay our plane full of passengers experienced while waiting on the airstrip in Diyarbakir. Destination: Istanbul. After what seemed like an inordinately long wait, the overhead speaker on the plane instructed the owner of a green duffel bag to disembark. I had chosen to travel with my old army-issue duffel bag because it was a pretty practical travel bag that could also be worn as a backpack. Other than a red bandanna wrapped around the handle (and a tiny little WWJD iron on patch), it was just a regular old army-issue bag. I don't know if it was just the fact that it was military or what, but before it got put in the plane's luggage compartment, they wanted to be sure about who it belonged to. After walking down the rolling staircase to the airstrip below, there sat my bag all by itself on the tarmac. A few guys met me at the bottom of the staircase, asked me to verify the bag was mine, and that was it. I got back on the plane (a little embarrassed for having been the reason for our delay), and soon after we were in the air.

Accompanying a medical team to Iraq was a privilege I would forever be grateful for. It was very surprising and exciting to have been invited in the first place. Maybe even a bigger surprise was that this wasn't the only invite I would receive. In the years to come, although we would all wish there were never the need for a disaster response in the first place, I was asked to and ultimately did participate with teams that provided medical care to both West Darfur, Sudan, and then Banda Aceh, Indonesia. Once again, due the willingness of my fire chiefs to allow me to be away for several weeks each time, along with the generous vacation time the fire service offers (augmented by a few of my coworkers donating a little of their hard-earned vacation time to help make it possible for one of their own to lend a hand across the globe), I was able to serve on these medical missions. One of my chiefs even kicked in some of his vacation time. I could only hope and pray that I would represent our department and the folks who contributed several hours from their own personal time off really well during these opportunities to serve. For both trips, I left the duffle bag at home.

CHAPTER 22

From Africa to Indonesia

Journal entry:

09/01/04, 11 PM, Wednesday night

Can you believe it? (I can't.) Right now, a physician from Oregon (Mike) and I are on our way to Sudan to work with the displaced people there. We will stop first in London and then fly on to Khartoum. I will keep this short for now but would like to say thank You, Lord Jesus! Thank you for everything. For Carol (she is such a great wife, and I know that I don't deserve her). For Hannah and Abbie and Philip. They are all so unique and such wonderful kids. Please, Lord, take care of Carol and the kids while we are away.

In 2003 and 2004, while many people like myself were half oblivious to the fact that this was even happening, several thousands of Sudanese Africans were being killed (murdered) and many, many thousands (ultimately 2+ million) more were being displaced from their homes and forced to live in surrounding villages or displaced people camps. African villagers of West Darfur had risen up against the government, accusing Sudan's leadership of oppression against non-Arabs.

Two rebel groups in particular, the Justice and Equality Movement (or JEM) and the Sudan Liberation Movement (or SLM) were leading the fight. In response, the government of Sudan recruited, armed, and backed bands of militia drawn from Arab nomadic groups known as Janjaweed. The Janjaweed nomads were essentially given free rein to plunder, pillage, kill, and burn the non-Arab Africans out of their villages. In short, they were given the freedom to perform genocide.

Journal entry:

09/03/04

I am now sitting in the waiting area of the Acropole Hotel in Khartoum. We arrived last night (actually this morning) at about 1:00 AM. Joe was here at the hotel, waiting to meet us. [Joe was one of the directors of the organization that had sent us to Darfur and would be in country, participating with the project for about the first week.] *Today we have been taking it easy and will be going on a little free tour of the city shortly. We plan (Mike and I) to fly to El Geneina* [the capital of West Darfur] *on Saturday the 5th. Joe will be flying over tomorrow. Thank you so much, Lord, for allowing me to come. My true desire is to get to know you better during this time and to hopefully make a difference for some people. Please help me to be REAL concerning you with Mike. He is a pretty cerebral guy, and I want to represent you well with him.* [Mike was an emergency room physician from Oregon. We had never met each other before this trip and would now be providing medical care and working together very closely in an environment unlike just about any other. Volunteers with the Disaster Relief Organization were made up of a pretty diverse mix of faith backgrounds. Mike, for instance, was associated with an organization known as the Church of New Jerusalem, or the New Church. Also called

Swedenborgianism. Members of this denomination inter-preted the Bible through the teachings of a Swedish gentle-man named Immanuel Swedenborg, who was born in the late 1600s. I knew enough about the New Church to know that Mike and I would likely be thinking quite differently concerning several issues of faith. Mike was a nice guy, and I could tell right away that we would have a good time working together. My hope was that we would also be able to embrace those faith issues that we held in common and enjoy a spiritual connection during the trip. Turns out we could.] *It was great—last night we had a little devotional together and prayed together. 6:30 PM, saw Sufi dancing, met Mohamed.*

09/04/04, 06:00 AM

Good morning! Yesterday evening was great. We went on a little tour hosted by the hotel. The old bus we started out on broke down, so we had to wait for another. Went to the sailing club, the palace museum, and ended up at a cemetery tomb where Sufi Muslims were danc-ing. It was really something to see. (A real mix of Islam and Africa). Apparently, Islam came here from Iraq. That's why the Muslim faith, but the dancing taking place definitely looked African. [The participants of this ritual prayer were all moving and dancing in a big circle while at the same time spinning round and round. I had heard of a "whirling der-vish" but never knew what it was. Several years later, I was informed that the spinning and dancing we were witness-ing was in fact a whirling dervish.] *A so-called "holy man" in the faith (who appeared to be blind) greeted me and kissed my hand.* [The gentleman standing next to me informed me this was quite an honor.] *Met a guy named Mohamed, who I think is a believer. He is from West Darfur. I have his email and want to communicate with him.*

Sunday, 09/05/-

Up early this morning to take the cab to the airport. Got off the ground at 08:45. Met a few docs at the airport with Doctors of the World and with Samaritans Purse—nice folks. Last night, met a journalist from Finland named Uri. He's married with two kids—very nice guy. Today met a gentleman named Roberto, who is the chief doctor for UNICEF in Sudan. He was pointing out how there are similar problems throughout all of Darfur. West Darfur just has all of the media attention right now due probably to the uncertainty of the situation and potential to get worse.

During our time in West Darfur, Mike and I would primarily be providing medical clinics for a few villages that had experienced significant population increases after folks from surrounding areas had been burned out of their homes by the Janjaweed. Working with us was a great guy from Canada named Lambert, who specialized in the maintenance and construction of freshwater wells. Our home base was located in the capital of West Darfur, El Geneina. From there, we traveled out to the villages and often stayed away for a few days at a time. Accompanying us on our trips out were a great team of Sudanese interpreters and drivers (all guys). Also, for some of our time, we were joined by a group of university students (both men and women) who assisted by screening many of those in and around the villages for malaria.

Tuesday, 09/07/-, 16:45

Up early this morning. Went to the village of Azerni. We were going to be involved with an evaluation of the needs. However, today was a food distribution day, so everybody was getting food. The people must go quite far to a pump in order to get water. One young man (Asam) was pointing out lots of men that he said were Janjaweed. Also lots of tents that he said belonged to Janjaweed. It sounds like what is going on here is just the same as what has gone on in the North, South, and Nuba mountains. [After only a few days in Sudan, I heard from several sources that the persecution taking place in West Darfur was also happening in several other parts of the country.] *Although there are some tremendous needs here for food, shelter, sanitation, and medicine, the people are a very happy people.* [In spite of the horrible circumstances that were taking place, we saw lots of beautiful smiles among the people.] *The kids are great. When they see you, they shout out Howaja* [sp?], *which means person from the west.* [The children would run up to you and call out what sounded like a little kid on the east coast of the States shouting, "How awe ya?"]

09/08/04

This is so unreal. We are in Sanidadi. First, we drove into the military camp, which according to a lot of the guys on the team was also full of Janjaweed. There were lots of horses and a few camels. Oh, by the way, a couple of the boys have said they want to be in our family and marry Hannah and Abbie. I told them they would have to wait a few years. [Our drivers and interpreters had seen pictures of my daughters, and although the girls were only fifteen and twelve years old at the time, a couple of the young men let me know they could come up with a pretty tempting number of camels in order to marry them and be part of our family. They might have even included a goat or two. Had the girls been a little older, we might have been able to make a deal.]

The team is sleeping under the stars next to a cement building that is the clinic. About twenty people, I think. [The females actually ended up sleeping in a thatched house.] *I have been eating whatever was provided, so Lord-willing (please, God), I'll stay healthy. We left Sanidadi on the 9th and came to Um Tagouk* [sp?] *Um Tagouk normally has a population of about 6,200, but I think with the displaced people, it's about 14,000, including the surrounding little villages. We were told by the school teacher that a few of the villages are still not secure from the Janjaweed. We met with the head honcho of the area, and he put us under his care and is providing two buildings for the men and women to sleep in. We held clinic along with the health professional (kind of like a PA), and I also tried to work on cleaning up the little pharmacy. What a mess.*

The little clinic in Um Tagouk was fortunate enough to have a small collection of medications, immunizations, and a few medical supplies, which I think were probably provided by the World Health Organization. Unfortunately, they had all been thrown into a little rodent-poop-infested shed. I worked off and on for a couple days, trying to clean and organize. I have always enjoyed providing medical care in an environment where you do the best you can even when resources are limited. We were definitely being given an opportunity to do just that in West Darfur. You just kind of had to deal with whatever came up. Although we had originally thought we would be exclusively providing care for those people who had been displaced from their homes, I'm pretty sure we had several Janjaweed included with our patients as well. I think it was on our first day of clinic in Um Tagouk that we had to ask one of our patients to leave his sword at the door.

09/10/-

Today is Friday, and the Holy Day as well as a market day. We held clinic even though it's the locals' day off, and they came. Also got some more work done arranging the pharmacy. It's been a productive day. Thank you again, Lord Jesus, for allowing me to be here. It really is an unbelievable experience. Please help us to make a difference. And as always, please take care of Carol, Hannah, Abbie, and Philip.

09/11/-

Just had an evening devotional with Mike and [we will call him Andrew] *also joined us.* [Although a Sudanese, Andrew was a believer. He was working with us and helping with logistics during our stay in El Geneina. He didn't give specifics about how he had come to know Jesus, but just said, "It was a miracle."] *Andrew read from his Bible and also prayed with us. What a great time. Also received an email from Mohamed in Khartoum.* [Mohamed was the guy I met while watching the Sufi whirling dervish.] *I think he is praying for us. How cool.*

Sunday, 9/12/-

Hello. Was able to talk to Carol, Hannah, and Philip today. Sorry, I missed Abbie. It was wonderful to hear their voices. Met with some folks from UNICEF, Department of Health, and the director of the hospital today. Ended up having futur (breakfast) with them. What a feast. Will spend the day around here tomorrow and then head for the field again. Sanidadi and Um Tagouk.

I found myself feeling really sorry for the young physician who had the huge responsibility of serving as director of the hospital in West Darfur's capital city. During our meal together, which I believe was held in the home of the "director general of health services"—that's right, it seemed pretty obvious that he was a very stressed-out guy. And with good reason. Mike and I had taken a tour of the hospital, and no lie, I think we might have had more supplies in the fire department supply room and on a couple advanced life support ambulances back home than he had in his entire hospital.

On those days, when we were at the Geneina base camp, our team would often be treated to the cooking skills of two lovely ladies, Fatina and Fatea. I was pretty amazed at the tasty treats they were able to whip up on their stove, which was actually just a pile of burning coal. Although they seemed to handle the coal fire without any problems whatsoever, our two great cooks were provided with a little Coleman-type stove a couple weeks into our stay. The food was simple but always really good. One day at the compound, in addition to being treated to one of Fatina and Fatea's delicious meals, we were also treated to one of the strangest things I've ever seen. Suddenly, while we were sitting in the little courtyard, hundreds and hundreds of locusts swarmed in and landed on and all around us. It was so unexpected and so weird. You literally had to brush them off. And then, as if this was something that happened every day, a few little kids came into the yard with buckets or bags and started to gather up the little creatures. According to Andrew, the locusts were going to become their next meal. (Sort of like John the Baptist in the wilderness.) And to think, I had actually heard a sermon or two where the preacher tried to make scripture a little more palatable by saying that John was actually eating the pods from a locust tree along with his honey. I can't say for sure what John was munching on, but I do know for sure that these kids and their families were intending to and were glad to be eating grasshoppers from heaven.

Journal entry:

Sunday, 09/19/-, 12:45

It's Sunday afternoon, and I just enjoyed a nice futur. [I'm not sure, but we might have called it futur, or breakfast, any time we had something to eat.] *Some kind of little round macaroni, diced tomatoes, creamed corn (sort of), and some little ribs of some kind. Our cooks Fatina and Fatea do a very good job.*

09/23/-

Just returned from Um Tagouk. Had a little eleven-month-old with severe respiratory distress. Brought her to the MSF (Médecins Sans Frontières) clinic. (Please, Father, help that little one to recover.) Also Mike brought a mom and baby to Geneina. She delivered last night at thirty-two weeks.

09/25/-

Unfortunately, both mother and newborn died. The wee one made it another day but then went to be with Father. [This mother was tragically one of West Darfur's several displaced refugees who contracted hepatitis E in 2004. Sadly, the death rate among those with the disease was much higher for pregnant females.] *Also just found out today that the little eleven-month-old with pneumonia also went to be with Jesus. Please, Lord, be with this father and with this couple.*

After having been in Sudan for just over three weeks, my time was now coming to an end. Mike was choosing to stay on for a bit longer, but I was scheduled to head for home. This truly had been a remarkable experience. I could only hope that the people we were privileged to meet and to care for were at least half as blessed by the help they received as we were by the opportunity to be there. Funny how that works but being given a chance to try and help even just a tiny fraction of the people of West Darfur had been without question one of the most fulfilling times of my life.

Journal entry (continued):

09/25/-

I am now sitting at the Geneina airstrip. Not sure if I will get a flight or not. We shall see. [Getting a ride on the 4 prop UN World Food Program plane from Geneina to Khartoum was kind of a hit-and-miss ordeal. You just went to the airstrip, put your name on the list, and hoped to be one of the chosen few. I knew of at least one person who had spent a whole day trying and never did make it on board. On this occasion, I had determined that it might be wise to try and utilize just about every polite phrase of the local language that I had been able to learn. I think that turned out to be a good idea.] *Well, I got on the plane and should be in Khartoum in about an hour. When we came to the airstrip this morning, the WFP gentleman put my name at the top of the standby list. (I sure am looking forward to seeing Carol and the kids.)*

09/26/-

Took a cab to the Acropole last night, but they were full. I'm glad they were. Called [Fred] *and ended up staying at the World Relief office. It's a great place. Just finished going to the souk and being shown around by a guy named Mohamed.*

No question about it, Mohamed is one popular name in Sudan. There were a few more Mohameds I had the pleasure of meeting but haven't mentioned. The gentleman who showed me around the souk was a very nice guy and a great guide of the city. He even gave me a couple telephone calls in the years that followed. Fred, whose real name actually isn't Fred, was a contact whose information we had been given and who worked with World Relief in Khartoum. I ended up spending a couple days at the WR apartment and even managed to watch a little TV while there. One of the shows we watched was a documentary about Washington State and in particular about the Seattle area (where I lived). It was showing very detailed graphics about all the devastation that would result if we were to experience the giant earthquake that many say "will" happen in our region at some point in the future. As bad as the results of the earthquake were, they were nothing compared to the look of things after the eruption of Mount Rainer, which would be woken up and made angry by the earthquake. And if the earthquake and volcanic eruption weren't enough, the tsunami resulting from all the other seismic activity would pretty much wipe our little piece of heaven off the map. Suddenly, West Darfur wasn't looking quite as horrible. Don't get me wrong, I'd rather take my chances with the earthquake, volcano, and tsunami than I would with the Janjaweed.

Although I have tried to keep a light pulse on what has been happening in Sudan over the years, I'm once again sort of half oblivious to the current situation, much like when I first heard about West Darfur. I'm pretty sure that terrible atrocities are still occurring in Darfur today and if not in Darfur then in Somalia or Afghanistan or Pakistan or Iraq or Syria and if not in these places then somewhere else (perhaps in our own neighborhoods or our own homes and among our own families). Folks are treating each other horrifically all over the world. As much as I would like to think that people are all inherently good at heart, I really don't think we are. Instead, I believe we desperately need some huge supernatural help from on high in order to get it right. It doesn't just come naturally.

Journal entry:

01/02/05

Well, here we are in 2005. And here I am on the way to Banda Aceh, Indonesia. We are responding to the terrible earthquake tsunami disaster. To be honest, I am surprised that I get to go. It is a privilege to be sure to be able to help. I know it's a bit hard on Carol and the kids for me to be gone. Please, Lord, take good care of them while I am away. (It's not like I take great care of them when I'm there.) Please help me to do better. I think this will be a wonderful group of people to work with. Two docs, one PA, three nurses, and I.

Saturday, 01/08/04

Well, it's been a pretty interesting few days. We are in Banda Aceh and have been here for a couple of days. We are trying to get to the town of Lamno.

On 26 December 2004, a massive 9+ magnitude earthquake—I believe the third largest ever recorded—shook the depths of the Indian Ocean. With its epicenter approximately 160 kilometers off the west coast of Indonesia's largest island, this undersea megathrust quake triggered a devastating tsunami, which first reached shore in northern Sumatra. The world's deadliest tsunami in modern history was ultimately responsible for death and/or destruction in as many as eighteen countries—the hardest hit being Indonesia and the Aceh province in particular, where hundreds of thousands were killed or displaced. After our team arrived in Medan, the capital of North Sumatra Province, we were met by an American couple who had been living and working in Indonesia for some time. They both spoke the language and would both be helping to coordinate the project while we were together in country. We were also joined by the most wonderful group of Indonesian interpreters that we could have asked for. They would be accompanying us to Lamno and proved to be absolutely invaluable members of the team. Not just because of their excellent skills in interpreting but also due to an undeniable love for people and willingness to help in any way they could.

Our first order of business was to find transportation to Banda Aceh, the capital city of the Aceh Province (431 km by air or 603 km by ground). Our interpreters ended up making this journey on a bus. It would have been easy if we'd all used this method to make the trip. However, it turned out that traveling by vehicle along the east coast of Aceh Province in Northern Sumatra on a dark road at night wasn't the safest thing for a Westerner to be doing at that time. Like so many world events that I had spent a lifetime being clueless about, there had been a situation taking place in Aceh that, although going on for nearly thirty years, had never fallen under my radar. In what started as a struggle for independence in 1976, rebels of the Free Aceh Movement (Gerakan Aceh Merdeka, or GAM) had been involved in an armed conflict to regain sovereignty of the Aceh region from the government. Probably the fact that northern Aceh was rich in gas and oil resources played a significant role in the ongoing insurgency. We had not heard any reports of aid workers running into problems on the coast road to Aceh, but still there was a civil war taking place, and hence the decision was made that American team members would not accompany our interpreters on the bus.

It was only a few days prior in December that the government had lifted an eighteen-month-old ban prohibiting any foreign journalists or aid workers from even entering the region. On that same December date, the GAM apparently declared a ceasefire, allowing aid to reach the victims. All the rest of the team were able to hitch rides on a helicopter for their trip north. All the rest that is except for Max and me. Max was one of our wonderful interpreters who I ended up working together with on several occasions over the weeks to come. Because there were no more spaces available on a helicopter and because I was not being permitted to take the bus, we had to find another way of getting to Banda Aceh. Our first mission together was to find a way north and meet up with the rest of the team. The US military was involved with delivering much-needed supplies into the Aceh Province. Some of these supplies were being delivered by airlift, which meant that military C130s (and probably some other types of aircraft) were making the flight north out of Medan. Our plan was to find out exactly where the planes were flying from, make our way to that location, speak with the captain of a plane, and see if we couldn't join them for one of the supply deliveries.

To make kind of a long story short, that's exactly what we ended up doing. It required a full day of speaking with lots of different people, several hours of waiting at a little military-type building at the airfield, a few more hours sitting outside on the ground next to the airstrip, watching and waiting for a plane we hoped to catch a ride on, then finally running up to the plane and trying to convince the captain and his crew that they should allow us to join them. Thankfully, they were feeling gracious that night, and after receiving a signal from the crew chief, Max and I ran up the rear ramp of a fully loaded C130 and found places to sit on top of the large piles of supplies that were being delivered to tsunami victims in the north. I might have even stretched out and caught a few—very few—z's during the flight.

> *I hope Carol and the kids are doing well. Talked to Carol the other day, and she told me that Hannah had run into the wall at the health department. Oh well, everybody was okay. Guess I'll close for now. Dear Lord, please give Carol and the kids a hug for me.*

Our oldest daughter, Hannah, was a brand-new driver during this time and apparently thought she had put the van in reverse when "oops" it wasn't. She kind of ran into a wall. When Carol told me about Hannah's little incident, I had to think back on some of the foolish mishaps I'd experienced as a young driver. Truth be told, there were times when I shouldn't have been allowed on the road.

> *Some interesting info about what happened: First the earthquake lasted about fifteen minutes. Many people ran out of the buildings. About fifty minutes later, the first wave hit. Prior to the wave, all the water went out from the shore, leaving fish on the beach. People ran to the beach to get the fish. This lasted approximately fifteen minutes. Warm black water then washed in. This was followed by the first wave, the first of three.*

From what the people we met and spoke with told us, absolutely nobody was expecting the tsunami and resulting destruction that it would bring. They were taken totally off guard and by surprise.

I could never have imagined the level of devastation we would be witnessing in Banda Aceh. Max and I were able to catch a lift from the airstrip into the city. During the ride, we passed by what were obviously bodies (lots and lots of bodies). They had been wrapped in plastic and laid next to each other not far from the road. We hadn't made it very far into town before seeing what looked like the results of a giant bomb having gone off. Block after city block were absolutely leveled. We saw what was left of large fishing boats, which had been thrown inland by the waves, ending up a kilometer from shore among the rubble of destroyed buildings. And then more rows of bodies. No question, it was like nothing I had ever seen. Our team spent a few days in Banda Aceh, waiting to secure transportation to the coastal town of Lamno, which would be our final destination. We were housed together with other aid workers who were already helping in the Banda Aceh region or who like our team were waiting to travel elsewhere. There was talk of making the trip to Lamno by helicopter, but in the end, we were able to secure a fishing boat. Our vessel brought us the eighty-kilometer distance south along the west coast of Sumatra to one of the coastal villages hit hardest by the tsunami. It was "very concerning" to say the least when we realized that some of our awesome interpreters would need to spend the night on the fishing boat along with all our supplies prior to an early morning departure. Apparently, we were unable to come up with some other source of security. As little as I knew about Indonesia, I vaguely remembered reading or hearing reports of piracy sometimes taking place. A boat loaded with a significant amount of medical supplies just seemed ripe for the picking. This was just one of many examples of the willingness of our Indonesian team members to do whatever needed to be done. Thank You, Jesus, they spent a safe and uneventful night on the boat.

Once in Lamno, we were able to set up clinic on the grounds of and stay in a home which was located directly across from the village mosque. In addition to holding clinic next to the mosque, we also sometimes set up shop at a few other sites throughout the area. And in addition to holding medical clinics, we were invited to partner with another aid organization (which I believe was out of California) and participated in an extensive measles immunization program for kids. I remember thinking the aid organization out of California must have had access to lots of financial resources because they had set up their headquarters in what was probably one of the very nicest houses (that hadn't been damaged by the tsunami) in all of Lamno. Not that I thought this was necessarily a problem, but at the same time, I really appreciated that the organization I had come to Indonesia with seemed to be very careful about not putting on the appearance of wealthy Westerners and were always more than willing to get down and dirty with the people they were serving. I'll never forget the day some of us went over to the big fancy house (those are just my words) for an orientation about the vaccination program. During our chat, the gentleman doing the speaking walked over to a fridge and pulled out an ice-cold Coke, which he began to enjoy in front of us. Now I'm not a big pop drinker but have come to realize there is a law of the universe that just can't be denied; when you're in a place like Iraq or West Darfur Sudan or Lamno Sumatra and temperatures are running somewhere near or above one hundred degrees Fahrenheit, an ice-cold Coke might just be the most delicious thing in the whole world. (We by the way didn't have any ice-cold Coke's back at our camp.) What that guy did was just not right—maybe even criminal. Having said that, it was great to be involved with the immunization program, and we provided a whole lot of vaccines to a whole lot of kids.

I kind of surprises me that I didn't make a few more journal entries while in Sumatra. Probably it just came down to being pretty busy.

Journal entry

01/21/-

Got to talk to Carol, Abbie, and Philip today— that was wonderful! The time is going so quickly. We have been busy doing clinic most every day. Sunday we will be working with an immunization program. That should be a fun change. [It was a lot of fun working with the kids and we ended up providing vaccinations at several different sites over several days.] *The team of interpreters here is great! They are all truly turned on to Jesus.*

There is no denying that I was so thoroughly inspired and impressed by this group of folks who had joined our team because they felt compelled to share some love with their brothers and sisters in the Aceh Province. Not brothers and sisters in the faith, however. Our interpreters (although believers in Jesus) had all grown up in the most Muslim-populated country of the world. They were now all choosing to leave their families for a time and come to a place that practiced the most orthodox version of the Muslim faith to be found in any other region of Indonesia. They came despite their differences because it was the right thing to do. For them, it was what Jesus would do.

When our stay in Aceh had reached its end and it was time to head back to the States, the first leg of our journey home included hitching a ride on a Navy helicopter, which had flown in from the Abraham Lincoln aircraft carrier. The Navy had been making regular visits to Lamno with deliveries of food and supplies. It was wonderful to see smiles on the faces of all those who ran up to the helicopter when it arrived and received the much-needed goods. It was just as great to see the smiles on the faces of the crew members who you could tell were so genuinely happy for a chance to help these people in a time of great need. I had just spent the last several weeks experiencing that very same feeling.

CHAPTER 23

A Huge Decision

The short story here is that in the years I worked as a medical officer, with the exception of those awesome opportunities to help with disaster response teams, I was for the most part totally separated from actually taking care of patients. I functioned as a nurse while working with the medical teams, but it was my paramedic certification that allowed me to meet the needed qualifications to go. As I was no longer working as a medic with the fire department, that certification would be expiring, and I wouldn't be able to renew it. With the loss of my certification would also come the loss of my ability to participate on and provide care with future teams. Providing patient care was the reason I ever joined the army and became a field medic or a nurse or went to paramedic school; it was to make that contact with the people who needed the help. I was incredibly grateful for my job as fire department MO but was also discovering that I really didn't want to make this a lifetime career. In addition to feeling like I wasn't doing the kind of work I was built to do, I also started to question if I was really the best guy for the job. I began thinking that if I was ever going to work with patients again, some changes would need to happen. As already mentioned, having a fifty-pound lifting restriction pretty much put the kibosh on performing as a medic. It more and more became evident to me that the department would probably be much better off with a medical officer who could not only perform the necessary administrative tasks but also function as a paramedic and or firefighter if the need arose. I had to accept the fact that I was not going to be that person.

So what to do? In the end, it boiled down to persuading the chiefs of the department that they would be better off with a medical officer who could do it all. Someone who could meet the one-hundred-pound lifting minimum that every other member of the department working in the field needed to meet. Not only did I think it would be better for the fire service to have a medical officer without any restrictions but also better for me to be taking care of patients and not sitting behind a desk and going to meetings. As a 91C in the Army, I had tested for and received a practical nursing license while in Colorado. I was able to transfer that license to New Jersey while we were living there and then to Washington State after we made that move. For some reason, I always felt the need to keep the license active even after getting out of the army and even though I had become certified as a paramedic. On the one hand, I felt a need to pay the annual fee and renew the license each year. On the other hand, I sort of felt like the license along with about three dollars would probably get me a cup of coffee. (Simply put, I didn't see a real reason for or a great value in maintaining the license but did it anyway.) Now, I was really glad that I did.

My thinking was that after leaving the department, I could work as a practical nurse while also completing a registered nursing program. This would allow the opportunity of providing patient care even with a fifty-pound lifting restriction. (Also, as an employee with the fire department, I had been paying into a disability insurance program. If the department were no longer willing and able to accommodate my fifty-pound lifting restriction, I would be permitted to take advantage of a small monthly insurance payment while working and going to school and still be able to pay the bills.) After much discussion, my chief did agree to rewrite the medical officer job description. The person hired into that position would now also be able to perform all the functions of a paramedic firefighter. I would be able to bow out gracefully and get back to performing the kind of work I was confident and comfortable doing.

To say that this was a "huge decision" is definitely an understatement. Giving up a very financially rewarding position with a wonderful organization and moving forward into a very uncertain future is not an easy or perhaps a very wise thing to do. And this with a wife and three kids to think about. Dear Carol had already experienced the ups and downs of being married to me and, despite I'm sure a whole lot of fear and trembling, graciously agreed to go along with this latest plan and to hang on for the ride.

Now here we are ten years later, and the ride continues. I tried to work and at the same time complete an independent study RN program over those first couple years but discovered that the going back to school part of my mind had pretty much turned to mush. It ended up being a significantly more difficult proposition than originally anticipated, and as a result, I chose to stop. Stopping school meant we would no longer receive any insurance assistance, but that was okay. I started working full-time and found that we could still enjoy a wonderful (yet very simple life) and always seem to have more than enough. Over these last ten years, I have been employed in a few different nursing settings to include primary care clinic, home health, progressive care unit, and in an urgent care clinic. I have developed a whole new appreciation for all the folks who work in each of these areas. Whether aids, medical or nursing assistants, nurses, practitioners, whatever—they all work their asses off. If ever I hear a paramedic or firefighter complaining about their work situation, I can only suggest they step back and consider all the folks out there who are in the medical field working very hard every day and yet not enjoying the wages and benefits that the fire service offers. If the urge to whine gets too great, I guess they could always just call for a "wambulance." I am currently working in an urgent care, and it is without a doubt the most fun and fulfilling job I've had since being a paramedic in the field. I think I may have finally "found what I'm looking for." As of the writing of this paragraph, with the exception of a short trip to Louisiana after hurricane Katrina and during hurricane Rita, I have not had the privilege of assisting with any further disaster relief responses. Those were some very special times.

Although there haven't been any international trips lately, Carol and I did in 2016 find ourselves being treated to the company of some delightful international visitors. Early in the year, our middle child Abbie finally flew the coup, and we for the first time became empty nesters. Perhaps to help us from going through withdrawals due to no kids being around for the first time in about twenty-seven years, God provided us with a few opportunities to host some foreign exchange students. The following is an excerpt from the Gates 2016 Christmas letter which Carol wrote.

March brought us the joy, honor, and privilege of hosting Nori Sato from Japan. Nori came to us via the exchange program from the local high school. Nori wanted to improve her English so she can help at the 2020 Summer Olympics in Japan. We look forward to seeing her (on TV) in 2020, helping with the tennis matches, a passion of hers is tennis. And I can attest that she is a good player.

In July we were privileged to have Sara from Spain with us for about ten days. We came to have Sara through a dear friend of mine from Hansville, who was a Spanish teacher in the local schools for many years. Sara is a university student who just wanted to visit the United States. She had written and illustrated a children's book to help her finance her trip to the United States, and we have a signed copy of that book. She is a very good artist. We so enjoyed her stay, and I learned so much more about Spain than just the "running of the bulls" in Pamplona.

September brought us our first guys. We had Simon from Denmark and Viktor from Poland for about ten days. Their host family had booked a vacation before they had agreed to take the boys for the school year, so they just needed someone to keep the guys for that short time. Simon and Viktor were on the football team, and so our feet did not touch the ground for those ten days. Their schedule was grueling. They got up early, went to school, had prac-

tice (which included watching the girls' volley-ball team practice) after school, then home to dinner (if they had not already had it at practice), homework, bed, and start all over again the next morning. We had them for just one game, and we found ourselves eating pizza at midnight!

It was such a treat to have each of these young people in our home. Even though they didn't stay for long, the friendships we gained will last forever. Carol and I are both anticipating many more opportunities to host exchange students in the future. It really is a lot of fun. I can only hope we are half the house parents that the wonderful folks were who invited me in when I was a teenager on the People to People trip.

My Friend Mr. Woodman

My family and I have been very fortunate to have lived in Northwestern Washington State in the Puget Sound region for over twenty-five years. A few miles north of our home in the Norwegian flavored town of Poulsbo rests the quaint little village of Port Gamble. Prior to its closing in 1995, Port Gamble was home of the oldest operating sawmill in North America. Although logging has dramatically declined in the Evergreen State, we are still fortunate enough to enjoy some of the rich tradition and heritage that has accompanied that industry. One happening that I always look forward to is the annual log show. As a little kid, we often travelled north to where my dad grew up and attended their log show—the Loggerama. I think we even had some distant cousins that participated in some of the competitions. Speaking of cousins, on one occasion, Pat and I accompanied our cousin Terry to the Loggerama, which by this time was probably known as the Deming Log Show. Terry was twelve or so years older than us. He was a favorite cousin and often visited our folks' house when we were kids. On this particular day (in the land of plaid shirts and spiked logging boots), he had decided to enjoy the festivities wearing only his red bathing suit. Pat and I were a little surprised and quite frankly a little uncomfortable at his choice of apparel, but hey, Terry was Terry. I guess we were a bit naive not to know that our cousin was gay. Dear Terry became a professional hairdresser and in later years owned a shop on Capitol Hill in Seattle. We were shocked and so very saddened when he told us that he was HIV-positive and had AIDS. On his last day on this earth, my mom and I had gone to visit Terry. It was very heartbreaking while at the same time a privilege and honor to be holding Terry's hand when he took his final breath. He has been greatly missed by so many. (I have been to several log shows since that one in Deming, and each time, I can't help but think about dear cousin Terry.) These logging events are held in different areas of Western Washington and typically include a demonstration and competition of some of the skills that loggers have historically become proficient at in order to perform their specialized jobs. Skills to include tree climbing, log rolling, axe throwing, maneuvering big logging trucks in reverse, and the like. The exhibitions now typically also include all kinds of vendors and in particular my personal favorite, chainsaw woodcarvers. Port Gamble's version of a log show is part of what is called Old Mill Days, and it was at one of these festive occasions that I first met Mr. Woodman.

My friend Mr. Woodman was born in Tokeland, Washington, a tiny little town out on the coast. (Tokeland, if you're wondering, was named after Chief Toke, a Native American chief of Chinnok/Chehalis ancestry that used to spend his summers in the area of what is now Tokeland. It honestly has nothing to do with taking a toke.) I should say that Mr. Woodman was not born but more accurately "born again" in Tokeland. Where he actually originates from I am not sure. I try not to be someone who judges by appearance but have to admit that I knew I was really going to like Mr. Woodman the first time I saw him. Since that day, Mr. Woodman has become a good friend to me. My kids are a little perplexed (probably more accurately a little weirded out) by this friendship, and think I'm pretty weird. The thing is, Mr. Woodman isn't actually human but really is a wood man. I mentioned that he was born again in Tokeland because that is where an artist found a piece of driftwood on the beach, and after some creative chainsaw carving a metamorphosis took place, he became Mr. Woodman. I realize that by definition I can't really call Mr. Woodman a friend. On the other hand, what is a friend? After doing a little searching for different definitions of friend and friendship I came across the following on a blog site called Beyond Evangelical, authored by a guy named Frank Viola. Although I really don't know any specifics about this author or about other things he has written, I did like the piece on being a friend.

Five Characteristics of a Close (True) Friend

1. *Rejoices in your joys and sorrows in your pain.* (True, I cannot know for sure if Mr. Woodman is sorrowing or rejoicing. He is, however, always ready and willing to listen, whether it be to my rants or to my raves. And he always has a thoughtful, understanding look about him, regardless.)

2. *Won't de-friend you if you disagree.* (Mr. Woodman has never ceased to be my friend regardless of whatever weirdness there might be going on with me. He has in fact never moved an inch from the place at our home where he resides.)

3. *A close friend stays in regular contact with you.* (I always know that I can depend on Mr. Woodman to be available at the front of our house any time day or night and even on weekends and holidays.)

4. *A close friend is someone whom you trust implicitly.* (I am absolutely confident that nothing I share with Mr. Woodman will ever be passed on to another. He can definitely be trusted.)

5. *A close friend will stand by you, defend you, even take a bullet for you when you're under attack.* (As mentioned, Mr. Woodman diligently stands guard at the front of our house, and I know he would provide me some protection even from a bullet. He's a big piece of driftwood for heaven's sake.)

You know how there are those people in your life who you are always delighted to see? The family and friends who always (or at least almost always) make you smile when you bump into them. I am incredibly blessed to have several of those people in my life. It makes me happy just to see them coming. Well, in a strange sort of way, that's kind of how it is every time I pull into our driveway or walk out onto our front porch and see Mr. Woodman. (I must mention here that I am very aware that it could be construed by some as odd, perhaps "very odd," that I have a large piece of driftwood for a friend. You must keep in mind, however, that I grew up in a house with Irish ferries living in the cupboard. Honestly, if you met Mr. Woodman I think you would like him.) So from time to time when I am hanging out with

Mr. Woodman and discussing world issues, although he has never actually spoken to me, I have gotten the impression that he likes to keep things pretty simple. He has impressed on me the importance of being thoughtful and prayerful when facing important issues. I think I once heard him say (in my mind), "Don't just do something—stand there." Also, on more than a few occasions Mr. Woodman's nonverbal advice to me has been to "talk to Jesus." Good advice from my good friend.

I think I would have benefited from having a friend like Mr. Woodman early in my thirty-plus years of blissful family life. Some extra added motivation to stop and pause and try to be genuinely prayerful about big decisions. Although Carol and I ultimately do make our big decisions together, there have been a few times along the way when she wasn't 100 percent in agreement with the direction I was trying to lead us, but agreed to go along for the ride anyway. I can't help but wonder what might have been had we chosen some different roads. Like what if I never insisted on taking the medic job on the west side of the mountains and instead we stayed in our little house next to the elementary school in Selah? What if I stayed working as a medic for a mom-and-pop ambulance slash tow truck company. (I say that with absolutely no disrespect and with a very special place in my heart for this organization.) I'm incredibly grateful for having had the opportunity to work for what was a relatively busy little emergency medical service in Yakima County.

Carol and I could have probably qualified for free government cheese with the salary I was receiving, but at the same time, I was being given a chance to take care of a really diverse mix of complex medical and trauma patients and also being forced to learn a lot in a short time. That was a good thing. I think every young medic could benefit from a similar experience, if nothing else just to help them appreciate how fortunate they are if they end up with one of the more lucrative medic jobs out there. As little as that first medic job paid, Carol and I always seemed to have more than enough. I think we were just happy and content to be getting along. I'll never forget the day early in the winter of '88 when our first child, Hannah, was just a few months old. Carol and I had her all bundled up in the stroller and were taking a walk along the Yakima River. The river walk happened to pass by a restaurant that we had been to and knew was pretty good. In spite of the fact that we were literally down to about $11.00 in our checking account, we chose to go in and each have a bowl of soup. On this day, the restaurant was serving steak and mushroom soup. This was without question one of the most delicious soups that I, and I'm pretty sure Carol would agree, she had ever eaten. And dear sweet Hannah slept for the entire time we were there. It was a beautiful, magical moment. I'm not sad that we left our little home in Eastern Washington, but I'm pretty sure that life could have been sweet had we stayed. (Who knows, we might have even ended up working for the Mission.) Or what if I had never been intent on persuading the chiefs of the fire department I was working for in Kingston that they would be better off with a medical officer who in addition to performing administrative tasks would also be able to function as a paramedic and take care of patients in the field? Was that the best decision for my family and for their futures? Have I often thought about the wages and benefits and overall wonderfulness of being associated with the fire department and its members? In answer to the first question, I can't really know for sure. In answer to the second question, oh yes. Do I wish that I never would have left? Sometimes I do. Like Mr. Woodman, I'm a pretty simple guy. Maybe not quite as simple as a chunk of wood but simple nonetheless. (Carol might argue the chunk of wood part.) Working as a medic never seemed terribly hard to me. It actually felt like it came sort of naturally.

Working as a medical officer on the other hand and having to participate with the team of folks who were trying to help shape what EMS would look like in the county (and even chairing the county medical officers division for a while) was for me very stressful. Coordinating and teaching our department fire academy's EMT program and feeling responsible for the quality of students that graduated the course also produced more stress than I am happy to deal with. Was I mostly just thinking about myself for wanting to leave the medical officer position? Absolutely. Now ten years later, if I could do it over again, would I have continued working in a position I really didn't like because it would ultimately be so much more financially rewarding for me and my family? Maybe I would. I guess therein lies the rub. No matter what I choose to do, whether it be a prayerful, thoughtful, carefully made decision, or not, I always have the option to choose. And with that comes the option to make a selfish choice. Hopefully, on a few occasions, there have been some decisions that weren't totally motivated by my selfishness. I do hope so.

Most everyone, especially if you grew up around the church, is familiar with the term *heathenism*. I for the most part always associated that word with folks who were either opposed to religion altogether or perhaps just in desperate need of being spiritually enlightened. Pretty much anyone who didn't believe in the God I learned about in the Bible. Sometimes the word would bring to mind pictures of people who were even hostile toward God. For me, at least as a child, that was like the ultimate bad thing. As the years have gone by and as I have had the opportunity to experience a little bit more of life, my thinking on this issue has changed some. It's no longer heathenism that I consider the "ultimate bad thing" but rather *hedonism* or hedonistic philosophy. As I understand things, God loves the whole world, whether the whole world knows it or not. Just like the song says, "Red and yellow, black and white, they are precious in His sight." He desires that everyone would come to know about his great love for them and has offered the opportunity to experience both the love and the new life that only He can give by way of an intimate and personal relationship. A new life that is available to anyone regardless of their past and regardless of their past beliefs. They can choose to get to know Jesus now, today, so-called heathen or not.

Hedonism, on the other hand, is a philosophy and way of think-ing that works very hard at making itself our most important goal and objective, regardless of what we claim to believe. Whether believer, nonbeliever, lover of God and man, hater of God and man, whatever. *Merriam-Webster* defines hedonism as "the doctrine that pleasure or happiness is the sole or chief good in life." Doesn't sound too bad at first blush, but another way to put it might simply be "selfishness." It's all about me and me feeling good. It is, I believe, the polar oppo-site of the kind of life that Jesus demonstrated by preferring others and considering them above Himself. It's the greedy, selfish kind of thinking that allowed for the banking crisis of the later 2000s and then ended up rewarding many of the responsible criminals. It affects all of us and every aspect of life, from the bank to the home to the church. It is, I believe, responsible for a prosperity theology found within the Christian world that teaches its God's will for believers to be wealthy.

Tell that to a believer in a developing nation where it's all they can do to find water. Or tell it to the disciples that were walking with Jesus and like Jesus were about as far from the life of luxury as you could get. What a crazy way of thinking. (It has, however, produced a fat wallet for a number of televangelists and leaders of churches who teach that sort of thing. Just suffering for Jesus, don't you know?) Although Mr. Woodman isn't a big talker and can sometimes be a little hard to read, I'm pretty sure that he agrees with me about the prosperity doctrine being an unbiblical and frankly asinine notion. As to how he feels about the many other controversial issues that have surfaced within Christendom over the last few decades, I am not certain.

In this age of post-modern, emergent, progressive, emerging, post-evangelical, post-something or other whatever movement that the church may or may not be experiencing and that modern-day authors are expounding upon, I'm thinking that I probably hold what would be considered an old-fashioned spiritual worldview. Turns out I'm a pretty conservative kind of guy. It would appear that we live in a culture where just about any historical biblical doctrine is open for complete and total reinterpretation, open to be deconstructed and then reconstructed. Sometimes, however, I believe it ends up being reconstructed in the image of the one doing the constructing. Rest assured though that according to the chosen recipients of these new and improved spiritual truths, the sources being used to derive their insights from on high are always of the oldest and most reliable, and the conclusions being drawn, exactly what the Bible has really been trying to tell us. We have just gotten it wrong until now. Questions concerning love, truth, sexuality, sin, heaven, hell, authenticity, and reliability of the Bible, the church, the return of Jesus, literally anything and everything we can think of.

The big problem for me is that regardless of the spiritual truth being delved into, two different so-called "scholars" or "experts" or "really, truly enlightened" can use all their skill and wisdom and spiritual connection with the Almighty and still come up with two totally different conclusions, and both be absolutely and without question sure that they are right. It's interesting that even in my relatively short walk on this earth (at least compared to eternity), there have been moments when I actually thought I knew some things. As the years have gone by, however, the *what I know* seems to be taking up much less space in me than the *what I thought I knew*. And the *what I've forgotten* is sadly taking up the biggest place in me of all. Like the blind beggar spoken of in the bible in John chapter 9 verse 25 who said "I was blind, now I see"; that's what I know for sure. (We will be taking a closer look at our friend in John 9 a little later.) Not that there aren't a few controversial areas of "ology" that I'm kinda certain about. For instance, many today are telling us that it's all about love. Love, love, love. If you can somehow package what you are doing in a "love" box, then it must be okay. The thing is, I don't believe love is just whatever we happen to say it is to meet our desires for the moment. It says in the Bible that "we have come to know and have believed the love which God has for us. God is love, and the one who abides in love abides in God, and God abides in him" (1 John 4:16, NASB). So *God is love.* Does that mean any thoughts or actions we place a tag of love on are automatically godly? I don't think so. In the book of 1 Corinthians, Paul says the following (and you may have received these words in a card or on a wall hanging, especially if you've been married), "Love is patient, love is kind and is not jealous; love does not brag and is not arrogant, does not act unbecomingly ; it does not seek its own, is not provoked, does not take into account a wrong suffered, does not rejoice in unrighteousness, but rejoices with the truth; bears all things, believes all things, hopes all things, endures all things" (13:4–7, NASB). And in Ephesians 5:25 it says, "Husbands, love your wives, just as Christ also loved the church and gave Himself up for her" (NASB).

The point is, love looks like something, but it doesn't look like anything we choose. For example, there are people who identify as "liberated" Christians and who (in the name of love) wholeheartedly believe it is healthy and God-honoring and according to scripture (using the oldest and most reliable sources, of course) that it is just groovy for married believers to have sexual partners outside of their marriage. Maybe I'm just naive, but it was quite a surprise for me when I first heard about this. I don't even need to expound on all the writings of the Bible, which at least in my mind so thoroughly teach this to be a screwy idea. Rather, just consider the world full of children of every age and from every color and religion and flavor who would tell you that having two parents who love each other and are faithful to one another is a good and wonderful thing. Kind of an obvious and natural conclusion, and they don't need to refer to any original texts or be Greek scholars to come up with that. Love is not "all about me."

When it's all said and done, I'm okay with trusting that Father God has the really difficult and confusing issues figured out. Some areas of disagreement that I may have argued once upon a time, I wouldn't argue today. There are lots and lots of things that I'm just not sure about. I am someone who really does believe that God loved the whole world so much that He provided us with a sacrifice for our sins by way of Jesus, the way, the truth and the life, and that by calling on Him we can have new life now and forever. It's amazing to me that in this post whatever it is church era that we are in, there are many even within the church who have determined that the gift of new life that God has offered us really isn't necessary anyway because everybody has the same eternal destiny, regardless. According to them, there is no place called hell, so not to worry, we are all going to spend eternity in heavenly places with our loving God. (And once again, they are making this claim due to their ability to understand and accurately interpret scripture. Finally, someone is getting it right.) Or are they? I am certainly no bible scholar (far, far, light years from it) and have no intention of arguing with those who question the existence of hell. I even hope that they are correct. At the same time though, I can't help but wonder why Jesus would have ever needed to offer Himself as a sacrifice to save us from the slavery of sin and from the penalty of death and destruction if there is no death and destruction to save us from? If these folks are correct, Hooray! It's a beautiful thing, and everybody wins. If, however, they are mistaken, then a very dangerous doctrine is being taught that it seems to me could literally make the difference between everlasting life and death for a whole lot of people.

I don't have the definitive answer, and to be honest, I won't know for sure until it's time to take off this earth suit and make the trip to eternity. I will have to admit though that this whole line of thought does make me carefully consider some things. It's impossible not to seriously think about all the truly wonderful people I have been privileged to meet and to know from around the world. Those who haven't met and don't know about my Jesus and about His love. What about them? Paul says in the book of Romans chapter 10 verse 14, "For whosoever shall call upon the name of the Lord shall be saved" (KJV). I believe that to be true. There is a prophetic scripture about the coming of the Messiah in Isaiah chapter 9 verse 6 that says, "For a child will be born to us, a son will be given to us; And the government will rest on His shoulders; And His name will be called Wonderful Counselor, Mighty God, Eternal Father, Prince of Peace" (NASB). (That's Jesus.) So His name is Jesus, Wonderful Counselor, Mighty God, Eternal Father, Prince of Peace. I can't help but wonder (and I realize this is heresy to probably many) if there won't be a whole lot of people in heaven who knew Him but hadn't yet discovered that the Prince of Peace or Eternal Father or Mighty God or Wonderful Counselor that they had come to know, was in fact Jesus. (Who knows, maybe I'll even be in heaven.)

I can wholeheartedly and without any hesitation say that getting to know Jesus really is the greatest, most wonderful thing that has happened in my life. Of course, I want people to know His name and to know Him. It would be unbelievably selfish not to share the good news about Jesus and His love. Having said that, the sad truth is, although I am more than happy to talk to people about the Good News, if the subject happens to come up, I am not very mindful about being the one to initiate that conversation. If I really believe to hold some kind of wonderful information that could make all the difference in a person's life, why wouldn't I make an effort to talk about it? For instance (and I know this sounds weird and is a really bad example), back in the seventies, if I had been turned on to some killer good weed, I wouldn't have hesitated and in fact would have been eager to share that good news. Now here I am today, believing to have been turned on to the Giver of Life and yet not always making the effort to share that news with my friends. This is definitely one of those areas of trying to "be real" that I struggle with.

As someone with a self-professed old-fashioned spiritual worldview, it seems to me that over the last twenty or thirty years, we have been witnessing a phenomenon taking place within the Church that has really left me confused. (Actually, this is just one of many things within the church that have left me confused, but oh well.) In what almost appears to be an effort at being more relevant to the world, some spiritually enlightened church folks have seen fit to include a few F-bombs or other choice expletives as part of their normal everyday vernacular. I just don't get it. As my wife, Carol, has been known to ask, "Is that the mouth you kiss your momma with?"

Although I believe there is scripture that directly discourages nasty talk which ultimately doesn't do anybody any good, it's probably just having grown up in the house I did that has caused me to think about this the way I do. Mom probably never spoke a foul word in her entire life. I honestly never heard my mother swear, ever. For that matter, I don't know if I ever heard her say an unkind word about anybody, ever. She really did have a supernatural thing going on. Dad was an old soldier who grew up in a logging community. He was definitely capable of verbalizing with the most verbal, but he rarely did, not that way. One time at about age fifteen, I overheard my dad having a conversation with another gentleman and was so surprised to hear the string of profanities that came out of his mouth. I confronted him about it later because it was just so uncharacteristic of the dad I knew. Without any hesitation or any sort of excuses, he apologized to me and also made the statement, "Talking like that is just a sign of ignorance." I don't know if that's always true, but it has forever stuck with me, and I rarely ever heard Dad swear again. I can still hear him saying things like "baldheaded Moses" or "for crying out in the sewer" (a weird twist on for crying out loud) or the classic and my personal favorite, "balls on a heifer."

When all was said and done (except for some fairly regular obscenities from brother Michael), I just didn't hear a lot of swearing from my family while growing up. Something else that also may have impacted my thinking on the words I chose was the time in the seventh grade while on the basketball court during PE class. I messed up the play we were running and made the unfortunate mistake of saying *shit*. I knew right away I was in for it but never expected the severity of penalty that was about to be administered. Apparently, the PE teacher (who I remember as being kind of a red-faced overly intense guy) wanted to make an example out of me. I was first sent into the shower room and instructed to do step-ups. That's where you rapidly and repeatedly jump up and down from a bench until you're told to stop, can't do any more, or throw up. It felt like I did about a thousand of them before being told to stop. Then just to make sure I really learned my lesson, the good coach pulled out his very large and intimidating wooden paddle (which I believe had holes drilled in it for added effect) and gave me a swat for each letter of the word. (A really, really hard swat.) Honest to goodness, the next day my butt was black and blue.

Public school has definitely gone through some changes since 1970. A teacher would likely lose their job for doing the same thing today. But I've never been bitter—the *flipflakkinblipbleepen* ***** *dirty word!* (Rest assured, I didn't ever say *shit* again in his class.) Not that I don't have a place in my vocabulary for the occasional *damn* or sometimes a resounding *bullshit*, I do, in spite of the coach. If, however, I'm ever feeling the need to spice things up and go to the next level, it helps to remember the limited and embarrassingly crude vocabulary of the two outspoken Scottish lassies that gave me an English lesson at the cafe in Rauzan. Remembering them effectively discourages me from wanting to swear. (And I'll tell you right now, I have never heard Mr. Woodman talkin' any unedifying bawdry.)

I do appreciate the very unique relationship I am able to enjoy with my friend Mr. Woodman. It's always great to see his calm and thoughtful face at the front of our house. For whatever reason, just seeing this friendly chunk of driftwood seems to motivate me to stop and breathe and simply be grateful and quite often to pray. (Good things.) As much, however, as I enjoy my friendship with Mr. Woodman, I am profoundly more appreciative and grateful to actually have a few beloved people in my life (the flesh-and-blood kind) who really and truly are close, true friends. (Don't worry, kids, your dad hasn't totally and completely lost it. I really do like people.)

CHAPTER 25

Pausing to Think

"If we pause to think, we will have cause to thank." These words can be found penned on a wooden plaque which has hung on our wall or sat on our mantle for nearly thirty-three years. Shortly after Carol and I were married, we were having coffee at a funky little cafe in New Jersey, which also had a small gift shop. When the plaque and its message caught our eye, we knew that it needed to live in our home. As life has continued to move us along with its good times, bad times, incredible times, disappointing times, take-your-breath-away times, heartbreaking times, and times that literally nearly killed you, we have found the words on the plaque to always be true. If we can just pause long enough to think and consider and remember and try not to freak out about the circumstances of the moment, we can see there's so very, very much to be grateful and thankful for.

I won't pretend that there haven't been times in life when I wasn't jumping and leaping and praising God and thanking Him for whatever was going on. There have been many. Those would be the times though when I have forgotten to stop and think. To stop and remember that I have been given a relationship with the Creator of the Universe. That He has actually allowed me to call Him my Father (my Abba, my Daddy) and that He really and truly loves us and wants the best for us. If that is true, and if I really believe that He is watching out for and involved with every aspect of my life, then what's not to be thankful for? I'm not thankful for my screw-ups and bad decisions along the way. Those have consequences and can sometimes be pretty painful (for me and for others). I am, however, so grateful that He loves me in the midst of my circumstances and in spite of my frequent screw-ups and bad decisions, and that He can and will and has worked those things out into something good. I have just needed to be open to the idea.

Back in 2001 while hanging over the back seat of our van, sweating bullets and experiencing the worst pain of my life as Carol drove us to the hospital, I didn't know what was going on, but I knew it was going to be okay. After finding out what was going on with my heart and aorta and then flying by helicopter from the hospital in Silverdale to the one in Seattle, I didn't know what the outcome would be, but I knew it was going to be okay. Throughout the hospitalization and subsequent surgery, although I knew things were going to change and be much different, I knew that still, it was going to be okay. It was going to be okay because no matter what, our Father God was there, and He loved us and He would work it out. I was thankful for that. During this whole experience, I think Carol would tell you that she also had a strange and wonderful peace about the whole thing, and for that, she was very thankful. (Probably both Carol and I knew that everything going on was totally out of our control so better to trust in and be thankful to God than to freak out.) The whole episode with the heart stuff was, I think, a good example of Carol and I being able to embrace the whole idea of stopping to think and finding cause to thank (despite the circumstances). In 2014 we went through another major life event, but unfortunately, on this go-round, we weren't able to grasp the whole concept quite so well.

It was like a Norman Rockwell painting. Sunday morning and all the kids were at the house on Father's Day. We were planning to all go out for breakfast and then as a family go to church. I was such a happy dad. (And then the painting fell off the wall.) Just before leaving for the restaurant, Hannah, our oldest daughter, decided it would be a good time to tell us the news. What news, you ask? Well, the news that she was expecting a baby. I didn't see that one coming.

Several months prior to our very memorable Father's Day, Hannah had been dating a young man who was stationed at the nearby naval base as a submariner. We had met Rasheem (RJ) on a few occasions and had even celebrated his birthday in our home. He and Hannah had, however, parted ways and, from what we knew about the situation, had not been going out for quite some time and were no longer even friends (at all). Hannah informed us that she had every intention of keeping her baby but that she and RJ had no intentions of being a couple (at all). We were led to believe in fact that the father of our future grandchild had no desire to be involved in the life of this baby (at all). It would be fair to say that I was doing a lot of thinking. Mostly though I was thinking about how I might be willing to spend the rest of my life in jail because I had beaten to death the person who had engaged in thoughtless, uncommitted, loveless sex with my daughter and as a result her life and all of our lives were being changed forever. (Don't get me wrong. We realized that Hannah was every bit as responsible for the situation they were in. I was, however, only thinking of killing him.) I was not finding any cause to thank, not even a little.

Both Carol and I were hurt. We were disappointed. We were angry. We were anything but thankful. I believe I even developed an ulcer. But *thankfully*, as time and as the pregnancy progressed, we both little by little came to our senses and were able to concentrate on how much we loved our daughter and on how much we were going to love this new little baby. I had to also come to grips with the fact that as a young man, the condition of my heart in regards to sex was probably not so very different from Rasheem's. I found myself praying for RJ's well-being rather than planning how I might end his life. While changes were taking place in our hearts, they were also happening in the hearts of both Hannah and Rasheem. Before our grandson was born, the kids had decided that they did indeed want to spend their lives together and that they wanted to be loving parents to their new baby. On February 11, 2015, Carol and I had the incredible privilege of being with Hannah and Rasheem at the birthing center when our beautiful grandson Kalib was born. Then on March 17 (St. Patty's Day), RJ, Hannah, Kalib, our family, and a few of the kids' closest friends celebrated the marriage of Rasheem and Hannah Halliday.

Granted—this was not the future I had envisioned for our first-born child. But you know what? It's not about me or about what I had in mind. It's now about doing everything we can to support this young family. I am so incredibly hopeful for their future together. Kalib is such an amazing and wonderful little gift. And the more Carol and

I have come to know Rasheem, the more we have grown to love him and to discover that he is genuinely a quality young man. (I'm so very happy about that because I really didn't want to have to kill him.) If we pause to think, we definitely have cause to thank.

CHAPTER 26

Unlikely Heroes

I think most people would tell you that they have had some sort of heroes in their lives. That remarkable individual you have either known personally or have read or heard about who you would consider a hero at least to some extent. Many of us have read about some of the extraordinary men and women of the Bible and may consider some of them heroes. You know the ones, the heavy hitters like Abraham, the founder of the Hebrew nation. Or Esther, the orphan who became queen of Persia and who played a huge role in saving those Jews of the empire from certain destruction. And David, the shepherd boy who became king and who is known for killing the giant warrior Goliath with just a rock and a slingshot. We can't leave out Paul, the ultra-orthodox who was well known for his persecution of believers. After an encounter with Jesus, Paul went on to author thirteen of the letters found in the New Testament of the Bible. These are not the folks that first come to mind when I think of my Bible heroes.

In the book of John in chapter 9, we're told of a guy who was born blind. While Jesus and his disciples were walking past this gentleman, the disciples asked who it was that had sinned to cause the blindness, the man or his parents. Jesus told them there wasn't anybody to blame but rather it was to show the power of God at work in him. Jesus made some mud out of spit and dirt, which he then applied to the man's eyes. He told the blind man to go wash in a particular pool. Our friend with the muddy eyes went to the pool and washed as Jesus had said to do. When he came back, lo and behold, for the first time in his life, he could see. Not surprisingly, when this fellow returned and was able to see, his friends and those who had known him as a blind man begging in the street were pretty amazed. They kept asking him how in the world a man born blind could now possibly be able to see. He responded by simply telling them what had happened. Jesus put spitty mud over his eyes, told him to go and wash it off in the pool of Siloam, and when he did, he could see, just that simple.

Not long after, the man found himself in front of the religious leaders who also started grilling him about what had happened. Once again, he explained how Jesus had put mud over his eyes, told him to go and wash it off in a pool, and when he did he could see. Just that simple. Rather than be excited about the fact that a blind man had been given his sight, the religious leaders were instead all freaked out about someone having performed a miracle on the Sabbath day of rest. Some of them even said that what Jesus had done couldn't possibly be from God because it wasn't in line with their interpretation of keeping the Sabbath. They decided that the man couldn't actually have been born blind so they called for his parents and started to question them. They asked his folks if indeed this was their son, if he was blind from birth and how it was he could see now. The parents confirmed that yes this absolutely was their son and yes he was born blind. As to how he was now seeing, they told the Pharisees to go ask their son, that he knew what happened and that he was old enough to speak for himself. The leaders, who absolutely did not want to concede that a miracle of God had just been performed by this person called Jesus, told the gentleman that "we know this man is a sinner" (this man being Jesus). It was the response of the once blind beggar that I so appreciate. He said, "Whether He is a sinner, I do not know; one thing I do know, that though I was blind, now I see" (John 9:25). Much like the man who was once blind, there is a whole lot that I don't know, a whole lot that I don't understand. What I do know for sure though is that there has been a change in my life. The same Jesus who gave sight to this man has allowed me to see that life is so much bigger and has so much more to offer than what I could have imagined. Even during those confusing times when I'm not sure what's going on in life (and there are plenty of those times), I can still say, "Though I was blind, now I see."

Another one of my favorite people in the Bible (perhaps the person who I can relate to the most) is found in chapter 9 of the book of Mark. It's the story of a father who brought his son to Jesus desperately in need of help. The boy was mute and had often experienced some sort of seizure-type activity that caused him to be slammed to the ground, sometimes being thrown into fires and sometimes into water. It sounds pretty horrible. The dad had already tried to get help from the disciples, but they were unable to do anything. In near hopelessness, he asked Jesus to please help them. Jesus told him that "all things are possible to him who believes" (verse 23). The man's response was so incredibly honest and genuine, and it's what rings so true with me. He cried out "I do believe; help me in my unbelief" (verse 24). That might just be the story of my life. I really and truly do believe. At the same time, I really and truly do need help in my unbelief every day. Maybe what I appreciate the most about the man who had been blind and about the boy's father is the simplicity of what they knew and what they believed. I love the fact that even people with a simple knowledge and an honest simple way of believing can still have a relationship with the Lord of the Universe. You don't have to be a Bible scholar or a giant of the faith. You can be a simple guy like me.

Now What?

There have been lots of ups and downs since when in the wee hours of the morning on the floor of my mom and dad's living room, through tears, I asked Jesus to please make Himself at home in my life. To please show me what His ways look like and to give me the help and ability to try and follow Him. Now nearly forty years later, my prayer really hasn't changed. I still wholeheartedly believe that Jesus is the giver of life, and I still desperately want to and need to know Him better.

I have an amazing wife who loves me. We have three great kids who, in spite of their mother's and father's totally challenged parenting skills, have grown up to be wonderful young adults. We have a son-in-law and beautiful little grandson who we couldn't love more (and another grandbaby on the way). Now as of May 27th 2017, we have added another quality young man to the family (a young man who we love very much) since our daughter Abbie and her fiancé, Justin have become man and wife. (Justin by the way has assured me that two goats will be forthcoming in return for allowing him to marry our daughter. I probably should have held out for a camel.) Carol and I both have work to keep us busy, and both enjoy the work we're doing. Not to wear out a word that gets used a lot among church people, but we have been very, very "blessed."

So now what? A few months ago, I turned sixty. Wow, how did that happen? The years have brought countless opportunities to try and live out the beliefs I have professed to hold true, countless opportunities to try and "be real." I don't know for sure what the future will hold, except that there will continue to be lots of ups and downs and challenges. We will be called on to make lots of decisions, and hopefully, we'll sometimes get it right. As the past has shown us though, we will also often blow it. The wonderful and amazing thing is, no matter what happens, no matter what decisions we make (good or bad, right or wrong), we will be living life with the knowledge that the Lord God of the Universe, the maker of heaven and earth, is and will be right there with us, through it all. I also know for sure that the journey won't be boring.

IN CONCLUSION

Being given the chance to look back on life and to remember some of the great adventures I've been allowed to experience has been an incredible gift. I never ever saw myself as someone who would try to pursue something like writing a memoir. Now after making the effort, I am so glad that I did.

But having said that, as much as I have enjoyed working on this little story, I really do need to clean out the garage now. Let's get real after all.

P.S. Jesus loves you.

PHOTOS

Our wee Lambs

A JOURNEY

Cyclo ride in Hue - 2000

China Sea - Vietnam

Getting ready to see Danang

Eating lychee nuts in Hoi An

Philip's new buddy

Outside Uncle Ho's house – Hanoi

A JOURNEY

Hue - ancient capital of Vietnam

Cu Chi tunnels

Mekong Delta

Gerhard and Roland in Konigstein Germany (during layover)

Gali Ali Beg Falls – Northern Iraq

Walls of Nineveh (Mosul)

Mine warnings – Northern Iraq

Kids of Kurdistan

Introductions at a technical school

Community Incubator – Kurdish hospital

V-80
Atom Infant Incubator

QALAH OF ERBIL
ERBIL IS THE OLDESTS CITY CONSTANTLY INHABITANT THE QALAH CONSISTES OF 3
QUARTERS TAKIYA, TOPKHANA, AND SARAY. THE QALAH HAS WITTNESSED ALL
EPOCHS OF MESOPOTAMIAN HISTORY AND PREHISTORY (FROM 7000 B.C. TILL
PRESENT) IT HAS BEEN FOR SOMETIME THE RELIGIOUS CENTRE OF THE
ASSYRIANS. THE GODDESS ISHTAR WAS PARAMOUNT GODDESS OF
THE CITY. SENNACHRIB THE GREAT KING OF ASSYRIA (705 – 681) B.C
SUPPLIED THE QALAH WITH WATER THROUGH A AVERY
SOPHISTICATED SYSTEM OF ACUEDUCT DERIVING
FROM BASTORA 22 KM. TO THE NORTH.
THE NAME ORBELYM WAS DERIVI FROM SUMERIAN TEXT
THE STATE ORGANIZAION OF ANTIOATIES AND HERITAGE IS
UNDERTAKING AN AMBITIOUS PROGRAME OF RESTORATION
AND DEVELOPMENTAIN THE QALAH

The sign we moved and then put back

Hard working Kurdish hospital nurses

Sufi Muslim service - Kartoum

Smiles in El Geneina

Howaja!

Meeting with tribal leaders

Getting to know the police and military

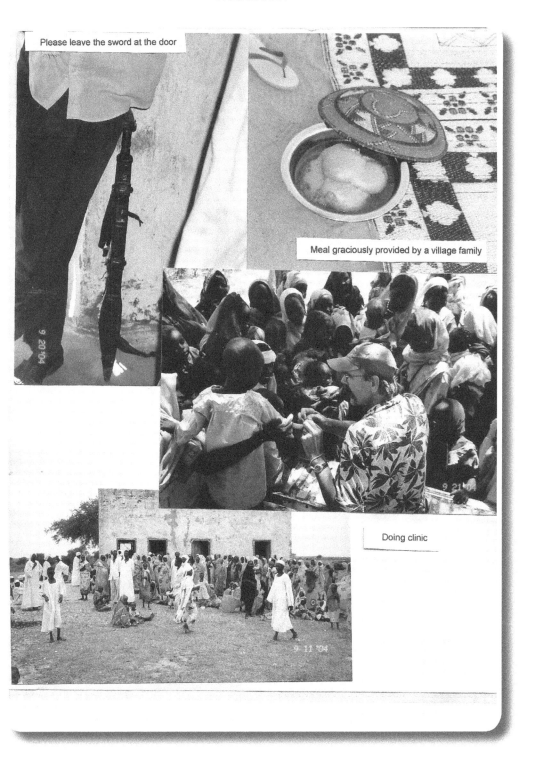

Please leave the sword at the door

Meal graciously provided by a village family

Doing clinic

Fatina and Fatea

Village kids

Feeding center in El Geneina

Dr. Mike and the guys

Cowboy in Africa

Janjaweed?

My ride back to Khartoum

Hanging with Mohamed and friends in Khartoum souk

Banda Aceh Indonesia

Hitching a ride on a C130

After the tsunami

Heavy machinery

Soldiers on patrol

More devastation

A JOURNEY

Boat ride to Lamno

Our clinic

Mosque next to the clinic

Trying to help

Vaccination program

Showing the kids a Paramedic Chicken

Working with a patient

Faces of Lamno

Some downtime with Dr. D

Wonderful people to work with

Hannah and R.J's most excellant day.

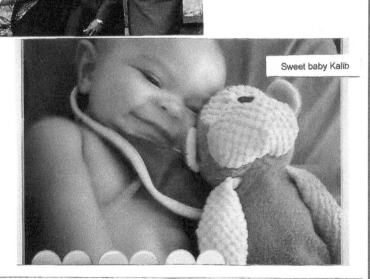

Sweet baby Kalib

Abbie and Justin's Best Day Ever

My friend Mr. Woodman

Tim enjoys life together with his lovely wife, Carol, and good doggie Ruca just outside of the quaint Norwegian-esque town of Poulsbo in the beautiful Pacific Northwest.

CPSIA information can be obtained
at www.ICGtesting.com
Printed in the USA
LVHW091934111221
705843LV00002B/50